The First World War

Exploring World History

Series Editors
John McNeill, Georgetown University
Kenneth Pomeranz, University of Chicago

As the world grows ever more closely linked, students and general readers alike are appreciating the need to become internationally aware. World history offers the crucial connection to understanding past global links and how they influence the present. The series will expand that awareness by offering clear, concise supplemental texts for the undergraduate classroom as well as trade books that advance world history scholarship.

The series will be open to books taking a thematic approach—exploring commodities such as sugar, cotton, and petroleum; technologies; diseases and the like; or regional—for example, Islam in Southeast Asia or east Africa, the Indian Ocean, or the Ottoman Empire. The series sees regions not simply as fixed geographical entities but as evolving spatial frameworks that have reflected and shaped the movement of people, ideas, goods, capital, institutions, and information. Thus, regional books would move beyond traditional borders to consider the flows that have characterized the global system.

Edited by two of the leading historians in the field, this series will work to synthesize world history for students, engage general readers, and expand the boundaries for scholars.

Plagues in World History by John Aberth
Crude Reality: Petroleum in World History, Updated Edition by Brian C. Black
Smuggling: Contraband and Corruption in World History by Alan L. Karras
The First World War: A Concise Global History, Second Edition by William Kelleher
 Storey
*Insatiable Appetite: The United States and the Ecological Degradation of the Tropical
 World, Concise Revised Edition* by Richard P. Tucker

The First World War

A Concise Global History

Second Edition

William Kelleher Storey

ROWMAN & LITTLEFIELD
Lanham • Boulder • New York • London

Published by Rowman & Littlefield
A wholly owned subsidiary of The Rowman & Littlefield Publishing Group, Inc.
4501 Forbes Boulevard, Suite 200, Lanham, Maryland 20706
www.rowman.com

16 Carlisle Street, London W1D 3BT, United Kingdom

British Library Cataloguing in Publication Information Available

Library of Congress Cataloging-in-Publication Data
Storey, William Kelleher.
The First World War : a concise global history / William Kelleher Storey. — Second
edition.
pages cm. — (Exploring world history)
Includes bibliographical references and index.
ISBN 978-1-4422-2680-7 (cloth : alk. paper) — ISBN 978-1-4422-2681-4 (pbk. : alk.
paper) — ISBN 978-1-4422-2682-1 (electronic)
1. World War, 1914–1918. 2. World War, 1914–1918—Environmental aspects. 3. World
War, 1914–1918—Technology. I. Title.
D523.S745 2014
940.3—dc23
2014008852

Printed in the United States of America

For Robin W. Kilson (1953–2009), humanista semper oppugnans bella imperiaque.

"Qua tibi lucem arte morer?" Virgil, Aeneid, *XII.873–4.*

Contents

Maps   ix

Preface   xi

 1 Introduction   1

 2 Empires, Technologies, and the Origins of War   5

 3 European Rivalries   13

 4 The Crisis of 1914   29

 5 The Western Front, 1914–1915   35

 6 The War in Eastern and Southern Europe, 1914–1915   51

 7 The World War in Africa, 1914–1916   63

 8 The War at Sea, 1914–1915   73

 9 The War in the Middle East, 1914–1916   81

10 The Offensives of 1916   93

11 Naval War and the U.S. Entry, 1916–1917   107

12 The Strains of Total War   115

13 The Offensives of 1917   129

14 Allied Empire-Building, 1916–1918   143

15 The War's End, 1918   151

16 The Peace Settlements   161

17 Understanding and Remembering the War   173

Notes   181

Sources on the First World War   187

Index   195

Maps

This book will include considerable discussion of geography. In order to help readers understand the discussion, I have provided thirteen general maps (listed below). Still, it is not possible for this book to provide a map for every battle. Fortunately, there are some good atlases of the First World War that can be consulted alongside this book. The most accessible is *The Routledge Atlas of the First World War* by Martin Gilbert, which is available in an inexpensive paperback edition. It is also possible to use the battlefield maps that are provided on the Internet site of the history department at the United States Military Academy at West Point. Go to http://www.westpoint.edu/history/SitePages/WWI.aspx. Fifty-two maps are provided, but the first click should be on "World War One Map Symbols," which explains how to read a military map.

MAPS IN THIS BOOK

Europe in 1914, p. 18
The Schlieffen Plan, p. 21
The Battle of the Marne, p. 40
The Western Front, 1915–1917, p. 42
The Eastern Front in 1914, p. 54
The Italian Front, 1915–1918, p. 60
Africa in 1914, p. 67
The North Sea, 1914–1918, p. 75
The Dardanelles Campaign, 1915–1916, p. 83

The Middle East, 1914–1918, p. 88
The Eastern Front, 1914–1918, p. 101
The German Offensives of 1918, p. 155
Postwar Europe, p. 169

Preface

PREFACE TO THE FIRST EDITION

This book has two purposes. The first is to provide a concise narrative history of the First World War for college students and general readers. The second is to present a global history of the war that highlights environmental and technological factors. Taking the environment and technology into account enriches our understanding of the social and political history of the war.

Many people have contributed to my understanding of the First World War. I began to study the war when I was an undergraduate at Harvard, where my tutors, Robin Kilson and Charles Maier, inspired me with their teaching and their writing. In graduate school at Johns Hopkins, my adviser, Philip Curtin, taught me what it meant to write and teach about global environmental history in ways that are socially and politically relevant. My post-doc adviser at Cornell, Sheila Jasanoff, helped me to understand the ways in which histories of technology and the environment could address fundamental questions about power.

My students at Millsaps College prodded me to write this book. In 2003 several students asked me to take a break from teaching my usual classes about world history to teach classes about the world wars. The wars, they claimed, were highly relevant to the current conflicts in the Middle East. I agreed with them, yet I found that the available survey books about the war—which I liked—tried their patience. For that reason, I have made this book as short as a survey of the war can be. I am particularly grateful to one student, MacDougall Womack, for persistent comments and questions. I also received excellent comments and questions from the audience members who heard me give presentations about the First World War at the annual meetings of the American Historical Association and the American Society for

Environmental History. I also gave several presentations about the war at Millsaps College, where colleagues and guests helped me to see my work in an interdisciplinary context. I am also grateful to my dean, Richard Smith, for supporting this project with a development grant and a sabbatical leave, and to Tom Henderson, the college librarian, for providing office space while I was writing. My greatest supporter has been my wife, Joanna Miller Storey, whose love and thoughtfulness stand in contrast to much that is described in this book.

PREFACE TO THE SECOND EDITION

After teaching with my own book for several years, it became clear that the approach of the war's centennial was inspiring a great deal more scholarship that needed to be taken into account in the second edition. The revision of the text benefited from the comments of a new set of anonymous reviewers. The most important revision has been to reorganize the book into more concise, thematic chapters. The second edition also adds more maps, to help students understand better the geography of the war. Once again, the book received support from Millsaps College. Students made many suggestions and a new dean, Keith Dunn, helped with development and sabbatical funds. My wife, Joanna, provided special support for this edition, especially by helping me to show our children the Western Front battlefields for the first time. One can only hope that their generation will not have to learn about the costs of war firsthand.

Chapter One

Introduction

The First World War was a social and political cataclysm. Nine million soldiers died and millions more suffered mental and physical injuries. The war cost billions of dollars, not only in military expenses but also in damage to property. The war emboldened democrats and feminists as well as communists and fascists. During the war, four major empires collapsed. Afterward, the peace settlements changed boundaries around the world. All these things were highly significant for world history. But the thing that most fascinates readers about the First World War is that it seems, in hindsight, to have been avoidable. The war originated in a small conflict in Eastern Europe that snowballed into a much larger conflict. This happened because of disagreements between two groups of allied countries that were committed to rigid military plans. At the outset they took steps that were too aggressive, since none of the participants predicted the war's awfulness.

The main lesson of the war—don't rush into a war, it might be worse than you think—seemed especially pertinent during the Cold War. In those days, it seemed that the alliance systems led by the United States and the Soviet Union were on the brink of nuclear war and that smaller conflicts in Africa, Asia, and the Middle East might escalate into a global holocaust. Many observers were surprised to see the Cold War standoff end rather suddenly in the late 1980s. Authors proclaimed an end to history. It appeared that liberalism and globalization had triumphed. The rigid communist bloc had disintegrated, but globalization made it possible for local conflicts to escalate into worldwide warfare. The Middle East remained a hot spot where interstate conflict was exacerbated by groups of stateless terrorists. On September 11, 2001, Al-Qaida employed the technologies of globalization to launch attacks on New York and Washington, DC. The United States replied by invading Afghanistan in an effort to destroy Al-Qaida and the Taliban. One year later,

1

the United States and its allies began to debate whether or not it was necessary to attack Iraq and what the consequences of such an attack might be. As it turned out, the campaigns in Iraq and Afghanistan that concluded recently ushered in many unintended consequences. Uprisings spread across North Africa and the Middle East, producing some governments that favor—and some governments that do not favor—democracy. Meanwhile, the most feared weapon of the First World War, poison gas, was used by the regime in Syria. Sadly, the First World War remains relevant one hundred years later.

The First World War has inspired more authors to write books and articles than most other topics. Why is there a need for another one? There are excellent survey histories written recently by Adam Hochschild, John Keegan, John Morrow, Michael Neiberg, David Stevenson, and Hew Strachan, as well as provocative works of reinterpretation by Niall Ferguson, Stéphane Audoin-Rouzeau, and Annette Becker. Two television documentaries, featuring the historians Hew Strachan and Jay Winter, have added greatly to public understanding of the war. Yet the new histories of the war either downplay or ignore the history of the environment and technology, two of the most vibrant new fields in the historical profession. This is not to mention that environmental and technological concerns are at the forefront of public debate in the early twenty-first century.

It helps that environmental and technological history have come a long way in the past several decades. It used to be that accounts focused on the ways engineers, inventors, and governments created, distributed, and regulated new tools and systems, as well as humanity's impact on the environment. In the 1970s and 1980s, historians began to focus more on cultural and social dimensions of environment and technology: how people imagine and represent the environment and technology, and how their understandings shape approaches to creating new tools and spaces. Recently, many studies have moved beyond the initiators of environmental and technological change to examine how ordinary users experience and shape environment and technology.

The people who participated in the First World War had an intense experience of environmental conditions and technological changes. The war's planners calculated how many soldiers, horses, and cannons could be moved to the front lines and then pushed through enemy territory. In their plans, they had to balance manpower, technology, and geography. The war itself was fought in a variety of environments. Today we tend to remember the trenches of the Western Front, but the war was fought in open spaces, too, as well as in forests, deserts, and mountains. The war also had an economic and ecological impact far beyond the battlefields. The soldiers who experienced the war reflected on the terrors of new weapons and on the degradation of life in filthy conditions. Artists, musicians, and writers described these conditions in order to make a variety of points against the war—and for it.

Most historians think that they should write about people first and material conditions, such as environment and technology, second. Traditionally, history is about human choices and the consequences of those choices, with the material world consigned to the background. Thus, historians have dismissed works that attribute influence to environmental and technological factors. Such ideas probably explain why historians of the First World War have shied away from environmental and technological history. This is unfortunate. It is no longer sufficient to write about the impact (or lack of impact) of technologies or environmental conditions on politics or society. Today, the best studies examine the ways technology, politics, and society are mutually constituted or "co-produced," a term coined by Bruno Latour and fleshed out by Sheila Jasanoff in a recent book, *States of Knowledge.* Accounts of co-production recognize that nature, objects, states, and societies are not separate categories that impact each other. Instead, they are linked interdependently.

This book is a short narrative history of the First World War that takes into account human decisions and experiences as well as environmental and technological factors. Like any survey history, this work depends on the more specialized publications of other historians. It must be said at the outset that the environmental impact of the war is only coming to be known. Very little research has been done on the ecology of combat zones on the land or on the sea. Likewise, history students await good books and articles about the environmental impact of wartime agricultural and industrial production. My own list of environmental factors extends beyond the impact of the war on specific ecologies. This book will consider the broader issues surrounding food, geography, manpower, and the ways people imagined the landscape. My list of technological factors includes the development of new weapons, which are considered in every history of the First World War, while I will also consider older technologies that remained important, too.

I will not argue that environmental and technological factors simply influenced people. Instead, I will show that human decisions and material conditions were inextricably linked and that the boundaries between the two are very blurry indeed. This book will not make a case that the war introduced radical environmental and technological transformations. Most of the key technologies of the war were refinements of technologies that existed already. Much of the wartime environmental damage associated with the rapid expansion of agriculture, forestry, mining, and industrialization continued previous patterns in a more intensive way. Battlefield landscapes and zones that were occupied and pillaged were severely damaged, but within a few decades people rehabilitated them to the point where they could be used again and even enjoyed.

The war changed the ways people thought about technology and the environment. Before the war, people who lived in Europe and its colonies generally regarded industrial technology as an instrument of progress, while during and after the war significant doubts crept in about the costs of progress. After the war, people did not abandon thoughts of technological progress, but they did have a keener sense of modernity's costs. New technologies pushed minds and bodies to the limits of their capacity, one of the most important intersections of human consciousness and material experiences during the First World War. In the run-up to the war, Europeans saw the landscape with a view to conquering it, dividing it, and ruling it. During and after the war, the costs of conquest became high. Soldiers experienced personal degradation, physical injuries, and mental collapse in the midst of technologically induced environmental conditions, which they remembered when they formed new identities in the postwar world.

Chapter Two

Empires, Technologies, and the Origins of War

It used to be that history textbooks about Europe described the period between 1815 and 1914 as an era of tranquility. It is true that during that time period the most powerful countries in Europe tended not to fight with each other. This tranquility contrasted strongly with the era of the French Revolution and Napoleon (1789–1815), when large numbers of Europeans fought and died for the sake of their nations and empires. In comparison, the period from 1815 to 1914 does seem relatively tranquil. The relative absence of warfare between nations allowed for a major burst in industrialization and technological development, which resulted in disruptions, to be sure, even as the overall standard of living rose in most places.

Yet this era cannot honestly be described as an era of complete tranquility. In the middle of the century, major conflicts were associated with the unification of the German and Italian nations. The Austro-Hungarian Empire and the Ottoman Empire fought to stave off disintegration. Meanwhile, Britain and France—as well as Germany, Italy, Japan, Portugal, Russia, and the United States—expanded their empires. For the most part, their colonies were obtained by shedding the blood of the native inhabitants and, to a lesser extent, the blood of their own soldiers.

The building of nations, empires, and industries was the main feature of European, Japanese, and U.S. history in the period from 1850 to 1914. The times seemed peaceful from the perspective of the industrializing countries, but much of the rest of the world found itself dominated by force. It was hard to resist the industrial countries, which enjoyed a temporary advantage in weapons, communications, and medicine. They harnessed the economies of their colonies in Africa, Asia, and the Pacific to serve their needs, while also

5

reaping profits from investments in parts of the world that were not formally colonized, such as China and Latin America.

Technologically driven dominance fostered a sense of well-being and superiority in the industrializing countries, even as their dominance brought new hopes and miseries to much of the rest of the world.[1] This seems to be a contradiction, but many scholars have concluded that it is not. The prevailing political idea of the nineteenth-century industrial countries was liberalism. Liberals believed in the freedoms guaranteed by such documents as the U.S. Bill of Rights, like freedom of religion and freedom of speech. Liberals also believed in free trade and tended to support laissez-faire economic policies— in other words, those policies that gave business owners a free hand to regulate their own affairs. Liberalism was associated with progressive causes, like the abolition of the slave trade and the emancipation of the slaves. Liberalism was also associated with revolutionary change. British liberals reformed Parliament in 1832 to make it more representative. Liberals on the European continent were associated with movements to overthrow monarchies and to form new nation-states like Germany and Italy. In the United States, liberalism was associated with the Republican Party and with the Union side in the Civil War. In Japan, liberals were led by the Emperor Meiji as they remade their country into a unified, industrializing powerhouse with a constitutional government.

Nineteenth-century liberalism is most often remembered for its positive political accomplishments, yet it had its darker side. Liberal thinkers believed that free markets and unregulated businesses produced the greatest good for the greatest number of people, but many people suffered through wrenching changes in agriculture and industry. Standards of living improved overall, but many people were still miserable. Many liberals turned a blind eye to industrial slums and to rural starvation, too. In the face of mass misery in Ireland during the great famines, or in the working-class neighborhoods of industrial cities like Manchester, liberals often adhered to their faith in free-market solutions, even when the free market did not appear to be helping. Liberals were even able to make themselves comfortable with the use of force to dominate less-developed countries. To liberals it appeared to be folly for Africans and Asians to resist empire-building, because the industrial countries had superior knowledge and technology. Liberal belief in free trade and free government might seem to contradict the spread of empires around the world, but the empire builders often thought that they were doing "the natives" a favor by showing them how to run things. Liberals thought that when Africans and Asians demonstrated that they had assimilated liberal ideas about good government—a process that some liberals likened to children growing up—then they might be ready to rule themselves.[2]

With hindsight, it is possible to see that liberal imperialism contained the seeds of its own destruction. In the colonies, Americans, Europeans, and

Japanese developed ideas about their own racial superiority that they began to employ in their relations with their neighbors. Many Europeans even began to think of themselves as separate races—a French race, a German race, and an Anglo-Saxon or English race—even though millennia of migrations and interactions between Western European countries made such claims historically and biologically preposterous. Familiarity with warfare against colonial "inferiors" also predisposed Americans, Europeans, and Japanese to think that their armies and navies could conquer each other's territories.

EMPIRES AT HIGH TIDE AND LOW TIDE

It seems extraordinary to us today that, only a century ago, most of the countries involved in the First World War were empires, but it must be borne in mind that empire has been the most common form of government throughout world history. Three of the principal countries involved in the First World War were governed by emperors: Austria-Hungary, Germany, and Russia. The Austrian emperor presided over a large territorial empire comprising more than a dozen nationalities, but he was limited in some ways by a constitution. The German emperor had fewer constitutional limitations over his homogeneous empire in central Europe, together with a handful of overseas territories in Africa and Asia. The Russian Empire spread from the Baltic Sea to the Pacific Ocean, and from the Arctic Ocean to the Black Sea, and the Russian emperor had the authority to override all of the constitutional limits that had been placed on him.

To the south, the Ottoman Empire had been fragmenting for some decades, and its sultan had recently been made a figurehead by a junta of modernizing reformers. Even so, the Ottoman Empire still held on to significant territories that stretched from the Mediterranean Sea to the Persian Gulf, including most of the modern Middle East. Another country, Japan, had a constitutional emperor and a small territorial empire, consisting mainly of Korea and Taiwan. Another small territorial empire was possessed by Italy, which had a constitutional monarch. And another country with a constitutional monarchy, Great Britain, possessed enormous territories overseas, some of which were already making the transition to self-government: Australia, Canada, New Zealand, and South Africa. France and the United States were both republics but still retained sizable colonial empires.[3]

At the start of the First World War, possibly the most interesting fact about world geography was that European empires had reached their maximum extent, controlling 84 percent of the planet's land surface. A hundred years before the war, the figure was much smaller. A hundred years after the war, colonial empires will probably be almost completely eliminated. But in

1914, Europe was at the height of its power relative to the rest of the world. Europe's acquisition of colonies had accelerated in the 1870s. The First World War would result in defeat for the Austrian, German, Ottoman, and Russian empires. Russia descended into violent revolution, while Austrian, German, and Ottoman territories were partitioned by the Allies. The British and French empires made a net territorial gain during the First World War, even as their economies were stretched practically to the breaking point. It would not be until the Second World War that their overreaching, plus discontent in the colonies, would result in moves toward decolonization.

In each case of an empire expanding its reach, there were particular circumstances that explain colonial domination. Europeans imposed themselves on vast territories in Africa, Asia, and the Pacific for many different reasons. European businesses exploited colonial resources and asked for support in obtaining land and labor. European settlers went out to start new lives for themselves. European missionaries and philanthropists sought to save souls and improve lives.

There were many specific circumstances that fostered European dominance in particular colonies. Some of them have been explained by authors who write about technology and the environment. Jared Diamond argues in his 1997 book *Guns, Germs, and Steel* that European countries were endowed with natural resources that enabled them to excel in the years after 1492, when their stronger economies made it possible for them to conquer much of the rest of the world. The Western Europeans believed that they were inherently racially superior, but in fact their superiority derived from the way they had adapted to natural resource endowments. The peoples of Eurasia simply had more plants and animals to domesticate, while these resources—as well as disease immunities—could be easily exchanged along a natural east–west corridor. Africa, the Americas, and the Pacific, which would come to be colonized by Europeans, did not have such a corridor, nor did they have a similar set of natural resources. Diamond's explanation helps us to understand that the European colonization of these regions was not somehow the fault of the colonized peoples for being inferior. His work does not shed much light on European empire-building in Asia, nor does he consider the many ways modern people have changed environments and natural resources.

A somewhat different explanation of European dominance was made in a 1981 book by Daniel Headrick called *The Tools of Empire: Technology and European Imperialism in the Nineteenth Century*. Headrick asked why imperialism intensified from 1850 to 1920, while the motivations to conquer other countries remained relatively consistent, generally speaking, from 1492 to the present. Headrick argued that, although motives remained consistent, the means of achieving those motives changed in the late nineteenth century. Before 1850, European technology was not vastly superior to the technologies available in the rest of the world. Key developments in the late nineteenth century, notably in medicine and metallurgy, gave Europeans particular, though temporary, advantages. Research on the causes of malaria, plus the manufacture of quinine, made it possible for Europeans to survive in many parts of the tropics that were previously thought to be "White Men's Graves." Steam engines and steel ships allowed Europeans to dominate the world's coasts and trade routes. The invention of the telegraph and the laying of submarine cables under the oceans made it more efficient to administer colonial governments and businesses, as did the development of better railways.

Headrick, like Diamond, places environment and technology at the center of his explanations of European dominance. From the standpoint of explaining the imperialism before the First World War, perhaps the most immediate developments were improvements in weapons. New weapons were used in Europe, particularly in the short wars that were associated with the unification of Germany and Italy. The struggle over the unification of the United States—the Civil War—was much bloodier, thanks in part to improvements in weaponry. The colonies conquered in the nineteenth century were also a significant proving ground for the new weapons. Firearms technology changed a great deal. The rifles used in the 1850s were muzzle-loaders that could be fired and reloaded from paper cartridges two or three times per minute. In the 1860s, most European armies switched to breechloaders, which could fire upward of a dozen shots per minute, with bullets that were starting to be loaded in metallic cartridges. By the 1890s, breech-loading rifles were equipped with magazines, which increased the rate of fire even more. And the new magazine rifles were firing bullets loaded in metallic cartridges with smokeless powder, which increased the velocity of the bullet while making it easier for the shooters to conceal themselves. Handguns developed along similar lines. The single-shot muzzle-loading pistols of the early nineteenth century were replaced by six-shot revolvers in the 1840s and 1850s. The first semiautomatic pistols appeared in the 1890s and were in widespread use by the First World War.

Smokeless powder, metallic shell cartridges, and breech-loading were increasingly features of artillery, too. But still the cannons recoiled after every shot and had to be repositioned, reaimed, and reloaded. Starting in the 1890s, new recoilless cannons were equipped with an oiled pneumatic slide for the barrel, so that a fired barrel slid back and popped forward without rocking the carriage out of position. A cannon that did not recoil and that could be loaded from the breech could be fired a dozen times every minute without reaiming.

In the late nineteenth century, rates of artillery, pistol, and rifle fire increased dramatically, but perhaps the most dramatic innovation in firing speed was the machine gun. The first machine guns were produced during the U.S. Civil War of 1861–1865. They were hand-cranked devices with multiple barrels that were capable of firing long, dense bursts of bullets. Their use was inhibited by their weight; they were so heavy that they had to be mounted on artillery gun carriages. In the 1880s, heavy single-barrel machine guns were invented by Hiram Maxim. These could achieve a rate of fire upward of five or six hundred rounds per minute. Their bulk required a team of several soldiers to serve them. The fact that their barrels were cooled by water meant that soldiers had to continuously drain and replenish the tanks. Even so, they were used to great effect in the colonial warfare of the 1890s. By the time of the First World War, several countries had adopted lighter versions of the Maxim design, while other designs that were even lighter and more mobile were becoming available.

Several wars around the turn of the century demonstrated that the new weapons were transforming the nature of combat. In 1898, a young British army lieutenant, Winston Churchill, participated in the battle of Omdurman in Sudan. This was an engagement that pitted the British army and its Egyptian allies, on the one side, and the forces of the Mahdi on the other. In one of his first books, *The River War*, Churchill described the futile charge of the "Dervishes," the followers of the late Islamic leader, the Mahdi, against the British positions. About fifty thousand Dervishes (or Mahdists), armed with outmoded rifles and bearing banners with verses from the Quran, lined up opposite a long line of eight thousand British and seventeen thousand Egyptian soldiers, who had their backs to the Nile River. The Mahdist forces began to charge across an open plain. At a range just under three thousand meters, the British and Egyptian forces opened fire. Remembering the charge of the Mahdists, Churchill wrote:

> Did they realize what would come to meet them? They were in a dense mass, 2,800 yards from the 32nd Field Battery and the gunboats. The ranges were known. It was a matter of machinery. The more distant slaughter passed unnoticed, as the mind was fascinated by the approaching horror. In a few seconds swift destruction would rush on these brave men. They topped the crest and drew out into full view of the whole army. Their white banners made them conspicuous above all. As they saw the camp of their enemies, they discharged their rifles with a great roar of musketry and quickened their pace. For a moment the white flags advanced in regular order, and the whole division crossed the crest and were exposed. Forthwith the gunboats, the 32nd British Field Battery, and other guns from the *zeriba* opened fire on them. About twenty shells struck them in the first minute. Some burst high in the air, others exactly in their faces. Others, again, plunged into the sand and, exploding, dashed clouds of red dust, splinters, and bullets amid their ranks. The white banners toppled over in all directions. Yet they rose again immediately, as other men pressed forward to die for the Mahdi's sacred cause.

The charge continued. As the Mahdists drew closer, British and Egyptian troops began firing at them from Maxim guns and rifles, too. Churchill continued:

> Eight hundred yards away a ragged line of men were coming on desperately, struggling forward in the face of the pitiless fire—white banners tossing and collapsing; white figures subsiding in dozens to the ground; little white puffs from their rifles, larger white puffs spreading in a row all along their front from the bursting shrapnel. . . . The tiny figures seen over the slide of the backsight seemed a little larger, but also fewer at each successive volley. . . . The empty cartridge cases, tinkling to the ground, formed a small but growing heap beside each man. And all the time out on the plain on the other side bullets were shearing through flesh, smashing and splintering bone; blood spouted from terrible wounds; valiant men were struggling on through a hell of whistling metal, exploding shells, and spurting dust—suffering, despairing, dying.[4]

By the end of the Battle of Omdurman, more than ten thousand Mahdist soldiers lay dead. Thousands more were wounded or taken prisoner. By contrast, on the British and Egyptian side, forty-eight were killed and several hundred wounded.

The new weapons made it very difficult for an army to rush an opponent's position. In order to attack successfully, armies would have to adapt their tactics. Ideally, attacking forces would need to have numerical superiority. They would also need to precede an attack with a heavy artillery bombardment. It appeared that the new weapons gave defenders a significant advantage. This was seen at Omdurman and time and time again in colonial warfare during the late nineteenth century. It was also seen as early as the U.S. Civil War and as recently as the war between Russia and Japan that took place in 1904–1905. Before and during the First World War, the new weapons proved to be formidable assets in the hands of defenders. Significant efforts were made to overcome the new weapons by developing new tactics and new technologies.

Chapter Three

European Rivalries

In the late nineteenth century, Britain was not the only country to harness new ideas and new technologies to expand its territory. France gained huge new territories in Africa that stretched from the Mediterranean to the Congo, as well as the present-day countries of Vietnam, Laos, and Cambodia. Asia's rising power, Japan, conquered Korea and Taiwan at the expense of the declining Chinese Empire. The United States defeated the declining Spanish Empire in a short, sharp war in 1898 that resulted in the transfer of Cuba, Puerto Rico, and other islands in the West Indies, plus the Philippines. To many people in the United States and Japan, the old empires of Spain and China seemed ripe for the picking. The United States made promises to nationalists in all their colonies that imperial rule would result in self-governance, but the United States also fought a brutal war against Philippine guerrillas who wanted to achieve independence quickly, on their own terms. Japanese rule in Korea and Taiwan was generally repressive and was deeply resented by Chinese and Korean nationalists.

The American, British, French, and Japanese empires appeared to be on the rise. Several empires, like the Chinese and Spanish, as well as the Austro-Hungarian, Ottoman, and Russian empires, appeared to be in trouble. None had embraced industrialization as early or as extensively as the rising powers. The Russians fought the Japanese from 1904 to 1905. The Japanese navy sank a large portion of the Russian navy at the battle of Tsushima while the Japanese army inflicted heavy casualties on the Russians at the battle of Mukden. Russia faced challenges within its borders, too, both from moderate politicians who wanted to put constitutional limits on the tsar and from socialist revolutionaries. National groups within the Russian Empire, including Finns, Poles, and Ukrainians, clamored for independence, while the empire's large Jewish population experienced—and resented—terrible periods of persecution known as "pogroms." Many Jews turned to Zionism, the belief in the creation of a separate Jewish state. Independence movements were strong in the Austro-Hungarian Empire, too. Ties of personal loyalty to the Catholic, German-speaking Austrian emperor no longer appeared likely to keep in check the national aspirations of the empire's Catholic Croatians, Czechs, Hungarians, Italians, Poles, Slovaks, and Slovenes, not to mention its Orthodox Serbs, its Bosnian Muslims, and a number of other ethnic groups who were Catholic, Orthodox, or Muslim.

THE GERMAN QUESTION

The new empire of Germany sought to find a role for itself in the era of industrialization and empire-building. Germany was industrializing rapidly and was exceeding all other nations in the quality and volume of its productivity. All the while, German agriculture remained highly productive. German universities were generally recognized to be the best in the world, while German literature, music, and philosophy were widely admired, too. Yet this was not enough for many Germans, who wished their country to have a colonial empire as well as a dominant army and navy. The First World War's origins stem largely from the rise of Germany to the status of a great power. For this reason Germany's rise requires careful explanation.

Before the 1840s, the German-speaking people of Central Europe did not have their own national government. Instead, Germany was divided into many different countries with many different sorts of governments. Between the 1840s and the 1870s, Germany was united by the government of Prussia, a state centered around Berlin in the northeastern part of Germany. Prussia was led by kings from the Hohenzollern family with the help of brilliant aristocratic politicians like Otto von Bismarck, who led the negotiations for Germany's new federal constitution.

Prussia united the small, German-speaking states of Central Europe into one federation by means of alliances and warfare. The final war of 1870 resulted in the incorporation of the southwestern state of Bavaria. This move was resisted by the French emperor, Napoleon III. The French were defeated by the Prussians, who seized the French provinces of Alsace and Lorraine, on the west side of the Rhine River. Major upheavals in France resulted in the collapse of Napoleon III's government. Napoleon's imperial government was replaced by a republic, while French nationalists nursed a grudge against Germany for seizing French territory. A French man, Robert Poustis, recalled, "When I was a boy, in school and with the family, we often spoke about the lost provinces—Alsace-Lorraine, which had been stolen from France after the war of 1870. We wanted to get them back. In the schools the lost provinces were marked in a special color on all the maps, as if we were in mourning for them."[1] This widely shared sense of grievance was palpable, and it even found its expression in imaginative geographical representations on maps. These imaginative representations flew in the face of some complex realities. Alsace and Lorraine contained many German-speakers as well as quite a few people who spoke both German and French. Like many parts of Europe, it was an ethnic and linguistic hodgepodge that became subject to strident nationalist claims.

After defeating the French and incorporating Bavaria, the German federation was renamed the German Empire. Germany faced two related problems, one internal and one external. The external problem had to do with geography and the frequently expressed aim of French nationalist politicians to regain Alsace and Lorraine. So long as Germany held Alsace and Lorraine, it could count on France to be an enemy. With an enemy on the western border, the Germans had to make sure that they had good relations with their neighbors to the east, in Russia, and their neighbors to the southeast, in Austria-Hungary. The Austrians at least shared a common language with Germany and, in many respects, a common culture. That was not the case with Russia. Russia became a central preoccupation of German diplomacy in the 1870s and 1880s. The German government worked to ensure that Russia remained friendly—or at least neutral. Relations with Britain were important, too. Britain possessed the world's largest navy, which could easily choke off Germany's access to the North Sea and the wider world. Britain had a long-standing policy of avoiding alliances with other countries. This made an alliance between Britain and Germany unlikely. It was also important for Germany to remain on cordial terms with Britain, so that Britain would not be driven to change its policy and ally itself with France.

Germany's external, geographical predicament was tempered by an internal political problem. In 1848, revolutions swept Western and Central Europe, with socialists playing prominent roles in the upheavals. Socialist threats to abolish private property and to have governments own farms and factories frightened the middle classes, who were prospering as Europe industrialized. In order to fend off socialism, middle-class Germans threw their support behind the unification of Germany under Prussian leadership, even though this meant that they would be governed by autocratic emperors and their supporters in the Prussian military. Government by soldiers and emperors was preferable to government by socialists—at least the emperor would not take away middle-class property.

The downside to this bargain for educated, middle-class Germans was that the new government was not fully accountable. The legislature was divided into two parts. The upper house comprised representatives of the states. The lower house was elected by all males over the age of twenty-five. The legislature had the right to approve the imperial budget and to regulate the size of the military. It authorized numerous national institutions, including the full range of national bureaucracies. But beyond domestic affairs its powers were limited. The legislature had no control over the army, navy, or foreign affairs, which were the prerogative of the kaiser. He continued to appoint all officers in the Prussian army, who swore an oath of personal loyalty to him, not to the imperial government. The imperial armed forces were dominated by Prussia, although leaders of the other states appointed their own officers. The Prussian king's chief minister, the minister-president, managed civil and foreign affairs, but even he had little influence over the generals, who answered directly to the king. As Prussia formed the new German Empire by federating itself with more German states, the king of Prussia became the German emperor, or kaiser, and his minister-president became the German chancellor. Each state retained its own government, law, and tax system, although a national tax was also put into place in most states. Most states also participated in national postal and telegraph systems. All state armies were commanded by the kaiser, who took control of collective foreign policy, too.

The Prussian system worked well enough so long as the kaiser was dependable. Dependability was certainly one of the traits of Kaiser Wilhelm I, who ruled from 1858 to 1888. He was an authoritarian who relied on his highly resourceful, conservative minister-president, Bismarck, to achieve German unification. After unification was achieved in 1870, Bismarck crafted a foreign policy that recognized Germany's geographic vulnerabilities. The enmity of France was guaranteed, so Bismarck secured treaties with Germany's other neighbors that aimed to isolate France and to protect Germany's southern and eastern borders. The key to security in the south and east was to prevent conflict between Austria-Hungary and Russia over former Ottoman territories in the Balkans. In 1873, Bismarck orchestrated an agreement between Germany, Austria-Hungary, and Russia called the Three Emperors League. This was not a formal alliance, but an undertaking on the part of Austria-Hungary and Russia to allow Germany to mediate their disputes. The league faded in the late 1870s but was renewed in 1881. In the meantime, in 1879 Bismarck negotiated an alliance with Austria-Hungary, the Dual Alliance, which expanded to include Italy in 1882 and then was known as the Triple Alliance. The Austrians and Russians were not willing to sign an alliance, but, to avoid war with Russia, in 1887 Bismarck negotiated the Reinsurance Treaty, which stated that if either Germany or Russia were attacked, the other country would remain neutral. Given the limitations of geography, the enmity of France, and the hostility between Austria-Hungary and Russia, this was the best possible diplomatic solution.[2]

German foreign policy was controlled by the kaiser, who delegated authority to the chancellor. Chancellor Bismarck served at the pleasure of Kaiser Wilhelm I. When Wilhelm I died in 1889, he was succeeded by his son, Friedrich, who died after only three months. Friedrich's son, the thirty-year-old Wilhelm II, then succeeded to the imperial throne. Kaiser Wilhelm II was aggressive and unbalanced. An accident at birth left him with a crippled left arm. He compensated for his physical disability by making public appearances in a wide array of fancy naval and military costumes; by making a point of excelling at riding, shooting, and other physical activities that were not easy with one arm; and by gaining a reputation as a domineering yet superficial conversationalist and speechmaker. He was overbearing and insecure—not the sort of dependable leader who could be relied upon to manage Germany's delicate internal and external problems.

Kaiser Wilhelm II clashed immediately with Bismarck over social policy. Wilhelm favored social reforms as a way of persuading working-class voters to turn away from socialism; Bismarck favored repression. In 1890, after socialists made gains in the elections to the legislature, Wilhelm fired Bismarck. Bismarck's successor as chancellor, Leo von Caprivi, persuaded Wilhelm that the Triple Alliance between Germany, Austria-Hungary, and Italy was inconsistent with the Reinsurance Treaty between Germany and Russia. They dropped the Reinsurance Treaty and strengthened the Triple Alliance. Almost immediately, Russia began to negotiate with France. France and Russia drew closer over the course of the 1890s, and by 1899 the two countries had signed a military alliance. They pledged to attack Germany if either country were attacked by Germany. Even if Germany or its allies mobilized their armies, France and Russia pledged to mobilize theirs.[3] The alliance between France and Russia was Bismarck's geographical nightmare come true: Germany was now surrounded by enemies working together.

This fundamental problem in diplomacy and geography came to dominate the thinking of Germany's military planners. It was related to a fundamental problem in manpower. The German army was recruited mainly from the countryside. The officers tended to be the sons of landowners while the enlisted men tended to be the sons of peasants. Composing the army in this way ensured that it remained conservative; including large numbers of city-dwellers might make it more liberal. When France and Russia threatened to surround Germany, one possible response would have been to draft more recruits from the city as well as from the country. Such a move did not meet with the approval of most German generals. Urban, middle-class officers were likely to be more critical of policy, while urban working-class men might "infect" the army with socialism. Fearing such a result, the kaiser and his generals tried to make do with the army they had. This decision meant that the German government had to encourage the military reliability of its allies, Austria-Hungary and Italy. And the army would have to plan and train as well as adopt new technologies in order to maximize its efficiency in strategy, operations, and tactics.[4]

In the minds of some prominent Germans, efficiency was a necessity for survival. A professor and popular lecturer from the University of Berlin,

Europe in 1914

Heinrich von Treitschke, wrote in the late 1890s that "Without war no State could be. All those we know of arose through war, and the protection of their members by armed force remains their primary and essential task. War, therefore, will endure to the end of history, as long as there is multiplicity of States. The laws of human thought and of human nature forbid any alternative, neither is one to be wished for." For Treitschke, war was a natural and positive state. His thoughts were echoed by the German general Friedrich von Bernhardi, who believed that war was a natural and positive part of human evolution. In his popular book *Germany and the Next War*, Bernhardi wrote:

> This aspiration [for the abolition of war] is directly antagonistic to the great universal laws which rule all life. War is a biological necessity of the first importance, a regulative element in the life of mankind which cannot be dispensed with, since without it an unhealthy development will follow, which excludes every advancement of the race, and therefore all real civilization. "War is the father of all things." The sages of antiquity long before Darwin recognized this.
>
> The struggle for existence is, in the life of Nature, the basis of all healthy development. All existing things show themselves to be the result of contesting forces. So in the life of man the struggle is not merely the destructive, but the life-giving principle. "To supplant or to be supplanted is the essence of life," says Goethe, and the strong life gains the upper hand. The law of the

stronger holds good everywhere. Those forms survive which are able to pro-
cure themselves the most favorable conditions of life and to assert themselves
in the universal economy of Nature. The weaker succumb. . . . The man of
strong will and strong intellect tries by every means to assert himself, the
ambitious strive to rise, and in this effort the individual is far from being
guided merely by the consciousness of right.[5]

Not all Germans believed this kind of rhetoric, in which warfare was
described as natural and positive. It is significant, though, that Treitschke and
Bernhardi were popular and had followers in the military. If enough people
came to believe that war was a natural and biologically essential activity,
then when a crisis came it would seem natural to take steps toward conflict.

PLANNING FOR WAR

When German generals realized that there was a real possibility of a simultaneous war against France and Russia, they began to develop a plan that
maximized the use of available manpower. Manpower—and the capacity of
the state to manage it—became the central resource concern of the war that
followed. Another key factor in war planning and war fighting involved
soldiers in responding creatively to the challenges of geography and technology. As we have seen, weapons such as quick-firing field artillery, machine
guns, and breech-loading rifles were making warfare more lethal. Already in
the U.S. Civil War and in the Russo-Japanese War, soldiers had responded to
the new weapons by digging trenches. Keeping armies in trenches for long
periods of time was expensive, while waging war without achieving objectives was unpopular. These problems were familiar to generals, politicians,
and intellectuals. Karl Marx's collaborator, Friedrich Engels, predicted in
1887 that there would soon be a devastating war in which eight to ten million
people would die. Helmuth von Moltke, retiring as Germany's chief general
in 1890, warned German legislators that wars between European states were
no longer going to be small. In the future, there would be a devastating
"people's war" lasting for years. The Polish banker Ivan Bloch warned spe-
cifically about the deadliness of the new weapons. He predicted that a future
war would feature trench warfare, high mortality, and economic ruin. Sadly,
Bloch concluded that the nations of Europe would appreciate the nature of
the problem and do everything possible to prevent war's outbreak.[6]

To make matters more challenging, the French had built heavy fortifications along their relatively short border with Germany and also in the vicinity
of Paris. By contrast, Russia, which then shared a long border with Germany,
was a vast country. In 1812, when Napoleon invaded, the Russians used their
geography as a weapon. They burned their own people's farms and towns,
calculating that Napoleon's army could not march all the way to Moscow

carrying their own supplies. The Russians were correct. Napoleon's army was defeated, and only a remnant made it back to Paris alive.

Germany's leading generals dreaded the prospect of a two-front war against Russia and France, but, in the event that this should happen, the German general staff made contingency plans. Before the 1890s, such plans were almost entirely defensive. The generals believed that it would prove impossible to break through France's defenses. Instead, they prepared to defend Germany from a French invasion. In the east, they planned to advance into Russian Poland and build fortifications. An advancing Russian army would hopefully be defeated, but pursuit into the Russian heartland was thought to be a bad idea. When the German generals imagined how to fight a two-front war, they concluded that geography forced them to fight defensively.

In 1891, as the French and Russians were drawing closer to each other, the new chief of the German general staff, General Alfred von Schlieffen, began to work on a bold new plan that would allow the German army to go on the offensive. First, the German army would throw most of its weight at the French, whose army could mobilize—or get to the battlefield—relatively quickly. Then, after defeating France, the Germans would transport most of their army to the east, where they would defeat the slow Russian army. German troops would have to be moved quickly to the border with France and then quickly to the border with Russia, a plan that depended heavily on railroads and telegraphs. This could be done according to complex timetables created by German officers. The trick lay in defeating France very quickly.

Schlieffen dedicated his tenure as chief of staff to imagining and planning for this two-front war. During the mid-1890s, he worked on the details of a plan to use heavy artillery to demolish French forts. Much to his chagrin, testing revealed that this might not work quickly enough. Next Schlieffen sketched plans for the German army to go around French fortifications by invading through Luxembourg and the south of Belgium. This would violate the neutrality of these countries and possibly draw Britain into the conflict—Britain guaranteed the neutrality of Belgium by treaty. Britain was likely to have practical problems with a German occupation of Belgium. Belgian ports were only a stone's throw across the North Sea from the east coast of England. The possibility of provoking the British caused the German generals some concern, but, as the British army was small, Schlieffen discounted it as a short-term threat.

As Schlieffen developed his plan, in 1905 he began to realize that he needed to strike France even harder than he had thought previously. Now most of the manpower of the German army would line up against France. The left wing, in the south, would withdraw from Alsace-Lorraine back to defensive positions in Germany while the right wing, to the north, would move through all of Belgium and Luxembourg, plus the southernmost corner of the Netherlands, and drive toward the coast. Near the coast, it would turn south in a giant hooking motion to surround Paris from behind. The French army would be surprised and defeated. Paris would fall to the Germans, who would then send most of their troops back east to face the Russians.

Schlieffen's plan was a gamble. The gamble was based on elaborate calculations about the movement of army units by rail and road, yet even with all the careful study there were few certainties. With training, the German army could be relied upon to mobilize quickly. With planning, the German railroads could carry troops to their destinations. But how hard would the French resist? Would the small Belgian army surrender? Or would it fight and thereby stall the Germans? Would Britain intervene more quickly than was thought possible? Britain and Belgium could only put small forces in the field, but they did not need to defeat the Germans in battle. All the British and Belgians had to do was delay the Germans. If the German attack slowed down even by a few days, the Russians might have time to capture Berlin.

The most important variable was the speed of Russian mobilization: how quickly could the Russians get an army into the field and across the German border? Schlieffen calculated that the Germans had forty-two days to defeat the French. The Austro-Hungarian army would help to pin down Russian

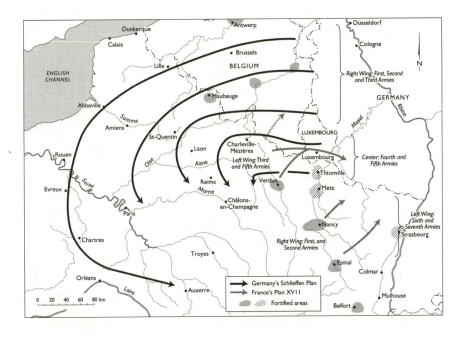

The Schlieffen Plan

forces, but only in the southeast. By forty-two days, the Russians would be on the eastern border of Germany, within striking range of Berlin. The massive attack on France made it necessary to leave only a small part of the German army in the east, where it would be used only for defensive purposes. With the Russians bearing down on Berlin, there was no room for error in France. A delay of a day or two could cost Germany its own capital city.

Schlieffen became obsessed with his plan's details. The key element involved sufficient manpower traversing geography, a basic environmental and technological problem. In a short period of time, was it possible to funnel enough German troops and supplies through Belgium in order to ensure a forty-two-day victory in France? The Belgians and French would destroy their railroads, making it necessary for German soldiers to advance on foot. Could the roads hold all of them? On the right or northern wing, Schlieffen planned to deploy thirty army corps, approximately one million men plus their equipment and horses. This was the figure thought to be necessary to defeat France, yet there were geographical limitations to their deployment. Each army corps consisted of two divisions, each with 17,500 men. In ideal circumstances, an army corps did not advance in one long column but in multiple columns running in parallel. If a corps had plenty of parallel roads, it could advance between twenty-nine and thirty-two kilometers in a day. If the corps started at dawn, by dusk the tail end of the column would have enough time to catch up with the head. In Belgium and northern France, parallel roads could be found within one or two kilometers of each other, but the front only extended three hundred kilometers. This left only ten kilometers of front for each army corps. Given that there might only be between five and ten parallel roads, a corps could not advance the full twenty-nine to thirty-two kilometers in a day and still have the tails of the columns catching up to the heads. Based on this evidence, the historian John Keegan concludes that Schlieffen's plan was a geographical impossibility. Schlieffen himself recognized that too few troops were assigned to the northern, right wing. He urged the addition of eight army corps, even though he knew that the roads could not carry them quickly enough. [7]

After Schlieffen's retirement in 1906, the German general staff was led by Helmuth von Moltke the Younger, so called because he was the nephew of the elder Helmuth von Moltke, who had died in 1891. Moltke the Younger diminished some of the military and political risks of Schlieffen's plan. In the original plan, the German army withdrew from Alsace-Lorraine in order to ensure the strength of the northern flank. Now Moltke hesitated to make Germany vulnerable to a French thrust across the Rhine and made plans to hold Alsace-Lorraine, reinforcing it with several divisions taken from the north. The original plan had the German army crossing through the southernmost corner of the Netherlands, an act that would have created another small but significant enemy for Germany. Moltke's revision to Schlieffen's plan eliminated this move. The north wing would not move through the Netherlands, only through Belgium and Luxembourg. With the north wing reduced in mobility and size, it was expected not to range as far into French territory, but it was hoped that its size was still sufficient to defeat the French. Even the revised plan was still offensive and inflexible.

From the 1890s to 1914, French and Russian planners also shifted from defensive to offensive operations. And like the Germans, they adopted inflexible plans that played down the realities of geography and technology. The French made plans between 1898 and 1909 that all involved deploying troops defensively along the French border, with the later plans placing larger numbers of troops near Belgium. The later plans also relied more heavily on the use of army reservists. In 1911, the leading French general, Victor Michel, proposed further modifications along these lines—completely incorporating the reserves with active-duty forces and planning for a preemptive strike into Belgium. Still, even under Michel, the French plans remained basically defensive in nature. But later in 1911, France's new right-wing government sacked the left-leaning Michel and replaced him with General Joseph Joffre. Joffre developed a plan, known as Plan XVII, that committed the French army to an offensive in order to recapture Alsace and Lorraine. Having restored French prestige, they would then punch into the center of Germany. From there it would be a long, deadly march to Berlin. The French army chose offense over defense for political reasons—right-wing politicians hoped to restore the glory of France. They hoped that they could make such a rapid advance that they could overcome the German army and the defensive firepower of the new weapons.

The Russians resisted French pressure on them to mobilize quickly. Russian generals recognized that the size of Russia and its relative technological backwardness would delay sending the country's active-duty troops into the field. Its reserve forces could take months. Between 1910 and 1914, the Russian army pledged to help France by mobilizing its most efficient units to attack Germany within sixteen days.[8]

As the French persuaded the Russians to make specific commitments to deploy troops, they also met with the British, even though the British were not formally allied with them. In 1911, France's chief general, Joseph Joffre, met with his British counterpart, Sir Henry Wilson, to discuss how Britain's small army might be included in Plan XVII in case war broke out on the continent. Wilson began to plan for a British deployment of six infantry divisions and one cavalry division to Belgium. Wilson did not make any definite commitments to Joffre, yet it increasingly appeared that Britain would join France against Germany. Many people in Britain saw France as a historic enemy. And many British people, with their ancient rights and liberties guaranteed by their government, were loath to ally themselves with

Russia's autocratic tsar. The British drift toward Russia and France can be explained, in part, by the kaiser's diplomacy. His desire to challenge British naval supremacy put a real strain on Anglo-German relations.

THE NAVAL ARMS RACE

Manpower, geography, and technology were the prime considerations as Germany, France, and Russia planned for war. One of the most sensible ways for Germany to overcome the challenges of geography and technology would have been to foster an alliance with Britain. The British government even approached the German government on several occasions. In 1895, Britain floated the idea of an Anglo-German partition of the Ottoman Empire; in 1898, as the French and Russians were moving close toward formalizing a military alliance, Britain and Germany had preliminary discussions about forming one of their own. Such an alliance would have made sense for a number of reasons. Britain's power at sea and its colonial empire would have complemented Germany's power on land and its dominance of central Europe. The countries had dynastic ties, too. The British royal family was of German descent. Kaiser Wilhelm II's mother was the daughter of Queen Victoria, who was married to a German, Prince Albert.

Yet family ties could only help so much. The kings and queens of Britain had influence in British politics but little real power. By contrast, Kaiser Wilhelm II controlled Germany's army and foreign policy, although, practically speaking, his superficiality enabled his generals and diplomats to run things on a day-to-day basis. If anything, Wilhelm's personality was an object lesson in the need to saddle monarchs with constitutional limits. One of Wilhelm's personal quirks was that he simultaneously envied and hated Britain. His animosity was personal. His left arm was deformed because of an accident at birth; he blamed his mother's physician, who was British. His mother was a pro-British liberal; Wilhelm rejected his mother by becoming an anti-British conservative. Wilhelm embraced German national romanticism, whose adherents typically believed that, while Germans improved themselves by cultivating the arts and philosophy, the British were a crass and materialistic nation of industrialists and merchants.

Wilhelm's anti-liberal, anti-British sentiments, coupled with his impulsiveness, kept Britain and Germany apart. During the late 1890s, without properly consulting German diplomats, Wilhelm publicly supported South Africa's Boers, many of whom were resisting Britain's efforts to incorporate their independent republics into a British-dominated South African confederation. As much as Wilhelm criticized British imperialism, he was like many prominent Germans in that he himself was an imperialist. But by the time Wilhelm II took power in 1888, there was not much left to acquire. Bismarck had initially been skeptical about controlling overseas territories, but in the early 1880s he persuaded Wilhelm I to acquire several colonies in Africa, including the countries known today as Cameroon, Namibia, Tanzania, and Togo. In the Pacific, Wilhelm I also acquired the northeast part of Papua New Guinea as well as several island groups to the north. Under Wilhelm II, Germany acquired several more islands in the Pacific. In 1898, he acquired a more significant possession: the port of Jiaozhou on the north coast of China, which Germany developed as a naval base. In 1899, Germany averted a naval clash with Britain and the United States over the islands of Samoa, when Wilhelm agreed to a partition.

Disputes over small islands in the Pacific were indicative of a larger problem: a naval arms race between Britain and Germany. Between 1890 and 1914, German naval policies challenged Britain's leadership at sea, thanks in large part to Wilhelm II. He had spent childhood summers with his English relatives at Osborne House, a royal residence on the Isle of Wight, near the Royal Yacht Club at Cowes. Wilhelm became an avid sailor. For several years after he became kaiser, he raced yachts at Cowes, where his membership was sponsored by his uncle, the future King Edward VII. The Royal Yacht Club lay only a few miles away from the Royal Navy's base at Portsmouth. Wilhelm's visits to the ships inspired him to build a great navy for Germany. In 1904, on the occasion of King Edward's visit to the German naval base at Kiel, Wilhelm reminisced with his dinner guests: "When, as a little boy, I was allowed to visit Portsmouth and Plymouth hand in hand with kind aunts and friendly admirals, I admired the proud English ships in those two superb harbors. Then there awoke in me the wish to build ships of my own like these someday, and when I was grown up to possess as fine a navy as the English." The German chancellor, Bernhard von Bülow, altered the transcript of the speech for the press. He removed the kaiser's anecdotes, lest the kaiser's juvenile remarks jeopardize the budget for naval construction.[9]

Naval ships had become very costly, thanks to a revolution in construction. In the eighteenth century, navies relied on wooden sailing ships. Large, triple-decker ships of the line, bristling with ninety cannons, fought the main battles. Faster, lightly armed frigates patrolled the seas and protected merchant vessels. During the French Revolution and the Napoleonic Wars, well-built frigates such as the U.S.S. *Constitution* began to dominate the seas. By the middle of the nineteenth century, sails were being replaced by steam engines; wooden hulls were being replaced by steel; and cannons peering through portholes were being replaced by gun turrets rotating on the main deck. The battleships of the 1880s and 1890s typically mounted four large guns with a diameter of eleven or twelve inches, two per turret, plus varying numbers of medium and small guns. At the end of the nineteenth century, the British navy dwarfed all other navies, while for the most part its ships were technically superior.

Battleships were costly to build, maintain, and operate, yet Wilhelm and his chief admiral, Alfred von Tirpitz, were determined to build a navy that would rival Britain's. In 1898, they persuaded Germany's parliament, the Reichstag, to fund the construction of twelve battleships. In 1900, they obtained a long-term commitment to build nineteen. The German construction program, coupled with the kaiser's support for the Boers, ensured that the British would respond in kind. A naval arms race began, shaped by a technological revolution in naval architecture.

As a rule, larger guns fire farther and more accurately than smaller guns. For this reason, around 1900 naval architects began to contemplate eliminating most of the smaller guns from battleships. In a battle, the most decisive shooting would be done by big guns at long distances. In 1905, Britain began work on a new, revolutionary battleship, the *Dreadnought*. The ship was bigger than most previous battleships, with a new hull design, heavy armor plating, and new engines with turbines that were faster and more reliable than the older battleships' piston engines. Most impressively, the *Dreadnought* mounted ten twelve-inch cannons on five turrets.

The *Dreadnought*'s trials at sea demonstrated its superiority to the old design. Between 1906 and 1913, the British produced thirty *Dreadnought*-style battleships, with increasingly powerful armaments: by 1913, the new battleships were mounting fifteen-inch guns. Britain also produced ten *Dreadnought*-style battlecruisers, ships that had weapons and engines that were similar to the battleships but had less armor. Less armor resulted in greater speed at the cost of greater vulnerability.

Germany responded by building its own *Dreadnought*-style battleships and battlecruisers. This posed a problem: the ships would be too large to pass through the Kiel Canal, which connected the North Sea to the Baltic Sea. The Reichstag funded the widening of the canal as well as the enlargement of previously authorized battleships. In 1908, the Reichstag passed another "Naval Law" that allowed for the construction of three *Dreadnought*-style battleships each year. All told, from 1906 to 1913 Germany built nineteen *Dreadnought*-style battleships and seven battlecruisers. Germany was not able to match Britain battleship for battleship, but now the German navy did pose a significant threat to British dominance at sea. Other countries got into the act, too. Austria-Hungary built four; France built seven; Italy built six; Japan built six; Spain built three; Russia built seven; the United States built fourteen. Argentina bought two from the United States; Brazil bought three from Britain.

Britain met the challenge from Germany, but the numbers of *Dreadnought*-style battleships do not tell the whole story. Many navies relied on smaller ships, too, including medium-sized cruisers and smaller destroyers. These could move more quickly than battleships and were better suited to protecting coastlines and trade routes. Smaller destroyers and a new type of ship, the submarine, could lay mines and fire torpedoes. These were weapons that posed a significant threat to all ships, including battleships.

All battleships were not created equal, either. Germany had fewer battleships, but they were better designed and better built than their British counterparts. German guns were lighter and made from better-quality steel. They fired shells propelled by better-quality powder that was contained in safer casings. German gun turrets were safer, too. German ships also had better armor than the British ships, as did the ships of Japan and the United States. Recognizing that heavy shells fired from long distances could hit the sides and also plunge onto the decks of ships, German, Japanese, and American designers armored the top decks, while the top decks of British ships remained relatively thin. German machinery and optics were superior, too. Even though many Germans thought that they had lost an expensive arms race against Britain, in fact their fleet was quite formidable. Used in the right ways, it could pose a significant threat to Britain.

The construction of the German navy damaged relations with Britain, a country that would have made a useful ally, given that Kaiser Wilhelm II's botched diplomacy had resulted in an alliance between France and Russia. To the east and west and now out on the North Sea, Germany faced determined enemies. Germany's main allies, Austria and Italy, were not completely reliable. Germany's geographic predicament fostered insecurity. Its industrial, military, and naval achievements made it formidable. And its leaders made it dangerous.

Chapter Four

The Crisis of 1914

In hindsight, it seems that by the decade of the 1910s, Europe was poised on the brink of a major conflict. Yet nobody could have predicted how, when, or where a conflict might break out. In fact, historians should be wary of making it seem like a conflict was inevitable. As it happened in the summer of 1914, the world war was touched off by a crisis over nationalist aspirations in the Balkans that spread because of a series of political miscalculations. The diplomatic crisis during the summer of 1914 has been the subject of detailed investigations by many scholars. Most agree that the war resulted from unfortunate decision-making on the part of civilian and military leaders who were rushed by the nature of war plans. The war plans, as we have already seen, were created as a way to harness manpower and modern technologies and apply them to the problems of geography and politics. At no point did these plans somehow determine that war would happen in 1914. Even so, awareness of these plans tended to rush decision-making in an era when there was not an international organization, such as a United Nations Security Council, where potential conflicts might be delayed and even defused by discussion.

The First World War began in Bosnia, an obscure province in the southeastern corner of Austria-Hungary. The province, home to Bosnian Muslims, Catholic Croats, and Orthodox Serbs, was acquired by Austria from the Ottoman Empire in 1878 and formally annexed in 1908. Nationalist Serbs resented the annexation, hoping to unite Bosnia with the neighboring, independent country of Serbia. On June 28, 1914, the heir to the throne of Austria-Hungary, Franz Ferdinand, and his wife, Sophie, visited the capital of Bosnia, Sarajevo. As Franz Ferdinand and Sophie were riding in their car, a nationalist Serb, Gavrilo Princip, shot them to death. Soon after, Austrian investigators learned that Princip had connections to the Serbian intelligence agency.

Austrians perceived that their empire's honor was at stake. On July 23, the Austrian government sent an ultimatum to Serbia, demanding that the Serbian government cease anti-Austrian activities. Austria also demanded that Serbia try those Serbs implicated in the plot against Franz Ferdinand, with Austrian officials supervising the proceedings. The Austrians expected a decision in forty-eight hours. These sorts of demands were thought likely to cause a war, but just a war between Austria and Serbia. The Serbs had some public support in Russia, but the Russian government did not have a reason to fear for its security if Austria attacked Serbia. The Austrian leadership might have confined the war to Serbia, had they not been concerned that the European alliance system might lead to war with Russia. Austria asked Germany for support, which it got: the kaiser promised Austria that it would have "Germany's full support." However, he did not believe that Russia and France would be drawn into the conflict; otherwise he probably would not have taken a vacation on the royal yacht immediately after giving Austria the "blank check."

Facing these demands from the confident Austrians, the Serbs might have capitulated or they might have given in to most of the demands and negotiated Austrian supervision of their courts. Instead, the Serbian ambassador to Russia sensed that the tsar and his advisers were becoming supportive. He wrote to his home government in the Serb capital, Belgrade: "The Russian Minister of Foreign Affairs [Sergei Dmitrievich Sazonov] sharply criticized the ultimatum of Austria-Hungary. Sazonov told me that the ultimatum contains demands that no state could accept. He said we could count on Russian help, but he did not explain what shape or form that help would take. Only the tsar could decide, and they have to cooperate with France as well."[1] On July 25, just before Austria's forty-eight-hour deadline was about to expire, the Russian government announced that it was taking preliminary steps to mobilize its armed forces, initiating what it called the "Period Preparatory to War." Russian soldiers were put on alert, while the reservists in some western districts were told to report for duty. This was not a full mobilization, but it emboldened the Serbians, who rejected the Austrian demands.

At this point in the narrative of events, it is worth mentioning that historians have disagreed about the ways in which a local conflict between Serbia and Austria escalated into a global conflict between the Entente and the Central Powers. The 1919 Treaty of Versailles, which ended the war, placed blame on German aggression. The treaty's punitive approach to Germany raised doubts, in the minds of some historians, that Germany could actually be blamed so much more than the other powers. During the Cold War, one school of historical thought tended to assign blame for the war's outbreak on the structure of the alliance system as well as on poor decision-making by politicians and generals in all countries. This was an especially compelling interpretation during the 1950s and 1960s, when two different alliance systems had the potential for an even more devastating cataclysm. Yet one German historian, Fritz Fischer, published a voluminous work in 1961 based on deep archival research that suggested that Germany was, in fact, heavily to blame for the war's outbreak. According to Fischer, German diplomats acted aggressively in support of Austria-Hungary, seeing the possibility of war as an opportunity to shore up the power of conservatives at home while building a stronger empire beyond Germany's current borders.[2]

The so-called Fischer Thesis stirred great public controversy in Germany, naturally enough. Many historians now follow the general thrust of Fischer's argument, while others have placed more blame on other countries. One of the most persuasive accounts to appear recently is Sean McMeekin's book *The Russian Origins of the First World War*. As the title would suggest, he blames Russia more heavily. McMeekin's research in recently opened Russian archives provided evidence that Russian leaders sought war in order to gain territory in the Balkans and the Middle East at the expense of their old enemy, the Ottoman Empire, while discussions between Russia and France were more aggressive than most historians realized.[3]

It appeared that Serbia and Austria-Hungary would go to war and that Russia might go to war against Austria-Hungary on the side of Serbia. In the next several days, Russia took steps to make ready about half of its army. This half-readiness had to be improvised—plans only existed for full mobilization against both Austria-Hungary and Germany at the same time. Troops were supposedly not made ready near the border with Germany, only near the border with Austria-Hungary. McMeekin argues that Russian mobilization was actually much more than partial—it took on an especially menacing appearance to Germany.

Partial mobilization did not satisfy the generals in Austria-Hungary, Russia, or Germany, all of whom wanted the strongest possible defense against external aggressors. Behind the scenes, generals pressed politicians for full mobilization, even as diplomats from many countries scrambled to initiate peace talks. Some of the strongest initiatives for peace came from Germany. Kaiser Wilhelm exchanged telegrams with Tsar Nicholas, while the German chancellor, Theobald von Bethmann-Hollweg, pressed his Austrian counterpart, Count Leopold Berchtold, to negotiate with Russia. Russia's mobilization was only partial, but it did still threaten to put millions of soldiers on the border with Austria-Hungary. Austrian generals sought to respond by fully mobilizing their own smaller army.

The problems of diplomacy and war planning were inextricably linked in Germany, too. The lead general, Moltke, worried that if Russia had some troops ready on the Austrian border they might throw off the complicated timing of Schlieffen's plan. As it was, the German generals feared that they might not be able to defeat France quickly enough to send troops back east and fight the Russians, who would be advancing on Berlin. If the Russians got a head start of even one or two days, Germany could lose the war. On July 30, Moltke went over the head of the kaiser and communicated directly with Austria's chief general, Baron Conrad von Hötzendorf, telling him that if Austria would order full mobilization, Germany would surely follow. This had not yet been decided by the kaiser, but it persuaded the Austrian leaders to order a full mobilization on July 31. Simultaneously, Russia's chief ministers and generals, together with the French ambassador, Maurice Paléologue, met with the reluctant Tsar Nicholas to persuade him to publicly order general mobilization. They made the argument that partial mobilization was proving impracticable from a military standpoint. They hoped for a general mobilization, even though they realized that Germany would interpret such an act as a provocation. Without an immediate general mobilization, the generals feared they might suffer greater losses in a war with Germany, especially if Germany sided actively with Austria-Hungary in a war against Russia over Serbia.

By this point, both sides had reached an impasse. On July 29, Nicholas decided to issue the order, but hesitated because of an exchange of personal telegrams with Kaiser Wilhelm. Wilhelm pressed Nicholas to refrain from intervening in Austrian actions against Serbia. On July 30, Nicholas's advisers persuaded him that any further hesitations would be dangerous to Russian forces. The next day, July 31, Nicholas ordered all Russian reservists to report for duty. At this point Nicholas sensed that, for diplomatic and technical reasons, mobilization could not be stopped. He sent a telegram to Kaiser Wilhelm stating that "it is technically impossible to stop our military preparations which were obligatory owing to Austria's mobilization," even though he also believed that "we are far from wishing war."[4]

Learning of Russian mobilization, the German government issued an ultimatum to Russia that proved to be the final straw: in twelve hours, Germany would begin to mobilize unless Russia stopped. A further note was sent from Berlin to Paris. Since France and Russia were bound to fight together against Germany in the event of German mobilization, then war between Germany and France was bound to happen if Russia did not stop its mobilization. Germany gave France eighteen hours to renounce its obligations to Russia and declare its neutrality. France and Russia ignored Germany's demands. On August 1, Germany declared war on Russia. On August 2, Germany gave Belgium a day to grant permission for German troops to cross its territory. The Belgians did not agree and German troops began to enter Belgium. That day, August 3, Germany declared war on France.

France did not have a formal alliance with Britain, just a cooperative relationship. For several years, the British and French military authorities had been involved in joint planning. In spite of these tentative plans, during the crisis of July 1914 the British cabinet had members who hesitated to enter the war on the side of France. The prospect of a French defeat, coupled with the prospect of German domination of Western Europe, did not sit well with British economic and political interests. Even so, some politicians still doubted whether a German victory over France would provide Britain a pretext for war. The German invasion of Belgium provided that pretext: Britain had signed a treaty guaranteeing Belgium's territory, and, more importantly, German occupation of Belgian ports threatened the east coast of England. On August 4, the British government gave Germany a day to cease operations against Belgium, or else Britain would declare war. Germany ignored the demands and Britain carried out its threat. The wealthiest and most powerful European countries were now at war. Out of all the great European powers, only Italy held back—for a time.

Europe's military and political leaders all worried that, if they delayed mobilization, other nations might get the jump on them. As Kaiser Wilhelm said in a telegram to Tsar Nicholas on July 31, "I now receive authentic news of serious preparations for war on my eastern frontier. Responsibility for the safety of my Empire forces preventive measures of defense upon me."[5] All major European countries had complex plans for rapid mobilization, while Germany and France were particularly committed to complex offensive plans. The timing of the plans pushed them toward quick mobilization. As John Keegan and other historians have shown, throughout late July and early August of 1914, leaders could have chosen to negotiate rather than to mobilize. And even after mobilization, the war plans could have been thrown away. The kaiser considered doing just this, in spite of his reputation for bluster. On August 1, Kaiser Wilhelm calculated that, if Germany did not attack France through Belgium, Britain would not enter the war, and that Germany could order most of its troops east to engage the Russians. The kaiser was probably right, but Moltke persuaded him that Schlieffen's plan was Germany's best hope for victory and that reversing the plan would be too complicated. Hesitation to implement war plans would result in negative consequences. As the French general Joffre explained to Adolphe Messimy, his minister of war,

> It is absolutely necessary for the government to understand that, starting with this evening, any delay of twenty-four hours in calling up our reservists and issuing orders prescribing covering operations, will have as its result the withdrawal of our concentration points by from fifteen to twenty-five kilometers for each day of delay; in other words, the abandonment of just that much of our territory. The Commander-in-Chief must decline to accept this responsibility.[6]

Political and military leaders gambled that they could win in spite of what they knew about the realities of geography and technology. The wars that had taken place between the mid-nineteenth century and 1914 had illustrated the costs of warfare in the industrial age while demonstrating the effectiveness of new weapons. It was common knowledge among Europeans that the new weapons gave advantages to defenders. Defenders had such an advantage that it was thought necessary for attackers to have as many as three to five times as many soldiers as defenders for an attack to have a chance at success. At no point did the Entente or the Central Powers have an advantage of three to one. The new weapons should have caused Europeans to hesitate before attacking each other. Such are the judgments made possible by hindsight.

Starting a war was made risky by the realities of defensive technologies. War was made more likely by geographical fantasies. The Schlieffen Plan assumed that the way to get around numerical parity between French and German forces was to attack through Belgium. Yet German planners downplayed a major problem: it was unlikely that sufficient forces could be pushed through the narrow Belgian and French frontier in time to outmaneuver enemy armies. Enough territory would be gained to ensure a conflict. Defensive technologies ensured that it would be difficult for the Belgians, French, and their allies to get it back.

The German leaders were not the only ones to engage in geographical fantasies. The leadership of every country in the Entente or the Central Powers aimed to gain territories, either in Europe or overseas. Overseas, military and naval technologies helped to make these fantasies possible. They remained fantasies, however, because territories were obtained at a time when anti-colonial nationalism was building in many places. At the end of the war, newly obtained colonies would be placed under international supervision—under the League of Nations—and almost all of them would become independent nations within fifty years. It would prove difficult for nations weakened by the world wars to hang on to colonial territories.

All of this lay in the future, and, of course, it was impossible to predict the future. This was true except in the case of Grigorii Rasputin, the disreputable faith healer who had become close to Russia's royal family. On the eve of war, and suffering from stab wounds received in an attempted assassination, Rasputin wrote to Tsar Nicholas: "Dear friend, I will say a menacing cloud is over Russia lots of sorrow and grief it is dark and there is no lightening to be seen. A sea of tears immeasurable and as to blood? What can I say? There are no words the horror of it is indescribable."[7] Rasputin used natural metaphors: a menacing cloud, a sea of tears, to describe the indescribable. Europe was starting a war in which natural metaphors would be used extensively to convey suffering and misery. In 1914, Europe's leaders were aware of the perils of launching a massive war. They all gambled against the odds. They all lost.

Chapter Five

The Western Front, 1914–1915

In the first week of August, millions of regular soldiers and reservists marched to train stations, boarded trains, and headed for the front lines. Many of these soldiers were optimistic, too. Enthusiasm for the war appeared to be widespread, at least in public. In hindsight, it is hard to credit this enthusiasm, but at the time it was palpable. Robert Poustis, who as a French schoolboy had imagined reclaiming Alsace and Lorraine, was now a soldier headed for the front in early August. He remembered that, when his train left the station, "Everybody was shouting and wanted to go to the Front. The cars, the railway wagons loaded with soldiers were full of tricolor flags and inscriptions: 'A (to) Berlin, à Berlin.' We wanted to go to Berlin immediately, with bayonets, swords, and lances, running after the Germans."[1]

Such fantasies of geographic mobility were indeed from an earlier technological era. In 1914, the bayonets, swords, and lances would be met by machine guns, breech-loading rifles, and quick-firing artillery. When movement occurred on the battlefields of the First World War, it often came at a high price.

For the most part the soldiers were cheered by crowds of people, but many intellectuals expressed their reservations. The Russian poet Anna Akhmatova conveyed her dread by using vivid environmental imagery in a poem, "July 1914":

> All month a smell of burning, of dry peat
> smouldering in the bogs.
> Even the birds have stopped singing, the aspen does not tremble.
> The god of wrath glares in the sky,
> the fields have been parched since Easter.
> A one-legged pilgrim stood in the yard
> with his mouth full of prophecies:
> "Beware of terrible times . . . the earth

opening for a crowd of corpses.
Expect famine, earthquakes, plagues,
and heavens darkened by eclipses."[2]

Akhmatova's dread was not shared by Poustis and his comrades. Inexperienced soldiers may have deluded themselves into thinking that their prowess would bring about a quick victory. By contrast, the British, French, and German soldiers who had fought in the colonies; the Austrian soldiers who had fought in the Balkans; and the Russian soldiers who had fought against Japan must have known about the damage that people could inflict upon each other with the new weapons. The generals were surely aware of the effects of the new weaponry, yet persisted in advocating offensive warfare.

The battlefields of the First World War may therefore be understood by deploying a concept from environmental history: sacrifice zones. A sacrifice zone is an area where people have been willing to sacrifice local natural resources in favor of some greater good, such as industrial production. For example, throughout much of the twentieth century the waterway ecologies near Houston, Texas, were thought worth sacrificing to the cause of petroleum refining and shipping. The same is true of the battlefields of the First World War. They became zones in which leaders deliberately sacrificed men, animals, trees, and land for the greater good. The side that could withstand sacrifices the most and still remain intact would win the war. The poet Akhmatova anticipated the scope and the symbolism of the sacrifices. She concluded her poem, "July 1914," with the following lines:

> Low, low hangs the empty sky,
> tender is the voice of the supplicant:
> "They wound Thy most holy body,
> They are casting lots for Thy garments."

THE WAR IN WESTERN EUROPE, 1914–1915

On August 4, 1914, German soldiers poured across the borders of Belgium and Luxembourg, headed for France. The northernmost soldiers, in the First Army under General Alexander von Kluck, faced a two-hundred-mile march in hard hobnail boots all the way to Paris, weighed down with sixty-pound packs. The German plan began to unravel almost immediately, thanks to the early resistance of Belgium's small army. Between 1888 and 1892, the Belgians had invested in fort-building along their rivers in order to impede invading armies. In 1914, the Belgians had the sturdiest and most heavily armed forts in Europe. For the Germans, the shortest path through Belgium and into France was blocked by the twelve forts surrounding the city of Liège, located at the site of a steep gorge on the Meuse River. On August 5, a German corps attacked Liège, only to be repulsed. Small German units were able to advance in between the forts to capture the city, but the forts still interfered with the German army's need to move all its forces forward to France quickly. The Germans tried new weapons against the forts. The first was a relatively new technology, the zeppelin, a long, cigar-shaped blimp that dropped bombs. When aerial bombs failed to breach the forts, the Germans moved forward enormous new siege cannons, the Krupp 420 mm howitzer and the Skoda 305 mm howitzer, whose heavy shells damaged the forts and persuaded the terrified defenders to surrender.

By the time that Liège's last three forts were destroyed on August 16, the Belgian government was withdrawing from Brussels, in central Belgium, to Antwerp on the North Sea. King Albert was leading his poorly equipped army in a series of rearguard actions, retreating across the country but standing to fight when good opportunities presented themselves. Belgian resistance slowed the German army and infuriated German soldiers. They not only blamed Belgian soldiers for fighting back and for destroying bridges and railroads; they also blamed Belgian civilians, accusing many of sniping when in fact few Belgian civilians were even armed. German soldiers took Belgian civilians hostage and shot hundreds of them. Several Belgian towns were looted and burned to the ground. In the worst incident, German soldiers destroyed the small university city of Louvain, famed for its architecture and its library. The fallout was terrible, not only for the Belgians. Word of the destruction spread throughout Europe. In Germany, where many were justifiably proud of their country's contributions to the humanities and the sciences, it was hard to condone acts of barbarism. The Allied countries were quick to publicize the atrocities in posters and stories. Such propaganda became highly significant as the war turned into a long test of wills between the Allies and the Central Powers.

The British and French responded to the German attack by moving aggressively themselves. The British shipped four infantry divisions and one cavalry division to France beginning on August 9—two more infantry divisions were sent by early September. The British Expeditionary Force, as it was called, was commanded by Field-Marshal Sir John French. It was put in place on the far western flank of the French army, at Mons, just across the Belgian border, by August 20. To the south, the French army set in motion their own war plan, Plan XVII, an attack across France's border with Germany. On August 7, three French divisions crossed into Alsace, taken by the Germans from the French in 1870. Three French divisions captured the city of Mulhouse, but by August 9 a larger German force pushed them back.

The next week, two French armies advanced into Lorraine. At first, the French encountered little German resistance. German troops fought a rearguard action, luring the French to move forward toward an equivalent German force. On August 20, a massive German counterattack drove the French out of Lorraine again. Sensing that German forces were strong in Lorraine—

and that they were also strong in Belgium—France's lead general, Joffre, ordered an attack up the middle, through the Ardennes Forest, which he presumed must have been defended lightly. It wasn't. France's eight corps marched through the hilly, wooded Ardennes only to encounter eight German corps moving directly toward them. The armies clashed on August 22, with both sides experiencing thousands of casualties. One attack was particularly telling. Some of France's most experienced troops, the Third Colonial Division, attacked a fortified German position repeatedly by charging it with bayonets. Out of the fifteen thousand troops who lowered their bayonets against the German cannons, rifles, and machine guns, eleven thousand were killed or seriously wounded. The old way of fighting was proving obsolete in the face of the new technologies.[3]

The French attack along the border with Germany was then completely stalled. To the north, in Belgium and the north of France, there was still plenty of movement. It still seemed possible that the German army could accomplish the goals set forth in the Schlieffen Plan: to capture Paris in forty-two days. On August 21—day seventeen of the invasion—the German Second Army crossed the Sambre River near Charleroi, close to the Belgian border with France. They were met by the French Fifth Army, whose units counterattacked across open fields, where they suffered terrible casualties at the hands of German machine gunners. Battles raged until August 23, at which point French forces began to withdraw to the south.

On August 23, the fourteen divisions of the German First Army—the great right wheel of the Schlieffen Plan—attacked the five divisions of the British Expeditionary Force at Mons, just north of the Sambre River. The British demonstrated that, even at a numerical disadvantage of 1:3, a defending force could inflict terrible casualties on attackers. Many of the British soldiers had experience in the Boer War, where they learned lessons (often the hard way) in how to attack and defend fortified positions. During the Boer War, British marksmanship had proved deficient; now improvements in training and in the design of rifles proved lethal. Against the massive German assault at Mons, every British unit held its positions. British casualties were heavy, at 1,600, but the Germans lost five thousand. Even so, the French Fifth Army, defeated along the Sambre River, had begun to retreat southward. The retreat forced the British to do the same. The two armies fought as they retreated. On August 26, three British divisions turned to fight at Le Cateau, digging shallow trenches and inflicting heavy casualties on the Germans before being forced to retreat again. On August 29, the French Fifth Army turned to fight at Guise. Despite some successes, the French retreated again. Technically, the French and British were losing—they were, after all, retreating. But this retreat was not a disorderly flight. For the most part it was an ordered, fighting retreat that delayed the advance of German forces.

Every delay of the Germans on the road to Paris gave the Russians more time on the road to Berlin. Schlieffen's hopes for German forces in the east had only been modest. He wanted the German army to delay the Russian army, buying enough time for Germany to conquer France and then ship enough soldiers back east to defeat the Russians. As it turned out, in August 1914 two Russian armies advanced toward Berlin more quickly than expected, but they were more than delayed by the German army—they were soundly defeated in several huge battles that took place in East Prussia. (These battles are described in chapter 6.) German forces succeeded in stopping the advance of the Russian army.

At the end of August, the German army abandoned Schlieffen's plan. In the east, the plan had overestimated the Russian army, which no longer posed such an immediate threat to Berlin. In the west, the plan had underestimated Belgian and French resistance and had failed to take into account the degree to which the intervention of the British would influence the outcome. The British Expeditionary Force (BEF) retreated to the area just east of Paris; the French Fifth Army, led by General Louis Franchet d'Espèrey, retreated south, too, just to the east of the British Expeditionary Force; the French Ninth Army under General Ferdinand Foch held positions to the east of the Fifth Army; while the French Sixth Army, commanded by General Michel-Joseph Maunoury, guarded Paris itself. By September 6, the French Sixth, the BEF, the French Fifth, and the French Ninth stretched in a line from Paris to the east, between the Marne River to the north and the Seine River to the south.

The German military leadership under Moltke decided that, instead of following the Schlieffen Plan and wheeling around Paris from the west, it was best to attack the retreating French and British forces now located in a line that stretched from the northern outskirts of Paris all the way east to Verdun, more than a hundred miles away. During the first week of September, German forces advanced in a line southward and encountered fierce French resistance orchestrated by Joffre. On the easternmost side of the front, Kluck's First Army moved south toward the French Sixth Army, which defended Paris; Karl von Bülow's Second Army moved against the main body of the French Fifth Army, just east of Paris. Joffre ordered the French Sixth Army to take a risk, moving them out from Paris to attack the eastern side of the German First Army. From September 6 to 9, the Battle of the Marne raged, with French units sustaining upward of eighty thousand casualties. To make up the shortfall in troops, French generals rushed more soldiers to the battlefield in taxicabs. As the battle continued, it became clear to British and French commanders that a gap was opening between the German First and Second armies. The BEF and the French Fifth Army pressed into the gap and began to cut off the two German armies, raising the prospect that they both might be encircled. Fearing that the British and French might

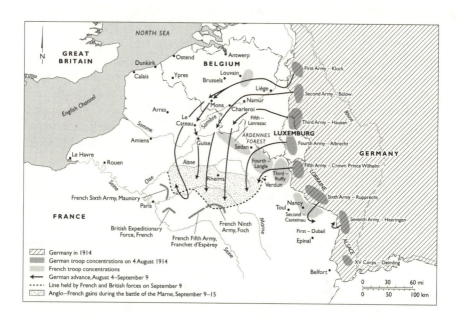

The Battle of the Marne

destroy his forces, on September 9 Moltke ordered a general retreat north, to the high ground along the Aisne River, where German soldiers dug into trenches. British and French forces followed in pursuit, reaching German positions on September 12 and 13, at which point they, too, were stopped by a successful defense.

In Belgium and France, the German army had failed to meet its objectives. Germany was now embroiled in a two-front war against France in the west and Russia in the east. This was the type of war that decades of German diplomatic efforts had tried to avoid. The hostility of the British tightened the vise. The British would not only support the French in the west, but they would also be able to shut down Germany's access to the North Sea. In hindsight, it seems that in September 1914 Germany faced an impossible situation. A swift victory by conquest now appeared to be out of the question. The best outcome for Germany would be a negotiated settlement, in which case continuing to fight hard would be rewarded.

To ensure a continued hard fight, the kaiser changed commanders. Moltke appeared to be suffering a nervous breakdown and was replaced by a court favorite, General Erich von Falkenhayn, who took steps to continue the German army's aggressive campaign. While German fortifications along the Aisne grew stronger, Falkenhayn ordered another German army, the Fourth, to move through Belgium toward the North Sea port of Antwerp, still controlled by the Belgians, and the French ports of Dunkirk, Calais, and Boulogne. Leaving the French Fifth and Sixth Armies to hold the line along the Aisne, the Second and Tenth Armies, along with the BEF, raced north to cut off the German advance on the ports, clashing with units of the German Fourth Army on the way. In the meantime, Britain sent an extra division, plus marines and naval units, to support the Belgians at Antwerp. German forces threatened to capture Antwerp just as they had captured every other Belgian city, so British and Belgian forces retreated south, to the town of Nieuport, where they linked up with British and French units that were moving northward.

The British, French, and Belgians now faced the Germans in the northern coastal region of Belgium known as Flanders. The Germans had moved their troops to the region in a final effort to outflank the Allies. The German decision proved fateful for reasons that are associated with the waterlogged Flanders environment. The region is low-lying, with much of it only a few meters above the level of the North Sea. The water table lies only one or two meters below the surface, and frequently the area is drenched by rainstorms. The three rivers that drain the area—the Yser, Lys, and Scarpe—are all prone to flooding. And to make the region even soggier, the soil consists mainly of a layer of sand over a layer of clay. For centuries, local residents dug canals and ditches and constructed dikes and polders in order to reclaim the land from the water. In wartime, these constructions were liable to be damaged, making it difficult for soldiers to move and to dig.[4]

Flanders presented soldiers with many environmental challenges, but, in one instance, it presented an environmental opportunity. In order to protect Nieuport, the only remaining port of independent Belgium, King Albert ordered the locks of the heavily channeled Yser River opened, thereby flooding the nearby countryside. This act of environmental warfare ensured that he preserved what was left of his country by submerging much of it. At the moment, though, this gesture prevented German forces from moving southwest toward Dunkirk and Calais.

During October 1914, battles raged around the historic textile-manufacturing town of Ypres, as the armies continued their efforts to move around each other. The Germans, who had moved into the lowlands first, occupied much of the higher ground, which was not only better to defend, but which did not lie so close to the water table. From the relatively high ground around Ypres, the Germans launched a series of offensives against the British. Once again, the generals ordered their troops to attack in massed formations across open fields, where they were cut down by rifles, machine guns, and artillery. It is thought that fifty thousand German troops died near Ypres in October and November 1914, compared to twenty-five thousand British troops. No army succeeded in overpowering or outflanking its opponents in Flanders, but the British and French did manage to push a bulge, or "salient," into the German lines just east of Ypres.

The armies now faced each other in a line 475 miles long that extended from the North Sea coast of Flanders to the French border with Switzerland. The terrain varied, from flat, waterlogged Flanders to the hills and woodlands of eastern France. All along that line, the armies dug trenches because it was proving less costly to defend than it was to attack. The remnant of the Belgian army—six divisions reduced to forty thousand soldiers—held the northernmost corner. The British army held the next thirty-five miles of front lines, with the remnant of the BEF being supplemented by the Royal Naval Division, an improvised unit of sailors and marines who had survived the siege of Antwerp. From that point south, the line was held by French troops.

By the time the winter weather was setting in, the Allies began to draw on colonial manpower, a key way in which the war was becoming global. British forces were supplemented by two divisions of infantry and two divisions of cavalry from India. The Indian army's infantry, the Meerut and Lahore Divisions, were each composed of three battalions of Indian soldiers and one battalion of British soldiers. British and Indian troops were all led by British officers. The officers and men were veterans of fighting in Burma and along India's Northwest Frontier, but they were unprepared for the battlefields of

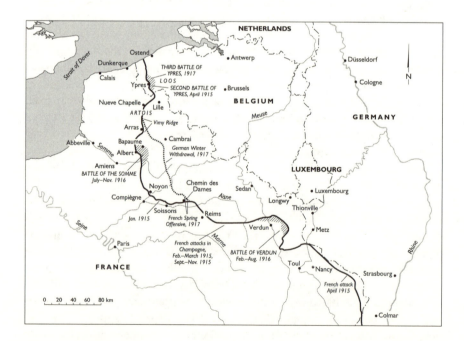

The Western Front, 1915–1917

Belgium and France, where they saw extensive service in 1914 and 1915. The Indian army had fewer machine guns than regular British units, and its troops lacked howitzers, mortars, and grenades, which were essential weapons in trench warfare. As a result, they suffered high rates of casualties at the front, while they had to cope with unaccustomed cold weather and low morale. The morale picture was complicated by religion. Some Muslim soldiers questioned their loyalty to a government that was now at war with the Ottoman Empire, whose sultan claimed leadership of all Muslims. Other factors also hurt the morale of the Indian army: units were recruited heavily from the Punjab in India's northwest, where a serious outbreak of plague in 1915 caused soldiers to worry about their families. Indian units had higher rates of self-inflicted wounds than British units, although Indian units were also involved in numerous acts of bravery under fire. British generals blamed the weather for morale problems in Indian units and at the end of 1915 transferred them to fight against the Ottomans in Iraq.[5]

All the armies suffered terrible losses in manpower and skill during the battles of 1914. The French army of two million men experienced 510,000 casualties, including soldiers killed, wounded, missing, and captured. Of those, 306,000 were killed. By comparison, the number of Belgian and British soldiers killed—thirty thousand for each country—seems significantly lower. Even so, Belgium is a small country with a small population, which meant that the losses were quite significant. As for Britain's small army, the killed soldiers were almost all regular soldiers, many of whom were veterans of colonial warfare. Their loss would be felt keenly in the coming years, when the British army came to rely heavily on recruits. On the other side of the fighting in France and Belgium, the German army lost 241,000 killed, a smaller number than the Allies but still quite substantial.[6]

In hindsight, such losses have seemed senseless to many historians and readers. It must be remembered that at the time there remained widespread popular support for the war. People in each country aided the war effort in the belief that their country was fighting on the side of righteousness. Such beliefs continued even as the war in Western Europe became bogged down in trench warfare.

There were certainly examples of civilians and soldiers who resisted the war. The most famous instance occurred on Christmas Day 1914, when many British and German soldiers put down their weapons and exchanged gifts. Such grand gestures of humanity in the face of inhumanity were uncommon. More common were the smaller gestures. Soldiers on both sides often reached certain understandings. For example, at supper time the artillery on both sides often took a break from shelling so that everybody could enjoy a meal. On the whole, though, as the war bogged down at the end of 1914, both sides prosecuted the war with vigor. This would continue through

1915, another year of great slaughter that saw officers on both sides experimenting with new approaches to trench warfare.

The main hypothesis of the British and French generals was that a massive attack eastward on one point of the German trenches would achieve a breakthrough. Once the German line was broken, cavalry and infantry would pour through the hole and envelop the Germans who remained to the north or south. (Even if this did not work, it was hoped that, at least if the British and French continued to attack, the Germans could not send many soldiers to the east, where they would contribute to the effort against Russia.) The Allied hypothesis made a number of suppositions that were incorrect. The main mistake was to believe that the Germans—with some of the world's best officers and engineers—would not respond cleverly to the challenges of trench warfare generally or to the simple tactic of massed assault in particular. Another mistake was to assume that, in the confusion of battle, Allied soldiers who did manage to break through would be able to communicate effectively with supporting units in order to safely push ahead.

Allied strategies found their match in German strategies. After the failure of the Schlieffen Plan, German leaders were content to wage a defensive war. This made sense for reasons that had to do with battlefield tactics as well as national strategy. In 1915, the German government hoped to push the Russians and the French to negotiate separate peace treaties. German proposals were sent through neutral countries. The proposals would have ended the war in exchange for major French and Russian territorial concessions. Neither country entertained these offers seriously, but the German leadership hoped that continued warfare would change their minds. Russian forces were attacked throughout 1915, but, in the west, German forces remained relatively static, in occupation of Belgium and a substantial portion of France. Strategically, this put a great deal of pressure on the French government. Tactically defense made sense, too. The new weapons of war favored defenders, while trenches, if constructed well, offered soldiers good protection. In 1914, German officers had been careful to site trenches on the highest available ground. Opposing trenches occupied by British and French soldiers were often found opposite on lower ground. Not only did this give the Germans a better view of the battlefields, but it also meant that German trenches could be built in better soil with fewer drainage problems.

Soldiers discovered that trenches could be challenging environments in which to live. One British soldier, Henry Williamson, remembered that "the condition of the latrines can be imagined and we could not sleep, every minute was like an hour. The dead were lying out in front. The rains kept on, we were in yellow clay, and the water table was 2 ft. below. Our trenches were 7 ft. deep. We walked about or moved very slowly in marl or pug of yellow watery clay. When the evening came and we could get out of it, it took about an hour to climb out. Some of our chaps slipped in and were drowned. They couldn't even be seen, but were trodden on later."[7] The trenches attracted rats, further compounding the effects of water-borne and lice-borne diseases. Near the trenches, decomposing bodies posed further environmental hazards, while they also changed the way soldiers viewed the landscape. A British officer, Roland Leighton, wrote to his fiancée, Vera Brittain, describing how his trench was on the edge of a lovely wood, surrounded by primroses. "Everything is such a grim contrast here," he wrote. "I went up yesterday morning to my fire trench, through the sunlit wood, and found the body of a dead British soldier in the undergrowth a few yards from the path. He must have been shot there during the wood fighting in the early part of the war and lain forgotten all this time. The ground was slightly marshy and the body had sunk down into it so that only the toes of his boots stuck up above the soil."[8] The beauty of the wood contrasted with the horror of a decomposed body being absorbed by the earth. The British lieutenant Siegfried Sassoon described the appearance of dead bodies in the Flanders mud in his poem "Counter-Attack":

> The place was rotten with dead; green clumsy legs
> High-booted, sprawled and grovelled along the saps
> And trunks, face downward, in the sucking mud,
> Wallowed like trodden sand-bags loosely filled;
> And naked sodden buttocks, mats of hair,
> Bulged, clotted heads slept in the plastering slime.
> And then the rain began,—the jolly old rain![9]

In spite of these depressing environmental conditions, some soldiers did attempt to add natural beauty to their surroundings. Lothar Dietz, a young philosophy student serving in the German army, wrote home to tell his family that he had been doing some trench gardening. Raiding several local gardens, Dietz recounted how "we fetched rhododendrons, box, snowdrops and primroses and made quite nice little flower-beds. We have cleaned out the little brook which flows through the valley, and some clever comrades have built little dams and constructed pretty little water-mills. . . . We have planted bushes of willow and hazel with pretty catkins on them and little firs with their roots, so that a melancholy desert is transformed into an idyllic grove."[10] Few trenches were designed in quite this way, but the Germans did earn a reputation for having the best-constructed trenches of the First World War.

It proved highly difficult for the British and French to rise up out of their trenches and assault German positions, yet there were several battles in 1915 in which they nearly achieved a breakthrough. In March 1915, a British attack on the German trenches at Neuve Chapelle almost worked. The British generals depended heavily on manpower from the two divisions of the Indian army, who made up half of the assaulting troops. The generals also developed a new tactic. Earlier assaults began with shelling the German trenches.

After a period of time, the shelling stopped and the British troops charged across open space toward the Germans. The trenches gave enough protection that significant numbers of Germans survived, rose to the top of the trenches, and began firing. The new British tactic at Neuve Chapelle began with a shelling, too, but, when the British troops emerged to run forward, British artillery continued to fire, shifting their targets to the German rear in order to interrupt the flow of any reserves. To ensure accuracy, artillery fire was directed by observers flying in eighty-five aircraft. The bombardment was massive, too. In thirty-five minutes, more shells were fired than in the entire Anglo-Boer War of 1899–1902. And the sound of the shelling remained continuous, causing German soldiers to hesitate before rising up to defend themselves.

Thanks to the planned coordination of imperial manpower together with artillery and aircraft, on the morning of March 10, 1915, the British and Indian soldiers surprised and overran the German trench at Neuve Chapelle, punching a hole in the German lines that was four kilometers long and one kilometer deep. Conditions on the battlefield were so confusing, though, and communications with the rear were so poor, that the British generals hesitated to follow up on the breakthrough lest their troops become trapped. Overnight the Germans were able to rush enough reserve soldiers to Neuve Chapelle to seal the breach. The anticipated breakthrough did not come.

Looking back on Neuve Chapelle, British generals concluded that they would have won if they had fired even more shells and used even more troops: massive assaults against trenches might still succeed if only enough artillery and infantry were put in place. Subsequent events proved them wrong, mainly because of the German response to Neuve Chapelle. The German generals studied the battle and concluded that one big, long trench packed with soldiers was indeed vulnerable to a breakthrough. To prevent breakthroughs, a second line of trenches was constructed. It was manned by plenty of troops and heavily fortified. The front line now received fewer troops. Their task was to remain alert at all times and to delay any attempted enemy breakthrough. Meanwhile, troops and artillery could be concentrated at the right points of the second line. Manpower, weapons, and terrain could be used flexibly, making a complete breakthrough unlikely.

The Germans were content to fight a defensive war on the Western Front in 1915, at least in part because in that year they were concentrating on knocking Russia out of the war. The main exception to their Western Front defensive strategy was their major assault on Ypres in April and May 1915. At Ypres the British trench lines bulged toward the German trench lines, creating a curved salient that, on both sides, took more soldiers to defend than a straight line. The purpose of the German assault was not so much to break through as it was to create a better defensive position, so it might still be said that the German attack was in keeping with their overall defensive strategy. They gambled that pushing back the Ypres salient would save more lives in the long run than would be lost in the battle, even though the British and French had fortified the salient heavily. They even had a well-built second line of trenches, of the sort that the German army had started to construct behind its own lines after Neuve Chapelle. The German army had another motive, too: they hoped that an attack on the British and French would hide the fact that they were transferring troops east to fight the Russians.

At Neuve Chapelle, the British attempted to surprise and confuse their opponents by the coordinated use of artillery, aircraft, and colonial troops. At the Second Battle of Ypres, as it came to be called, the attacking Germans surprised the French and British by unveiling a new weapon, poison gas. The French and Germans had already used small amounts of tear gas on each other on two occasions, in spite of the fact that the use of gas was outlawed by the Hague Convention, signed by all the powers in 1899. On April 22, 1915, at Ypres the Germans released chlorine gas from five thousand canisters. The gas drifted in an oddly colored mist toward trenches on the north side of the salient that were defended by two divisions of French soldiers, many of whom were from Algeria (the colonies were providing troops to the French army, too). The Algerian and French soldiers, not knowing what to do in the case of a gas attack, stood on guard at the top of their trenches. The chlorine gas inflamed their eyes and lungs, causing victims to drown in their own mucus. Hundreds died within minutes; thousands fled back from the trenches, opening a gap of eight kilometers in the French line. Four German divisions advanced but, just like the British troops who had moved forward at Neuve Chapelle, they were unable to coordinate their assault with reserve troops and did not achieve a complete breakthrough.

The Second Battle of Ypres turned into a slogging match that resembled Neuve Chapelle in many ways. The British Second Army, including a brigade of Canadians, counterattacked on April 22. For several days, the battle raged. Four more German divisions attacked along the central and southern portions of the salient. The German generals ordered another gas attack, this time against the British and Canadians, on April 24. Soldiers began to cope with the gas by pouring water or urine over handkerchiefs and then placing the wet cloths over their mouths—soldiers breathing through these rudimentary masks survived because chlorine is soluble in water. The battle continued until the end of May, by which point the British and French had withdrawn from the outer ring of the salient to positions five or six kilometers to the rear. The Germans had succeeded in reducing the size of the salient, but they did not eliminate it. They also failed to take advantage of the major breakthrough achieved by the surprising use of gas.

Soldiers and civilians in Britain and France condemned the new technology as barbarous and rushed to design and manufacture gas masks. The use of gas seemed, at first, to be a propaganda victory for the Allies, but very soon after Second Ypres the Allied armies formed units of chemical engineers and assigned them the task of developing their own poison gases. Gas attacks became a fixture on the Western Front for the next three years, even though many believed that gas attacks were an inhumane and unethical method of killing. The most famous description of the new technology came from a young British officer, Wilfred Owen, serving on the Western Front later in the war. His poem about gas, "Dulce et Decorum Est," uses vivid description and soldierly irony to condemn the war.

> GAS! GAS! Quick, boys! An ecstasy of fumbling,
> Fitting the clumsy helmets just in time;
> But someone still was yelling out and stumbling,
> And flound'ring like a man in fire or lime. . . .
> Dim, through the misty panes and thick green light,
> As under a green sea, I saw him drowning.
> If in some smothering dreams you too could pace
> Behind the wagon that we flung him in,
> And watch the white eyes writhing in his face,
> His hanging face, like a devil's sick of sin;
> If you could hear, at every jolt, the blood
> Come gargling from the froth-corrupted lungs,
> Obscene as cancer, bitter as the cud
> Of vile, incurable sores on innocent tongues,—
> My friend, you would not tell with such high zest
> To children ardent for some desperate glory,
> The old Lie: Dulce et decorum est
> Pro patria mori. [11]

There was no glory in a death that was inflicted by a distant enemy using industrial technologies such as chemical weapons. Even so, the use of the weapons spread. The dreadful new gas technologies were used by the Allies for the first time in their massive September attacks on German positions in Artois and Champagne. The attacks had been planned in July, at an Allied conference in Chantilly. The British opposed an immediate offensive, believing that they would not be producing a sufficient amount of shells until 1916. By contrast, the French generals pressed hard for an offensive. From a French perspective, the sooner the Germans were beaten the better. The Russian and Serbian governments—who were represented at the conference—registered their concern that any less pressure on the Western Front would result in more German troops on the Eastern Front. The British government gave in to pressure, hoping that the shell shortage could be made up by the use of gas. It proved hardly a match for the elaborate defenses that the Germans were constructing in order to maximize their lesser manpower and their defensive weapons. During the summer of 1915, German soldiers and laborers dug a second line of trenches, positioning them well on higher ground and providing for superior fields of fire. The frontline trenches were shored up, too, while machine-gun emplacements were dug in between. German artillery drilled on the best ways to stop an Allied assault at various points along the double line of trenches.

The Allies still thought that they might be able to achieve a breakthrough. On September 25, 1915, the French Second and Fourth Armies attacked the German Third Army's trenches along a twelve-kilometer front in Champagne. At the same time, the British First Army and the French Tenth Army attacked the German Sixth Army along an eighteen-kilometer front near Loos and Vimy in Artois. The attacks on Loos and Champagne demonstrated the difficulties that forces faced when trying to seize heavily defended trenches that were surrounded by barbed wire. One British soldier, Charles Lippett, recalled that "as we approached this wire I could see the bodies of men hanging on it, obviously dead or badly wounded, and there were no gaps in it at all. Our artillery had not cut the wire, even firing 18-pounder shells at it."[12] At Loos the British also unleashed canisters of chlorine gas, which blew back into their own lines when the wind shifted directions. The new weapon proved difficult to control, inspiring engineers in the following months to design ways of dispersing gas in artillery shells.

The Allied assaults in Champagne and Artois, which were much larger than the assault on Neuve Chapelle, resulted in weeks of bloody fighting and shelling. The French lost a staggering two hundred thousand casualties; the British and Germans lost around sixty thousand each. Very little ground was won or lost. The commander of the British Expeditionary Force, Sir John French, was relieved of command, to be replaced by Sir Douglas Haig. The French commanders began to reconsider the wisdom of massive assaults, while they were frustrated by German skill at holding the French soil taken in 1914. At the end of 1915, the Allies had made little headway on the Western Front, while on the Eastern Front Germany was meeting with success, not only in defending German territory but in taking territory from the Russians.

Chapter Six

The War in Eastern and Southern Europe, 1914–1915

In the summer of 1914, the governments of Eastern and Southern Europe wanted war. The Serbs sponsored the assassins who provoked Austria-Hungary. The Austro-Hungarians, backed by the Germans, issued unreasonable threats against the Serbs. The Serbs received backing from the Russians, based on fictive notions of pan-Slavic Orthodox kinship. The Russians mobilized first, forcing the hands of the others. The Italians offered their allegiance to the Central Powers and to the Entente Powers, to see which one would promise the most territories.

All the associated blustering, posturing, and saber rattling lost sight of fundamental economic and political weaknesses. With the exception of Germany, all the countries mentioned above were in the earliest stages of industrialization. Their leaders seemed not to grasp the risks of war in 1914. By the end of it, the Austro-Hungarian Empire would be dissolved into its constituent nations. Russia would undergo a communist revolution and civil war. Italy would undergo a period of revolution and instability, culminating in the rise to power of the fascists in 1922. Germany actually won the First World War in Eastern Europe, through the surprising defeat of the Russian Army in August 1914, followed by successful campaigning in 1915 and 1916. Yet the necessary problem of having to fight both Russia and its allies in the west drove Germany to the breaking point, too. All this is clear from hindsight. Nationalist visions of mobility and the belief that new weapons would end the war quickly were still prevalent in 1914.

GERMANY'S SURPRISE VICTORIES IN THE EAST, 1914

For the Russian army, the road to Berlin lay through East Prussia, the east-ernmost German province that is today the northern part of Poland. East Prussia was defended by the German Eighth Army, whose 150,000 soldiers were commanded by Maximilian von Prittwitz. On paper, his forces were outnumbered by the two armies that Russia sent. Russia's First Army, commanded by Pavel von Rennenkampf, had 200,000 soldiers. They invaded East Prussia from the east. Russia's Second Army, commanded by Aleksandr Samsonov, had 150,000 soldiers. They invaded East Prussia from the south. Their numerical superiority would seem to have guaranteed their victory, but there were significant problems with the readiness of some of these troops. Other Russian units had to be left behind to occupy the conquered towns of East Prussia. By the time the forces made contact, it is likely that the German Eighth Army outnumbered each Russian army. The French had urged their Russian allies to invade Prussia with more than two armies. In fact, the Russians deployed four armies against Austria-Hungary. Historian Sean McMeekin explains this decision by pointing out that the Russian government had greater hopes of imperial expansion in Galicia, along the border of Austria-Hungary, where Slavic languages were spoken, rather than in East Prussia, where most of the inhabitants were ethnic Germans.[1]

There were further factors that favored the Germans. The majority of the German soldiers were from East Prussia. For this reason, they were inclined to fight tenaciously to defend their homeland. And the two Russian armies faced a geographical challenge. According to military dogma, it is always best to concentrate units into one force rather than divide them in two, because dividing increases the probability of defeat. Yet the two Russian armies were separated by the Masurian Lakes and by the surrounding woodlands, Europe's last primeval forest. It was simply easier for the two armies to move separately. That was a geographical and logistical mistake; separation proved disastrous.[2]

German forces met the invasion by attacking first at Stalluponen on August 17, when a German army corps pushed back Rennenkampf's First Army and captured three thousand prisoners. German generals feared that they had overextended themselves and ordered their forces to fall back to Gumbinnen, where they were followed by Rennenkampf's pursuing forces. As the Russian First Army approached Gumbinnen on August 20, German forces attacked along a line that stretched more than twenty-five miles. German attacks succeeded initially, at the cost of thousands of soldiers killed, wounded, and captured on both sides. Counterattacking Russians captured six thousand German prisoners. The resistance of the Russian First Army, coupled with the possibility of being surrounded by the Russian Second Army, advancing from the south, persuaded Prittwitz to retreat west, toward the Vistula River.

When Germany's commanding general, Moltke, learned of Prittwitz's retreat, he fired him. Moltke replaced him with a retired general, Paul von Hindenburg, who was to be assisted by another general, Erich Ludendorff, who had led troops aggressively in Belgium during the German assault on the fortresses near Liège. Ludendorff and Hindenburg were helped by an ingenious colonel, Maximilian Hoffman, who analyzed the movement of Russian forces and took advantage of the ways the two Russian armies were divided over a large geographical area—a divide that was anticipated by the war-gaming of a generation of German staff officers. As in the practice war games, the German generals withdrew their forces away from the Russian First Army, checked in the east, by using the north–south railways to move troops quickly south toward the Russian Second Army under Samsonov. More than distance, lakes, and forest separated the two Russian armies. Samsonov and Rennenkampf disliked each other personally. They were also unlucky in their radio communications. Radio was still new at the time. It allowed the rapid transfer of battlefield information in real time, but in 1914 both the Entente and the Central Powers were still learning how to use the technology. Both sides had radio codebooks, but radio operators had difficulty keeping up with the volume of messages. Radio operators became careless about sending radio communications without using code. Uncoded messages between Samsonov's and Rennenkampf's headquarters indicated that Rennenkampf would not come to help Samsonov. This kind of intelligence seemed too good to be true. Hindenburg and Ludendorff doubted it, but Hoffman persuaded them that such was the enmity between Samsonov and Rennenkampf that they probably would not help each other.

Trusting Hoffman, Hindenburg and Ludendorff began their assault on Samsonov's Second Army. Samsonov had spread his troops thin, over a front of nearly one hundred kilometers. Denser German units made contact with the Russians on August 23. Battles raged up and down a front near the town of Tannenberg. Moltke was concerned enough by reports from the east that he dispatched three corps of infantry and one division of cavalry from France. But by August 26, it became clear that German forces were destroying the overextended Russian left. German forces began to encircle the Russians. Instead of moving his forces to the flanks and fighting against encirclement, Samsonov ordered his troops to attack northward. They became completely encircled. By August 31, nearly the entire Russian Second Army was killed, wounded, or captured: only ten thousand of the original force escaped. Samsonov got lost in the woods. It appears that he killed himself rather than report such a catastrophic defeat to Tsar Nicholas.

After the massive victory at Tannenberg, Hindenburg and Ludendorff swung the German Eighth Army to the north to attack Rennenkampf's Russian First Army. Between September 5 and 13, the two armies fought a series of large engagements in the vicinity of the Masurian Lakes. Rennenkampf,

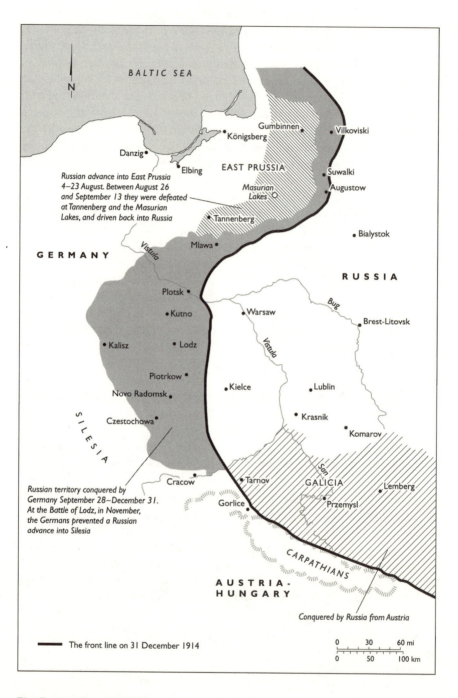

Russian advance into East Prussia
4–23 August. Between August 26
and September 13 they were defeated
at Tannenberg and the Masurian
Lakes, and driven back into Russia

Russian territory conquered by
Germany September 28–December 31.
At the Battle of Lodz, in November,
the Germans prevented a Russian
advance into Silesia

Conquered by Russia from Austria

The front line on 31 December 1914

0   30   60 mi
0   50   100 km

The Eastern Front in 1914

fearing that he would be encircled like Samsonov, ordered a fighting retreat east toward the border with Russia. At the Masurian Lakes, the Russian First Army suffered 125,000 casualties, while the German Eighth Army withstood forty thousand. The Russians launched a counterattack on September 25, which, after three days, pushed German forces back to the Masurian Lakes. Even so, the battles of August and September 1914 proved disastrous for the Russian army. The German army inflicted a major defeat on the Russians, even though, according to the Schlieffen Plan, it was the job of the Eighth Army merely to fight a delaying action against the Russian invaders.

AUSTRIA-HUNGARY FALTERS AT THE OUTSET

Germany's Austrian allies also found themselves fighting a two-front war. On the whole, the Austrians were less successful than the Germans in balancing the constraints of manpower and geography. It seemed to most of the leaders of Austria-Hungary that honor demanded an invasion of Serbia. This was in spite of two recognized facts: that Serbia was unlikely to invade Austria-Hungary, while massive Russian forces were. Survival required an adequate defense against the Russians, but Austria's leading general, Conrad von Hötzendorf, divided Austrian forces into a northern group to resist Russia and a southern group to invade Serbia.

Conrad's southern army, commanded by Oskar Potiorek, attacked Serbia with four hundred thousand soldiers, just enough to get across the border and inflict significant damage but not enough to defeat Serbia's army, which also had about four hundred thousand soldiers. The Serbs were well-armed veterans of previous wars in the Balkans. They enjoyed the support of the local populace, plus a superior knowledge of Serbia's rugged, mountainous terrain. When the invasion began on August 12, the Serbs allowed the Austrians to capture low-lying territory along the Sava and Drina Rivers. Serbian forces occupied higher ground near the Vardar River and lay in wait for the Austrians to attack. When they did, on August 16 and 17, Serbian forces held their ground and forced Conrad to divert several divisions from the north. Even with these reinforcements, the Austrians were forced to withdraw. They renewed their offensive in November and December. At one point they even captured the capital, Belgrade, but once again Serb forces drove them out. At the end of 1914, the Serbs and Austrians had fought to a draw, with each side suffering tens of thousands of casualties.[3]

Conrad's decision to commit troops against Serbia jeopardized the Austrian forces that were poised to attack the Russians in the north. There, in what is today Poland, geographical conditions were quite different. One million Austrian troops advanced northward through their part of Poland, with their backs to the Carpathian Mountains and hemmed in by the Vistula River to the west and the Dniester River to the east. And from the Russian part of Poland, 1.2 million troops spread themselves in a 250-mile arc stretching from Lublin to Lvov (then called Lemberg). This land is a relatively flat, open space, which worked to the advantage of the Russian attack. The armies hurtled toward each other over the plains. Their initial clashes around Kras-nik, near Lublin in the north, resulted in an Austrian victory, but Russian forces regrouped and pressed the attack. Massive battles were fought all along the front, in which generals attempted large-scale flanking movements against each other. By mid-September, the Russian army was winning. It had suffered a quarter of a million casualties, but the Austrians suffered twice that number. Depleted Austrian forces retreated in disarray toward Cracow, surrendering a hundred miles of their territory.

Austrian forces were pressed hard enough that Germany began to provide support. In October, German and Austrian forces attempted a coordinated assault. Thirteen German divisions under Hindenburg and Ludendorff marched toward Russian Warsaw, only to pull back when it seemed that they risked being surrounded by a larger Russian army. At the same time, thirty-one Austrian divisions advanced north from Cracow, only to be driven back again by the Russians. The Austrians counterattacked throughout November, losing more ground than they gained, including many of the passes in the Carpathian Mountains, but German attacks in the vicinity of Lodz pushed the Russian army back toward Warsaw again. In December, with German help, the Austrians did succeed in pushing the Russian front northward from the Carpathians.[4]

VICTORY ELUDES THE CENTRAL POWERS, 1915

The fighting on the Eastern Front can be hard to follow. On both sides, large armies maneuvered against each other across large spaces. Both sides scored victories and both sides experienced defeats. The eastern campaigns were important for Germany, in that the German army had successfully defended East Prussia from Russian invasion. Even so, the German army was also forced to draw reinforcements from France, a move that diminished the likelihood of a German victory. Still, Germany remained in a strong position.

By contrast, the war was already taking a toll on Austria-Hungary and Russia. Industrial production was having trouble keeping pace with the con-flict, so that the Russian army began to ration artillery shells by the end of 1914. The manpower situation was even more alarming. Between August and December 1914, the Russian army lost 1.5 million of its 3.5 million men. Russia could still draw on its large population to make up the difference, but already at the end of 1914 replacement soldiers lacked training. One general, Alexei Brusilov, wrote in his memoirs that at around this time, at the battle of

Przemysl, he realized that this "was the last [battle] in which I can say that I had an army that had been properly taught and trained before the War. After hardly three months of war the greater part of our regular, professional officers and trained men had vanished, leaving only skeleton forces which had to be hastily filled with men wretchedly instructed who were sent to me from the depots; while the strength of the officers was kept up by promoting subalterns, who likewise were inadequately trained. From this period onward the professional character of our forces disappeared, and the army became more and more like a sort of badly trained militia."[5]

Austria, too, was beginning to show signs of strain. In 1914, its army of 3.4 million men experienced 1.3 million killed, wounded, and captured. These figures were slightly lower than Russian losses, but Russia had a larger population of potential replacements. Another issue hampered Austro-Hungarian recruitment: the Empire had significant minority ethnic groups who were keen to achieve independence and were not enthusiastic about the war effort. Austria's manpower crisis began very early in the war.[6]

During the winter of 1914–1915, the Eastern Front saw increased German participation and the relegation of Austria-Hungary to the level of a junior partner. The German generals recognized that transferring more troops from France to the east reduced the possibility of a victory in the west, but they were also getting the sense that a weakened Russia might be knocked out of the war. In February 1915, in freezing conditions, two German armies advanced along the border of East Prussia with Russia near the Masurian Lakes. The Russians offered a stout resistance and kept the Germans from breaking through. Even so, Russian casualties amounted to two hundred thousand. Another winter offensive to the south combined German and Austrian forces in an effort to relieve 120,000 Austrian defenders besieged in the fortress at Przemysl, to the west of Lvov. This effort failed. The Russian army counterattacked successfully along a long front, ensuring the capture of Przemysl in March 1915. In the process, the Russians sustained several hundred thousand more casualties, as did the Austrians. The manpower crisis deepened for both empires.

In May 1915, German reinforcements were nearly able to deliver a knockout blow to the Russians. Along the Carpathian front, a well-supplied German and Austrian force of twenty-three divisions attacked nineteen Russian divisions that lacked sufficient rifles and shells. Russian troops defended their positions by digging trenches and laying barbed wire, but their defenses were superficial compared to the ones that could be found on the Western Front.

Trench warfare only developed in specific zones of the Eastern Front where there were unusually dense concentrations of armies. For the most part, though, soldiers on the Eastern Front experienced a war of movement. Why were the fronts so different? At any given time, the Eastern Front was about twice as long as the Western Front, with roughly the same number of troops. The vast space and the relative lack of good roads and railroads also made it more difficult to reinforce trench positions quickly, which was more easily done on the Western Front. In the west, trenches remained the best protection for armies against modern weaponry; in the east, geography and technology ensured that most battles still involved maneuver, much as they had in the Napoleonic Wars.[7]

In the spring of 1915, the Central Powers pushed the Russians hard. In their May 1915 assault in the Carpathians, the Germans and Austrians broke through in the south near the town of Gorlice, capturing hundreds of thousands of Russian prisoners and forcing the Russian army to retreat. The Germans and Austrians pressed forward from the west and from the south, in some instances employing chlorine gas against Russian soldiers. By August 1915, the Central Powers had captured Warsaw and most of Russian Poland.

This was a major defeat for the Russians. Many Russian officers and soldiers blamed the Jews—the western borderlands of the Russian Empire were known as the Pale of Settlement, home to millions of Jews. The Jewish residents of the area had been subjected to numerous pogroms, or murderous persecutions, during the reign of Nicholas II, whose government tolerated and even encouraged civilian and military attacks on Jewish settlements. In 1915, these attacks began again. Jews were suspected of aiding the Germans and Austrians, whose governments were somewhat more tolerant. While Russian soldiers attacked the Jews, the Russian government ordered the forced migration of Jews from Lithuania, which lay in the German army's path to Petrograd. Jews were accused of treachery, even though many had volunteered to serve in the Russian army in order to prove their loyalty.

The pogroms were a deplorable activity for an army that was growing desperate in defeat. Out of desperation and a desire for vengeance, the retreating Russian army laid waste to the countryside. By comparison to Russian misdeeds, the German occupation seemed mild, although that was not saying much. To many Germans, Poland was the anti-Germany. According to German stereotypes, Poles were disorganized and primitive, their country ripe for colonization by superior Germans. Under German occupation, Poles, Jews, and other nationalities were allowed some latitude to maintain their cultural heritages. They were also required to provide Germany with labor as well as grain and animals. Under German occupation, Poles suffered from malnutrition as well as from strict, colonial-style justice.[8]

Russia's situation seemed dire enough that, in September 1915, the tsar took personal command of the army, a mistake in light of his limited talent. There was only one bright spot for Russian strategy: geography was on its side. Russia was a vast country, so the Russian army was able to trade space for time. Retreating from the Polish bulge to form a straight north–south line also gave the Russian army less of a front to defend. The Russians were down but they were not out. During the final months of 1915, they offered strong resistance to German pressure along the new front that stretched from the Baltic Sea straight down to the Carpathian Mountains.

The successes against Russia allowed the Central Powers, Germany and Austria, to renew the attack on Serbia. The Germans and Austrians were joined by the Bulgarians, who entered the war in September 1915 to settle old scores with Serbia: Serbia had taken Bulgarian territory in the Balkan War of 1913. In October 1915, Bulgarian forces attacked Serbia from the east, while a joint German and Austrian force attacked from the north. The Serbs fought back as well as they could. They appealed for help to the British and French, who sent three divisions to Salonika, near Bulgaria's border with Greece, where they were effectively pinned down by the Bulgarian army, by malaria, and by unfavorable geography. Serb forces—which had already suffered significant casualties in the battles against the Austrians in 1914— along with King Peter and his government were forced to retreat across a mountain range in winter to the Adriatic coast, where they were evacuated to Italy and to the island of Corfu.

THE ITALIAN WAR, 1915

Bulgaria's entry on the side of the Central Powers was offset, to a degree, by the entry of Italy on the side of the Allies in May 1915. Some people in Italy hesitated to support the entry of their country into a war that held significant risks, but King Emmanuel III, his prime minister, Antonio Salandra, and a significant number of leading politicians and intellectuals saw war as an opportunity to bind together a nation that was divided along regional and class lines. The Italian leadership also hoped to gain more territory. During secret negotiations in early 1915, the British and French promised the Italians that at the end of the war they could have a share of Austrian territory. The Italian leadership rose to the bait and entered the war—initially only against Austria—even though the Italian army of twenty-five divisions lacked suffi- cient artillery and was not trained well enough for major offensive opera- tions. Under the leadership of Luigi Cadorna, the Italian army planned to defend its mountainous border with Austria while attacking through the mountains toward Austrian Trieste.

The geography of the Italian border with Austria hardly favored attackers. The region, which is part of the Alps, is highly mountainous and easily defended. There were only a few geographical options for an Italian attack on Austria. In the west, there were several mountain passes that could be at- tacked, while in the east attackers could cross the Isonzo River, which runs north–south along the former border between the two countries. The river starts in the mountains, then flows down a narrow corridor, which, as it nears

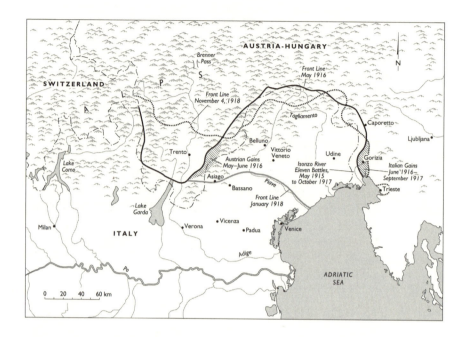

The Italian Front, 1915–1918

the sea, is low-lying and prone to flooding. In 1915, the Isonzo and the surrounding mountains were the scene of three major assaults by the Italian army. All were repulsed at great loss: each side sustained more than a hundred thousand casualties. Along the Isonzo, relatively large forces tried to push through a narrow space that was easily defended by concentrating troops, digging trenches, and using weapons that were especially suited to defense such as rifles, machine guns, and artillery. The Italian army was handicapped, too, by having large numbers of enlisted soldiers who were illiterate and poorly trained. Many were unfamiliar with their government's war objectives, too, making it difficult to sustain their morale.[9]

In this way, the Isonzo came to resemble the Western Front. Yet the Italian front was different in that much of the fighting took place in nearby mountains. Some troops on both sides had grown up in the mountains and had trained as part of special alpine units, but for the most part the soldiers had little prior experience of mountain conditions. It took great efforts to move men and equipment short distances, especially at night, when men might not notice a sheer drop until it was too late. The weather, ranging from intense heat in the summer to freezing conditions in the winter, presented major challenges. All year the soldiers experienced major precipitation. In the mountains, it was difficult to dig entrenchments. Instead of digging, engineers used dynamite to blast trenches out of glaciers and rock. When the rock was hit by shellfire, it exploded into dangerous fragments. The Italian soldier Virgilio Bonamore described a summer night on a mountain:

> A terrible night. Towards midnight a fierce thunderstorm breaks out. In the meantime, the first platoons of the 23rd arrive to take our places in the trenches. We stand waiting, up to our knees in water, for the order to leave. Rain pours down nonstop. It's cold, pitch dark and I'm drenched to the bone. At 2 a.m. we set off. We can't see a thing, so we hold on to each other's cloaks. After a few hundred meters, we stop in torrential rain on a muddy path, about 20 centimeters wide. We stand, unable to move, right on the edge of a sheer drop. It is indescribable torture. I shake convulsively with cold, I can feel the water dripping down my skin, but if we move one more step, we'll fall straight to our death. We stay standing like this, in the rain, in total stillness for at least three hours. [10]

As the quotation from Bonamore suggests, the war in Italy took place in one of the world's most dangerous and spectacular environments. While the war on the Western Front became a stalemate, too, the campaigns in Italy took on a particularly dogged quality, thanks to these harsh mountain conditions. Italy's lead general, Luigi Cadorna, enforced iron discipline. Officers and soldiers found retreating were typically executed. There was also a high degree of mistrust between educated officers and ordinary soldiers, who were often laborers and peasants. Through twelve assaults near the Isonzo, the Italian army remained cohesive. It was not until 1917 that the Italian army, like the French and Russian armies, began to buckle under the strains of total war.

Chapter Seven

The World War in Africa, 1914–1916

Historians have tended to focus on the First World War in Europe. Europe was, after all, the continent that suffered the greatest casualties and political upheavals during the war. Then why is it called a "world war"? Initially, the British called it the Great War, and the French used a phrase that meant the same thing, *la grande guerre*. "World war" comes from the German *Weltkrieg*, which means "war of global significance" just as much as it means "war around the world." In any event, the First World War did have a global significance that went beyond Europe. Fighting took place in Africa, Asia, and the Middle East, as well as on the world's oceans. Casualties in these theaters tended to be less than in Europe, so the relationship between the First World War and global imperial expansion has tended to be downplayed by historians. This is understandable, but it is also a mistake.

There are several ways imperialism and the First World War need to be examined as part of the same global historical trends. We have already seen that the principal weapons used on Europe's battlefields during 1914 to 1915 were developed and tested during an era of imperial expansion. We have also already seen that the Allied armies depended to a considerable extent on colonial manpower. For decades the British had kept their army small, planning to use Indian troops in case of emergency. In 1914, such an emergency happened. Britain deployed most of its regular soldiers to France. Heavy casualties required replacements, while Allied leaders sought a greater overall British commitment. The British government appealed to civilians to volunteer. Thousands did, but, while they were training, several divisions of Indian army soldiers arrived in France and fought on the Western Front. They were joined by other troops from around the empire, especially the Canadians, while a substantial number of old and new British troops were Irish. The French, too, incorporated colonial troops into their effort on the

Western Front. In the first week of the war, the government shipped ten thousand West African infantrymen to France. Training camps were segregated from the civilian population, but on August 21 the African troops took part in their first combat as fully fledged members of the French army. And like the rest of the French army, they suffered heavy casualties: 600 total casualties and 250 deaths. Units from French colonies continued to play a significant role on the Western Front until the war's end. [1]

At the start of the war, the colonies were not only providing significant numbers of troops for Britain and France—they were supplying laborers, too. In both Britain and France, the manpower needs of the army and navy, together with the manpower needs of farms and factories, meant that labor was scarce for other activities that supported the war effort. Ships and railway cars needed to be loaded and unloaded. Roads needed to be built and maintained. Trenches and graves needed to be dug. Trees needed to be cut down. Britain and France recruited hundreds of thousands of laborers to work behind the lines of the Western Front. They came from British and French colonies in Africa, the Caribbean, and Asia, as well as from China, all places where networks of labor recruiting already existed to supply the mines and plantations with labor. Many of the men who joined the Allied forces supported the war effort and hoped that in return for participation their countries might receive a greater degree of freedom. Laborers typically came voluntarily in order to earn money, but some were subject to coercion, particularly those recruited from Africa. Colonial laborers were often subject to the same restrictions in France as they experienced at home. Many were kept in segregated camps and were prohibited from mingling with civilians and soldiers. [2]

Over the course of 1914–1919, manpower and resources were more and more important for the European powers because their choice to continue fighting resulted in social and economic strain. Many of these social and economic strains existed before the war and were actually related to war objectives and imperialism to a significant degree. We have seen how German liberals chose orderly Prussian domination over socialist revolution. Many German liberals sought trade opportunities in the colonies, while others sought to create settlements that transcended the home country's social divisions. Those divisions—class divisions, ethnic divisions, and religious divisions—troubled both liberal and conservative Germans who hoped to build a powerful nation-state. While the new Germany became an industrial and cultural powerhouse, there were increasing signs of anti-Semitic, anti-Polish, and anti-Catholic sentiment. French civilians who resisted the 1870 occupation of Alsace and Lorraine were ruthlessly suppressed by the German army, who engaged in summary mutilations and executions of suspected resisters, while also destroying much property. The Pan German League, founded in the 1890s, advocated the occupation and settlement of Poland and the expulsion of the Poles, many years before Hitler. One of the league's founders, Karl Peters, was a famous explorer who had engaged in atrocities in East Africa; he traveled in anti-Semitic circles, too. Germany's imperialism in Eastern Europe and in Africa was all of a piece, rooted in insecure nationalist fantasies of conquest, combined with a willingness to engage in mass destruction.[3]

Germany claimed its colonies in order to compete globally with Britain and France, both of which had long histories of colonial domination and administration themselves. These countries had their share of racists and ruthless colonial campaigns, too, although neither had ambitions for European acquisitions like Germany did. In Africa, German administrators generally followed the pattern of the British and French in that they tended to govern coastal regions directly, with German personnel, while relying on collaborating "headmen" to govern remote regions in the interior. Christian missionaries were relied upon to introduce "civilized" practices and to provide intelligence about African people. Like other colonies, German colonies were expected to produce raw materials for the mother country. Those who resisted development, civilization, and administration would be put down by colonial armed forces, led by German officers and manned by African soldiers. The Germans followed the general pattern of colonialism in Africa, but they tended to be more efficient than their British and French counterparts.

THE WAR IN WESTERN AFRICA

The most successful German colony was tiny Togo, a narrow strip of land in West Africa with a million residents governed by several dozen German administrators and officers. The colony exported palm kernels and other raw materials produced mainly by peasant farmers, who were helped by German investments in the development of railways and roads. Africans were not represented in the government, although in the interior district administrators worked with appointed African chiefs to collect taxes and maintain justice. Corruption was common, as was corporal punishment, but in 1914 the German government was considering reforms. Togo also contained the most important strategic objective in Germany's African colonies: the radio transmitting station at Kamina, located 120 kilometers to the north of the coastal capital, Lomé. The radio transmitter linked Germany to its other African colonies, while also providing a connection to ships in the South Atlantic. On August 12, 1914, the British moved to seize the transmitters. Two companies of Britain's Gold Coast Regiment invaded from present-day Ghana, firing the first British shots of the war as they captured Lomé. The Gold Coast Regiment then marched north, encountering occasional resistance from lightly armed German forces. More British forces approached from the east, while

French forces were coming from their colony Dahomey, to the west. On August 24, the German governor ordered the destruction of the radio station. The next day, he surrendered the colony. The Allied victory in Togo may seem insignificant in light of the colossal struggle in Europe, but, in considering the transfer of territories during wartime, it must be remembered that even though Togo was smaller than most African colonies, it was still bigger than Belgium and Alsace-Lorraine put together.[4]

To the east of Togo, Germany's colony in Cameroon was substantially larger—in fact, it was about the same size as Germany—with a population of three million. In Cameroon, German companies were granted concessions to produce raw materials. Peasant farmers produced for the market, too, with the same negative and positive inducements experienced by farmers in Togo: taxes had to be paid, while railroads and roads made commerce attractive. Interior districts were administered by German officers and appointed African chiefs, while the coastal towns were ruled directly by German authorities. Cameroon was a model of efficiency, with a budget that was routinely balanced, a rarity in an African colony. But like Togo, it was surrounded by British and French colonies and cut off from Germany by the Allied navies.

Germany had greater military success in Cameroon, in west-central Africa. The Germans kept four thousand troops in Cameroon, three-quarters of whom were Cameroonian. In 1914, they enjoyed success in spite of being badly outnumbered by the approximately twenty thousand Allied soldiers who invaded from the nearby British, French, and Belgian colonies. They came in September 1914, when British West African units seized the coastal capital, Duala, and French forces pushed into southern Cameroon. German troops escaped to the northern plateau, where they held out against the Allies throughout most of 1915. Running low on ammunition, in February 1916 they marched to the southeast and escaped into the Spanish colony of Río Muni. From there they went to Spain's offshore island, Fernando Po, where they spent the rest of the war, preparing for a time when a German victory in Europe would allow them to take power in Cameroon again.[5]

THE WAR IN EASTERN AFRICA

In early 1916, the prospect of a German victory was not so far-fetched, either in Europe or in Africa. While the Germans were defeated quickly in Togo and slowly in Cameroon, they remained in charge of German East Africa, a colony with tremendous economic potential. There, in the two decades before the war, German administration and trade focused on the coastal towns, home to Muslim Swahili traders, whose commercial networks reached far into the interior. German administrators, merchants, and soldiers worked

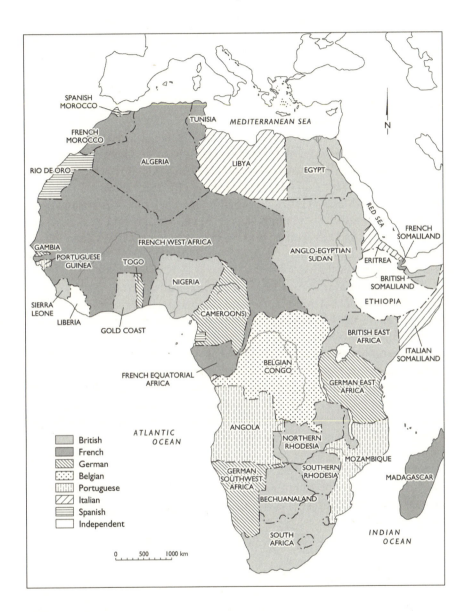

Africa in 1914

together with Swahili merchants, constructing two major railways to support trade with the interior. Swahili boys were able to receive a German education. German was made the language of administration in the interior forests and grasslands, where German authority was centered in military outposts. Local people were affected adversely by two ecological disasters at the turn of the century: a rinderpest, or cattle disease, that killed off many herds, and a spread of trypanosomiasis, or sleeping sickness. Grievances over payments for rubber and cotton led many African people to join a millennial movement, the Maji-Maji, which caused most of the southern half of German East Africa to rebel against Germany. German troops suppressed the rebels ruthlessly, killing two hundred thousand people and substantially depopulating large areas of the countryside.

East African resentment toward German rule meant that when war broke out in August 1914, German territories appeared to be vulnerable. In addition, the German colony was surrounded by enemy colonies. It was bordered on the west by the Belgian Congo, with British Northern Rhodesia (Zambia) and Nyasaland (Malawi) lying to the southwest, and with British East Africa (Kenya and Uganda) to the north. To the south, Mozambique was governed by the Portuguese, British allies who did not enter the war right away. On the coast, the British controlled the island of Zanzibar, while Britain's Royal Navy dominated the Indian Ocean.

The German governor of East Africa announced his desire for his colony to remain neutral, but his orders were ignored by the commander of the German cruiser the *Königsberg*, which played cat and mouse along the coast, sinking British vessels until the Royal Navy put it out of action almost a year later. Orders to remain neutral were also ignored by the military commander, Colonel Paul von Lettow-Vorbeck, who prepared his 260 German officers and 2,500 African troops for action. Lettow-Vorbeck began hostilities by raiding the border with British East Africa, defended by an equivalent force of settlers and African troops. In November 1914, the British landed eight thousand Indian troops at the port of Tanga, only to be repulsed by Lettow-Vorbeck's smaller force. Tanga was a significant embarrassment for the British. Afterward, during 1915, the East African front remained relatively quiet, except for some minor skirmishing. The Allies only resumed major operations against Lettow-Vorbeck in 1916.

THE WAR IN SOUTHERN AFRICA

German rule in South-West Africa (known today as Namibia) was like German East Africa in that it was more than twice the size of Germany itself, but South-West Africa's mainly arid environment ensured that the population was only about two hundred thousand, compared to Germany's sixty-five million. Of those, fourteen thousand settlers immigrated to South-West Africa, attracted by farmland in the vicinity of Windhoek, in the interior. Their settlement was made possible by a genocidal war that the German army fought between 1904 and 1908 against the Herero, local pastoralists who revolted against German rule. A German campaign reduced their number from seventy-five thousand to fifteen thousand and accounted for many of the deaths of thousands of their Nama and Baster neighbors, too. During the campaign, the German army suffered two thousand casualties. As the war against the Herero was coming to a close, the Germans discovered diamonds near Lüderitz, which produced a boom in mining while encouraging the development of towns and transportation. Labor was hard to find, on account of the recent genocide. The remaining Herero, Nama, and Baster were typically required to work on settler farms, so mineworkers had to be recruited from the Ovambo people in the far north.

The colonial situation in German South-West Africa was complicated by relations with the British colonies in South Africa, which were recovering from the Anglo-Boer War of 1899–1902. The British had won the war by defeating Boer forces in the field and by rounding up Boer supporters and placing them in concentration camps, where many died from disease and malnutrition. Boer resentment was mitigated, in part, by the creation of the Union of South Africa in 1910. Under the terms of this political arrangement, which unified the colonies and chiefdoms of South Africa under one government, the Boers were given a disproportionate share in the European-dominated government, while the discriminatory "native" policies of the former Boer republics were allowed to remain substantially in place. This favorable treatment led many Boer resistance leaders to reconcile themselves to British rule and even to participate in the new government. The elections of 1910 were won by the South African National Party, led by two former guerrillas, Louis Botha, a landowner from the Transvaal, and Jan Smuts, a Cambridge-educated attorney from the Cape. Their most significant achievement was the Natives Land Act of 1913, which pushed the African majority onto segregated rural reserves and prevented them from renting from the Europeans, who owned most of the land outside of the reserves. Given this treatment, African responses to the First World War were highly variable, ranging from pledges of loyalty, to small strikes and rebellions, to indifference.[6]

The outbreak of the war forced many Boers to consider the extent to which they were loyal to Britain. On the one hand, in the 1900s the British government was willing to contemplate a greater degree of independence for its white colonies, while it appeared that British South Africans were now more appreciative of Boer desires. Yet some Boers felt sympathy with Germany, the country that had supported their efforts during the war against Britain. Before, during, and after the war, quite a few Boers had migrated to South-West Africa and found the German colony to be congenial. The vast majority of Boers stayed home, and quite a few retained a deep hatred for Britain. Some Boers were even willing to fight on the side of Germany, based on the principle of "my enemy's enemy is my friend." And some Boers were willing to become reconciled to Britain to a degree but were not quite ready to fight and die for the British Empire.

The test of loyalty came when Britain declared war on Germany on August 4, 1914. Britain's settler colonies were not completely sovereign: Ireland was considered part of the United Kingdom, while Australia, Canada, New Zealand, and South Africa had representative parliaments that managed their own internal affairs. The British parliament assumed that its declaration of war brought the entire empire into the war, but in South Africa politicians debated the extent of their participation. Many South Africans of British descent supported the war, while Africans, Boers, and Indians held various opinions. The Boer leaders of the dominant South African Party, together with Botha, the prime minister, and Smuts, the minister of defense, debated with their more reticent colleagues in the cabinet about Britain's request for South African forces to invade German South-West Africa. After a month, the cabinet decided to grant Britain's request, but only if the South African parliament agreed and only if volunteer troops were used. During the cabinet deliberations, several well-known Boer military and political leaders began to plot a coup against British rule. When South Africa declared war, they declared independence and led five thousand Boer cavalrymen on raids in rural areas in hopes of sparking a widespread rebellion. Botha led loyal Boer units against them and over the course of the month succeeded in capturing or killing almost all of the rebels.[7]

Botha's next mission in 1914 was to lead South African forces against the Germans in South-West Africa. The Germans were particularly vulnerable. Their two thousand troops and three thousand reservists were not well prepared for war against fellow Europeans. South Africa could put numerically greater forces into the field, while Britain's navy controlled the coast. The navy landed small South African forces on the coast at Lüderitz. The Germans yielded the mining town to the South Africans, but at Sandfontein, on the border with South Africa, a force of 1,700 Germans captured three thousand South African troops. To the north, another small German force, with five hundred troops, skirmished with ten times as many Portuguese soldiers in Angola, their colony to the north, and succeeded in driving them away from the border region. (Portugal was allied with Britain, although not actively involved in the war.) But German successes were to be short-lived. Once the South African government succeeded in suppressing the Boer rebellion, it could turn its full attention to South-West Africa.

In early 1915, South Africa had seventy thousand men in its armed forces, with more than half of them ready to deploy to South-West Africa. Environmental conditions in South-West Africa limited the mobility of South African forces. Water was particularly scarce, and, as the South Africans took control of the port of Swakopmund and began to advance on Windhoek, the capital, in the interior, they found that the Germans had poisoned the wells. New wells proved slow to dig and yielded little water. Water even had to be transported by ship and overland by motor vehicles. The South Africans hoped that their advance would follow the rail line from Swakopmund to Windhoek, but the Germans destroyed it. South African forces were forced to rebuild it, as there was insufficient water and hay for mules to pull transport wagons, and in any case the Germans had placed landmines on the roads. German forces executed strategic retreats, avoiding large-scale battles. It was only in May 1915 that South African forces, led by Botha, were able to capture Windhoek and its radio transmitting station. The Germans remained in control of the rest of the country but were forced to surrender in July. Combat casualties were very low compared to other theaters of the war, amounting to several hundred lost on both sides. Botha's government allowed the German reservists to return to their farms, in the expectation that a South African administration of South-West Africa would depend on loyal settlers dominating the majority African people, just like at home. [8]

These underlying similarities meant that German settlers in South-West Africa had little to regret about their conquest by South Africans. The lives of individual settlers remained substantially the same. Even so, German national ambitions for an African empire were largely thwarted by 1916. South-West Africa, Togo, and Cameroon fell quickly to the Allies, who relied mainly on settler and African soldiers. In East Africa, the efforts by colonial forces to oust the Germans met with significant resistance that would prolong the fighting until the very end of the war. For the Allies, the war presented an opportunity for them to continue the expansion of their empires, a process that was more or less continuous with the empire-building that had begun in the 1870s. For African people, the war did not usher in massive changes so much as it intensified and extended processes that were already under way.

Chapter Eight

The War at Sea, 1914–1915

Britain and France's ability to defend their empires depended on the willingness of people in remote countries to serve their interests. While some challenged imperialism, most imperial subjects remained loyal or at least neutral. Morale in the colonies preserved Allied interests. So did Allied navies. To administer far-flung empires, Britain and France depended on their navies, and, as we have seen, the Germans also understood the connection between navies and empires, even if their empire was smaller. At the same time as the kaiser was acquiring colonies such as Togo, Cameroon, Tanganyika, and Namibia, he was also embarking on an ambitious naval building program.

The world's navies were in the midst of a technological and tactical revolution. Much attention was paid to the construction of dreadnought battleships, the enormous ships that mounted large, long-range cannons. Naval officers prepared for big naval battles in which fleets of battleships, cruisers, and destroyers sailed against each other, firing and maneuvering. But when war came, a consideration of geography, technology, and the nature of the war led naval officers and their governments to fight differently. In the First World War, there was only one large battle between fleets, the Battle of Jutland, fought between the British and German fleets in 1916. This battle was exceptional. Instead of fighting big battles, the Allied fleets devoted themselves to economic warfare, blockading Germany's access to the sea. And the blockading fleets refused, for the most part, to approach close to Germany, where they might be trapped. Instead, Allied blockade efforts focused on sealing the northern passages that run between Scotland and Norway, a geographical strategy that choked off Germany at low risk.

Allied commanders were averse to risk because their battleships were so costly to build, one of the most peculiar features of the technological history of the First World War. Admirals also worried about the vulnerability of their battleships to new weapons, such as mines, submarines, and torpedoes. These fears were genuine. In response to the blockade, the German government pressed the construction of all these weapons. Submarines armed with mines and torpedoes sailed past (or under) the Allied blockade, in an attempt to build a blockade of their own around the British Isles. Navies on both sides engaged in grim economic warfare that killed both sailors and civilians. As on land, geography and technology made it difficult for combatants to achieve glory in combat.

THE SURFACE WAR, 1914–1915

There were, of course, some exceptions. At the war's outset there were a number of small naval battles on the surface that harkened back to the supposedly glorious days of "fighting sail." In 1914, Germany ordered several of its cruisers into action around the world. As we have seen, one German cruiser, the *Königsberg*, helped to defend the coast of German East Africa until it was sunk in 1915. Another cruiser, the *Karlsruhe*, sank Allied shipping in the South Atlantic before engine trouble caused it to explode in November 1914. In China, Germany kept a naval squadron at Tsingtao. When Japan entered the war on the side of the Allies, the German commander, Vice Admiral Maximilian Graf von Spee, ordered his ships out to sea rather than be destroyed in port by Japan's Imperial Navy. Before the Japanese approached Tsingtao, Spee sent his fastest cruiser, the *Emden*, to the Indian Ocean, where it sank thirty ships and even shelled the city of Madras (today called Chennai), on the east coast of India. The ship was trapped and sunk by an Australian cruiser in November 1914. In the same month, Spee's five other cruisers sailed across the Pacific toward the coast of Chile, where they engaged a squadron of British cruisers, sinking two of them; this was Britain's first naval defeat since the Napoleonic Wars. When the British Admiralty learned of the defeat, they were perturbed enough to dispatch six cruisers, including two fast battlecruisers, to South American waters. Spee sailed his ships around Cape Horn, intending to attack Port Stanley in the Falkland Islands. When he approached the harbor, he was surprised to discover the British cruisers. The British, superior in guns, speed, and numbers, chased and sank four of the German ships on December 8, 1914. Four months later, the British cruisers trapped the fifth one off the coast of Chile.[1]

The cruiser actions highlighted the ways the German navy operated at a considerable geographical and technological disadvantage. Their cruisers depended on coal, yet Germany lacked coaling stations around the world. Prewar plans for supply ships to rendezvous with cruisers proved too difficult under wartime conditions. Yet the prevailing naval technologies also made it difficult for the Allied navies to achieve successes that were significant. The

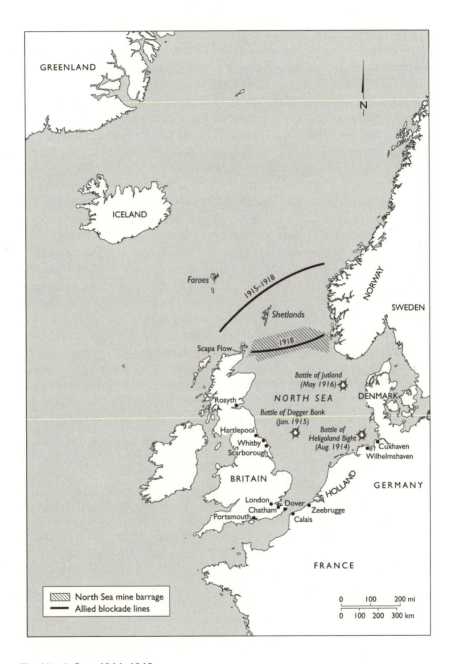

The North Sea, 1914–1918

operations of 1914 demonstrated that British cruisers could ultimately prevail over German cruisers, but the battles had little impact on the course of the war. The British navy's greatest success of 1914 was actually its escort of the ships that carried troops and supplies across the English Channel to France in August 1914, a feat of logistics that was not particularly glorious. At the end of that month, a small force of British submarines and destroyers attacked German patrols off Heligoland, near the coast of Germany. When German cruisers raced out, Britain's battlecruiser squadron intervened, sinking three German cruisers and a destroyer before breaking off the battle. The British were surprised by the quick naval raids that the Germans launched against several English seaports during the fall of 1914. In January 1915, the German navy ordered a squadron of battlecruisers to sea, hoping to lure and trap British ships at Dogger Bank, but the British had cracked Germany's naval codes and were lying in wait with their own squadron of battlecruisers. In a short, sharp battle on January 23, 1915, the British sank one German battle-cruiser and badly damaged another. The German losses at Dogger Bank and Heligoland lent weight to the position taken by the kaiser: German battle-ships should not venture into the North Sea, lest they be lured and trapped by the larger British navy.[2]

In 1914 and 1915, the British navy contained the German navy on the North Sea. The story was similar in the Mediterranean. The British, working with the French, exercised a somewhat loose control in the fall of 1914 that tightened in May 1915 when Italy joined the Allies. The Austrian navy posed a threat from its bases along the Adriatic coast, but it was so badly outnum-bered that its ships remained at their moorings for the next four years, except for several raids.

While on the Mediterranean, Adriatic, and Aegean the Allied navies were superior to the forces of the Central Powers, the Germans did carry out one successful operation with two cruisers, the battlecruiser *Goeben* and the light cruiser *Breslau*. The two warships eluded Allied patrols on their way to Istanbul, which they reached at the end of August. The German government donated the ships to the Ottoman Empire as part of its effort to recruit another ally. The German cruisers were reflagged as Ottoman ships but re-tained their German officers and crews. The donation played an important part in the Ottoman decision to enter the war on the side of the Central Powers in October 1914. The German ships also played an important part in defending Istanbul from attack by the British and French from the west and the Russians from the north and east. While the Russian navy controlled the Black Sea, its inferior ships were not a match for the *Goeben* and the *Bres-lau*.

Russian naval forces improved over the course of 1915, yet at no point were they able to contemplate action against Istanbul. This was mainly for reasons that had to do with geography and technology. Istanbul is situated at the eastern opening of the narrow, fortified waterway that connects the Black Sea to the Aegean. Not only were the German cruisers still formidable—so were the fortifications along the straits. The closure of the straits had serious economic consequences for Russia. Merchants in Russia's southern ports were not able to export grain to markets overseas, nor were they able to import needed war supplies. Russia's northern ports remained open for commerce, but ice closed them for most of the long winter. While Russia controlled its coastal waters, including the Black Sea, it was effectively blockaded by the Ottoman Empire's decision to join the Central Powers.[3]

The Russians had ports on the Baltic, to the north, but the German navy controlled the outlets to the North Sea. Even so, the Germans had little success on the Baltic. The Germans chose to send their best ships to the North Sea, leaving a smaller force of old ships on the Baltic. The Russians, who had lost many ships in the Russo-Japanese War of 1904–1905, had a numerical advantage on the Baltic, but everyone recognized that, should the Germans choose to shuttle ships from the North Sea to the Baltic, the Russians would face a formidable enemy. They responded by employing their ships in defensive positions, particularly around the capital, St. Petersburg, and by laying extensive minefields. The Baltic became a stalemate that was different in one key respect from the North Sea, where the British successfully blockaded Germany: the Germans were still able to use the Baltic Sea to transport goods. Sweden became a key trading partner with Germany, supplying the Germans with iron ore and other essential goods.

THE SUBMARINE WAR, 1914–1915

Before the war, the major powers focused on building battleships, but, within a few months of the war breaking out, the constraints of geography and technology weighed heavily on naval decision makers. Germany's disadvantages could best be overcome by using a technology that had been underestimated before the war: the submarine. Before the war, the British and French navies had experimented extensively with submarines. In 1914, they had fifty-five and seventy-seven, respectively. The Germans began their submarine experiments later, and in 1914 the German navy had only twenty-eight U-boats.

Before reading too much into these numbers, it is important to remember that submarines were still in the earliest stages of design, while naval leaders had not yet thought carefully about their possible roles. Some admirals regarded submarines with contempt, as vessels that snuck about dishonorably. One British admiral declared that they were "un-English" and were "the weapon of cowards who refused to fight like men on the surface."[4] For the most part, admirals tended to imagine that navies would use submarines to sink other naval vessels. This was, in fact, what started to happen in September 1914, when a British submarine sank a German cruiser and a German submarine sank three British cruisers. In January 1915, a German submarine sank a British battleship in the English Channel. On account of the submarine attacks, the British fleet shifted its main base from Scapa Flow in the Orkney Islands, just north of Scotland, to harbors in Scotland and Ireland. It was only after nets, mines, and other defenses were installed around Scapa Flow that the fleet returned there in early 1915. Even then, British admirals—and their German counterparts—hesitated to commit their battleships and cruisers to offensive action, fearing that they might be sunk by submarines.

After the initial encounters of 1914, it began to seem that at sea, as on land, there was a stalemate. British and German naval strategy shifted away from offensive actions by their fleets to economic warfare. The British navy used less expensive ships, such as old cruisers and armed ocean liners, to blockade the northern approaches to the North Sea in an effort to cut off supplies to the soldiers and civilians of the Central Powers. The Germans, for their part, began to use submarines against merchant ships that were on their way to Britain, creating a blockade of their own. The German submarine campaign opened in February 1915.

Submarine warfare was complicated by several factors. Germany announced that all ships approaching the British Isles were subject to sinking, but the German fleet did not have enough submarines to sink every merchant vessel. Instead, the German government hoped to sink enough ships to scare away the rest. The submarine was as much about creating public perceptions of risk as it was about sinking ships. As a strategy, submarine warfare had tremendous potential to inflict economic damage on Britain. Even so, the submarine had technological limits that helped to produce a public relations problem. Submarines were small relative to other ships. They achieved success mainly through surprise, yet the element of surprise was limited by the rules of warfare at sea. By convention, naval vessels that intended to sink merchant vessels were obliged to warn the crew and give them enough time to climb aboard lifeboats. This rule required submarines to rise to the surface and notify the merchant vessel's crew that they would be sunk. This rule worked well enough when large, heavily armored surface vessels approached merchant ships, but submarines were small and vulnerable to attack. In some cases, merchant captains decided to take their chances in efforts to ram and sink submarines. The Allied navies even armed some merchant ships, calling them "Q-ships," and used them to lure submarines. Captains of British merchant vessels even flew the flags of neutral countries. Submarine captains responded to these tactics by not rising to the surface to give warnings. Submariners earned the support of the kaiser, who announced "unrestricted submarine warfare." The kaiser permitted submarine captains to fire their torpedoes from under the water, without warning, at any ship in the vicinity of the British Isles.

Neutral countries such as the United States found the attendant loss of civilian life to be outrageous. The German government responded by stating that the British blockade of Germany was directed at neutral shipping and innocent civilians, too. While this may have been true, the British blockade tended to result in the loss of property, while unrestricted submarine warfare tended to result in the loss of life, too, compounding Germany's propaganda problems. In May 1915, a German submarine sank the passenger ship *Lusitania* off the coast of Ireland, killing 1,201 civilians, including 128 Americans. The U.S. president, Woodrow Wilson, demanded that Germany cease unrestricted submarine warfare. The kaiser complied. Once again, German submarines rose to the surface before sinking ships. Once again, German submarines were attacked by armed merchant vessels. Faced with the choice between losing more submarines and U.S. intervention on the side of the Allies, the kaiser chose to end all submarine warfare in September. The campaign had been a political failure even though it had resulted in the sinking of nearly a million tons of shipping.[5]

The suspension of submarine warfare did make it possible for the United States to remain neutral. One other neutral country, Portugal, decided that in any case its shipping and colonial interests were best protected by entering the war on the side of the Allies. Portugal had an alliance with Britain that dated to the fourteenth century. Portugal declared war in March 1916. During 1917 and 1918, fifty thousand Portuguese soldiers served under British command on the Western Front, while Portuguese forces were also active in Africa. The Portuguese switch from neutrality to belligerency was significant, yet not as significant as the switch of the United States. This would only happen in April 1917, after another year of quasi-neutral support for the Allies was met with new German provocations.

Chapter Nine

The War in the Middle East, 1914–1916

In the intensive war that developed in Europe in 1914 and 1915, both sides grasped for any advantage. The Allies had a significant advantage in that they could draw on the human and material resources of their colonies. These included the overseas empires of France and Britain as well as the Russian provinces in the Caucasus and Central Asia. Colonial order became more imperative than ever. The Allies took steps to ensure their prestige as rulers, while the Central Powers took steps to try to undermine that prestige and cause dissent. Even so, the Central Powers' efforts could not take the form of major incursions and invasions, simply because the Allied navies dominated the world's oceans and had a chokehold on the North Sea and the Mediterranean, where the Central Powers had their naval bases.

Allied power at sea made it possible for them to turn the First World War into an extension of the colonial warfare that had occurred during the previous five decades. British Empire forces, along with their Belgian, French, Japanese, and Portuguese allies, captured German territories in Africa and Asia. Britain, France, and Russia all pressed their advantage on the Ottoman Empire, which entered the war on the side of the Central Powers in November 1914. Ottoman territory, stretching throughout the Middle East, was now up for grabs by the imperialist powers.

The Ottoman Empire, thought to be the "sick man of Europe," resisted well at first, provoking concerns about Allied imperial prestige. Successful Ottoman resistance in the Dardanelles and Iraq, together with successful German resistance in East Africa, made for the only bright spots in the Central Powers' war effort outside of Europe. Germany's introduction of submarine warfare prevented the Allies from receiving all their raw materials, but it also produced outrage in the United States. Prestige was closely bound to the ability of a country to control and protect the distribution of raw materials. As such, the war at sea and the war in the colonies was an extension of nineteenth-century imperialism.

EMPIRES AT WAR IN THE DARDANELLES

When the Ottoman Empire entered the war on the side of the Central Powers, it blocked Russia's access to the Aegean and Mediterranean seas. Ottoman forces launched a winter assault into the Caucasus Mountains, a campaign in which tens of thousands of soldiers were killed in battle or froze to death. Pressed by the Ottoman entry into the war, Russia appealed for help to France and Britain. Geographic considerations inspired the Allies to attack the Dardanelles from the Aegean Sea, to the west. Britain's First Lord of the Admiralty, Winston Churchill, had visions of the fleet steaming through the straits, capturing Istanbul, knocking the Ottomans out of the war, and flanking Germany and Austria from the south. Churchill was a graduate of the Royal Military Academy at Sandhurst and a veteran of campaigns against amateur soldiers in South Africa, the Sudan, and the Northwest Frontier of India. He believed it would be possible for the Royal Navy to mount a successful assault on the Ottoman Empire. Churchill seriously underestimated the Ottomans, who had a professional, modernizing army that was receiving considerable help from the Germans.

At Churchill's direction, in February and March 1915 the British and French navies attempted to push a fleet of ten battleships through the narrows, in spite of warnings from senior admirals that naval gunfire could never defeat the Ottomans' well-built fortifications. The geography of the Dardanelles gave defenders a heavy advantage. Allied naval gunners had to hit Ottoman guns directly to put them out of action, but an Ottoman hit on an Allied battleship's steering or hull could put numerous Allied guns out of action. The technology of land-based artillery also made it easier to hit a ship. A land-based cannon fires a shell in a high trajectory. A miss splashes in the water and is easily spotted, enabling the observers and battery commanders to adjust their fire accordingly. By contrast, a naval gun fires in a flat trajectory. When it misses at sea, it is relatively easy to spot the splash and make adjustments. But when it misses on land, its flat trajectory means that it might miss by a lot, while the target and the actual site of impact is often obscured by dust and smoke. To further help the defense, the Ottomans laid mines and employed mobile howitzers to chase minesweepers. The mines, combined with the artillery and the fortifications, made it virtually impossible for the Allied navies to reach Istanbul.

The Allied admirals' pessimistic assessment of the fortifications proved correct during a pitched battle on March 18, 1915, when Ottoman mines, protected by mobile field artillery, sank three battleships and disabled three

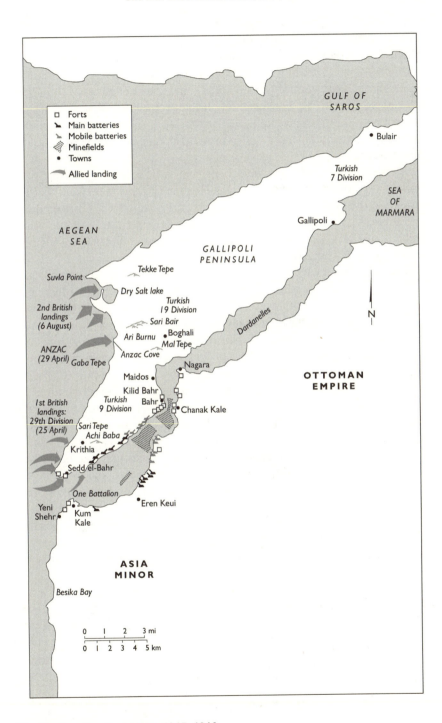

The Dardanelles Campaign, 1915–1916

more. The Allied fleet was forced to retreat. Evidence was piling up that it would be difficult to defeat the Ottomans, yet in March and April 1915 the Entente Powers negotiated what was called the Pact of London, which was signed on April 26, 1915. The pact was a secret agreement in which France and Britain pledged control of Istanbul and the straits to Russia, while Italy was enticed to join the Entente through the promise of what is today the southern part of Turkey, in addition to territories in southeastern Europe that belonged to Austria-Hungary and Albania. Imperialist visions of conquest remained robust.

In order to achieve these objectives, the Allied navies yielded to the armies. On April 25, Allied troops landed on the Gallipoli peninsula near the entrance to the straits. At the tip of the peninsula, Cape Helles, fifteen thousand soldiers from Britain, France, and their colonies came ashore, while fifteen thousand troops from the Australian and New Zealand Army Corps (ANZAC) landed at Ari Burnu, a point on the northwest coast that was subsequently named Anzac Cove. Allied troops met heavy resistance from the Ottoman army everywhere, yet most military historians agree that, with better planning and execution, the Australians in particular might have seized key positions. Instead, they made several key errors. For example, the Australians landed one mile north of their planned beachhead. Disordered ANZAC soldiers encountered determined and well-led Ottoman troops who nearly drove the invaders back into the sea.[1]

The ANZAC and other Allied forces dug in, and Gallipoli became the scene of trench warfare. What caused the stalemate? During and after the campaign, journalists, historians, and official inquiries have pointed to poor strategic planning. The idea that all of European Turkey and the Balkans could become a long and successful southern front was preposterous, given the constraints of resources and geography. At the operational level, it was virtually impossible for a navy to break through the heavily fortified Dardanelles, while military operations, such as the landings at Anzac Cove and the attacks at Lone Pine, never mounted sufficient force. The infantry tactics that were often used, with soldiers fixing bayonets, jumping out of their trenches, and charging forward into enemy machine-gun fire, revealed a certain misplaced optimism, given the experiences of soldiers in Europe in 1914.

All the accounts written during and immediately after the Gallipoli campaign criticized the strategic, operational, and tactical failures and blamed then on senior officers and politicians. And following the journalist and official historian of the Australian forces, C. E. W. Bean, many recent historians have represented individual soldiers as heroes, in contrast to the British leadership, who are blamed for sending inadequate resources to win the battle.

Much historical work has focused on poor leadership, from the British cabinet on down to field commanders. Yet if we shift focus to environmental factors, the campaign looks somewhat different. The campaign originated in the British government's faulty strategic assessment of geography—not somehow in the geography itself—while Allied defeat at the hands of the Ottomans can be understood by examining the ways each side applied manpower and technology to topography. These are modifications to the conventional military and political histories, although, as they relate to geography, they might be claimed as environmental. Another environmental aspect of the story involves the experiences of the soldiers themselves. The troops who fought at Gallipoli experienced dangerous and degrading circumstances. The Ottoman experience at Gallipoli is only beginning to be understood. By contrast, Allied troops depicted their horrid environment in a wealth of writing and art.

At Gallipoli, environmental conditions tested the limits of human endurance. Troops suffered from exposure to heat and cold. They experienced water shortages and intestinal diseases, while at the same time sharing cramped quarters with flies, lice, and corpses. The vileness of Gallipoli highlights a key point about the campaign and about campaigns in the First World War more generally. They are remembered for their degradation, which soldiers experienced and depicted with reference to environment and technology, and contrasted with the nineteenth-century belief, held by British, French, and Ottomans alike, that modern civilization held out the prospect for something better.

In Allied accounts of the fighting around the Dardanelles, personal degradation was often described by reference to the hostile environment. Many particularly recalled the misery of living with swarming insects. Private Harold Boughton of the London Regiment remembered:

> One of the biggest curses was flies. Millions and millions of flies. The whole side of the trench used to be one black swarming mass. Anything you opened, like a tin of bully, would be swarming with flies. If you were lucky enough to have a tin of jam and opened that, swarms of flies went straight into it. They were all around your mouth and on any cuts or sores that you'd got, which then turned septic. [2]

Another soldier, A. P. Herbert, composed a poem entitled "Flies" about the indignities visited by the insects upon decomposing corpses:

> The flies! Oh, God, the flies
> They soiled the sacred dead.
> To see them swarm from dead men's eyes.
> And share the soldier's bread. [3]

Insect pests, dread diseases, and poor sanitation filled the battlefield with environmental hazards and produced the most degrading deaths. Seaman Joe Murray of the Royal Naval Division remembered:

Dysentery was a truly awful disease that could rob a man of the last vestiges of human dignity before it killed him. A couple of weeks before getting it my old pal was as smart and upright as a guardsman. Yet after about ten days it was dreadful to see him crawling about, his trousers round his feet, his backside hanging out, his shirt all soiled—everything was soiled. He couldn't even walk. So I took him by one arm and another pal got hold of him by the other, and we dragged him to the latrine. . . . We tried to keep the flies off him and to turn him round—put his backside toward the trench. But he simply rolled into this foot-wide trench, half-sideways, head first in the slime. We couldn't pull him out, we didn't have enough strength, and he couldn't help himself at all. We did eventually get him out but he was dead, he'd drowned in his own excrement.[4]

In order to compensate for the hostility of the environment, British troops, wherever they went, tended to give places names that reminded them of home. This practice was true at Gallipoli, too. The British trenches at Cape Helles were given such names as Piccadilly Circus, Regent Street, and Hyde Park Corner, a reflection of ironic nostalgia for home. It is also a reflection of long-standing British colonial practice to name places after home as part of the process of appropriation: witness New York, Melbourne, and Wellington, to name but a few.

This practice was, of course, simultaneously ironic and nostalgic. Nostalgia for particular places in Britain and Ireland could also be found in other sorts of depictions that mention places at home. The song most strongly associated with the British army in the First World War is "It's a Long Way to Tipperary." The fact that Tipperary is in Ireland (then a part of the United Kingdom) was not such a concern in the British army. The song mentions Piccadilly and Leicester Square as well, and, besides, even the units from towns and counties in England and Scotland were heavily supplemented by Irishmen, a key way Britain relied on colonial troops during the war. The main thing to remember about the song, though, is that it helped soldiers in the British army to think of a landscape at home while serving far away.

In poetry, too, British troops reflected on their homes. Most famously, the poet Rupert Brooke, on his way to Gallipoli, wrote the following sonnet.

> If I should die, think only this of me:
> That there's some corner of a foreign field
> That is for ever England. There shall be
> In that rich earth a richer dust concealed;
> A dust whom England bore, shaped, made aware,
> Gave, once, her flowers to love, her ways to roam,
> A body of England's, breathing English air,
> Washed by the rivers, blest by suns of home.
> And think, this heart, all evil shed away,
> A pulse in the eternal mind, no less
> Gives somewhere back the thoughts by England given;

Her sights and sounds; dreams happy as her day;
And laughter, learnt of friends; and gentleness,
In hearts at peace, under an English heaven.[5]

Notice how even the structure of the poem moves away from England. The first half is in the classic English form of the Shakespearean sonnet, rhyming ABAB CDCD, while the second half is an Italian or Petrarchan sonnet, rhyming FGH FGH.

Such reflections on location were different from the practice of the Australians and New Zealanders, who tended to name geographical features descriptively or even after soldiers. For Australians and New Zealanders, Gallipoli came to be remembered more as a special occasion for their nations—the first time their soldiers fought outside of the British Empire and on the world stage. More Australians and New Zealanders died in France in 1916 to 1918, but Gallipoli was first and for that reason is still special. In Turkey, the Gallipoli campaign is remembered as an important step in nation-building. It is particularly remembered as the place where army major Mustafa Kemal gained recognition as a leader—he was the first president of Turkey, from 1923 to 1938, during which time he embarked on modernizing reforms. At Gallipoli, Kemal and his fellow soldiers resisted the Allied imperialists successfully, although in the early 1920s the memory of Gallipoli would be overshadowed by events that were even more significant for Turkey's nationhood: Kemal's success in driving out the British, French, Greeks, and Italians.

In January 1916, the Allies recognized that they had been defeated by the Ottoman army. The Allies gave up on trench warfare at Gallipoli and evacuated the peninsula. This was not the only defeat for the Allies in the Middle East. In the Ottoman territory of Iraq, then still called Mesopotamia, the Ottomans inflicted what was, in some ways, a worse defeat on the British.

EMPIRES AT WAR IN IRAQ

The British had two reasons for being interested in Iraq. In the years before the war, the British navy, led by Winston Churchill, began to convert its battleships from coal to oil. Oil-powered engines were capable of greater speeds, and speed, as we have seen, was a principal goal of the British navy—in designing battle cruisers, the admirals had even been willing to sacrifice armor for speed. There was another sacrifice involved in the switch from coal to oil: plenty of coal was produced in Britain itself, while oil supplies had to come from sources overseas. Depending on oil from overseas ran the risk of it being cut off by hostile powers. The large oil fields of the day lay in the United States, the Dutch East Indies (Indonesia), and the region around the Caspian Sea. It would be difficult for the British to secure

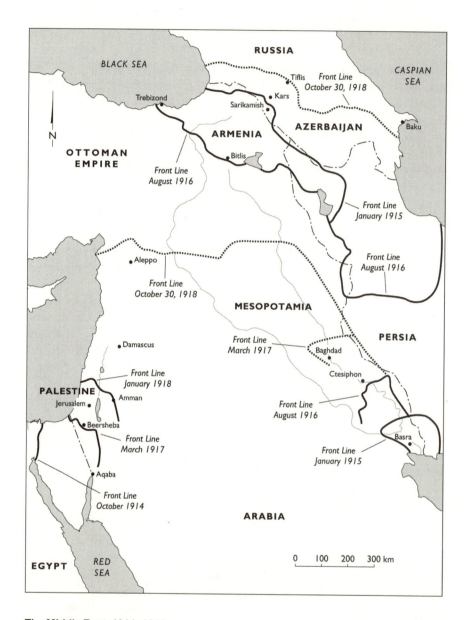

The Middle East, 1914–1918

access to these sources. Oil exploration had only just begun in the Persian Gulf during the years before the war. The oil fields on the southern, Arab side of the gulf were not yet discovered, but it was then at least becoming clear that there was abundant oil on the northern shores, in Persia (Iran).

Persian oil was starting to be exploited by the Anglo-Persian Oil Company, which had obtained a concession from the weak Persian government. The Persian government was so weak, in fact, that in 1907 Russia declared a protectorate over northern Persia and Britain declared a protectorate over the southwest. The British protectorate was managed by colonial officials from British India, who supported the development of Anglo-Persian's large refineries on the offshore island of Abadan. When Churchill began to build oil-burning battleships, he took steps to secure this oil supply for Britain. In 1913, Churchill persuaded the British parliament to acquire a majority share in Anglo-Persian. When the war broke out, Churchill was keen for the Indian government to take steps to secure the oil supply from Ottoman attack.

Concerns about oil were not the only motive for the British invasion of Iraq. Oil and battleships were bound up with British imperial power during the war, a power that was under threat in the most important British colony, India. The Indian government had special concerns. A significant proportion of India's population was Muslim and disinclined to fight against fellow Muslims in the Ottoman Empire. To complicate the picture further, the figurehead Ottoman sultan, Mehmet V, was the caliph—the successor of Mohammed and leader of all Muslims. When the Ottoman Empire joined the Central Powers and went to war against the Allies, Mehmet V called for all Muslims in British, French, and Russian territory to rise in a holy war, or jihad, against their rulers.

The call for a jihad failed, but British administrators were conscious of the need to maintain British prestige when it came to the war effort against the Ottomans. British defeats would not only play into the hands of propagandists from the Central Powers. In prewar India, there had been a rising tide of nationalism. Few Indians called for independence yet, but many Indian leaders hoped for greater self-government. Their hand would be strengthened by British defeats as well as by pleas for help from India.

Concerns about prestige, coupled with the desire to secure an oil supply, persuaded the British cabinet to request that India send troops to attack the Ottomans in Iraq. In the fall of 1914, troops of the Sixth Indian Division secured southern Iraq, driving Ottoman forces out of the port of Basra and the town of Qurna, where the Tigris and Euphrates rivers flow together. They also secured the oil fields in Ahwaz, Persia, the source of oil for a pipeline that ran to Abadan, near the gulf. Reinforced by the Indian Twelfth Division in the early months of 1915, British forces in Iraq rose to nearly thirty thousand to form an army that had significant manpower but that lacked equipment and medical supplies. British officers led Indian soldiers in successful campaigns to take Amara, up the Tigris River, in June 1915, and to take Nasiriya, up the Euphrates River, in July. In doing so, the Indian army not only had to overcome Ottoman defenders who built fortifications along the rivers. They also had to find their way across the hostile landscape of southern Iraq, where floods, swamps, and heat impeded their advance. And finally, local Arabs resented both the Ottomans and the British, and engaged in sniping and ambushes against both sides.

Nevertheless, the capture of Amara and Nasiriya and the securing of the oil fields at Ahwaz represented successes for the British at a time when the Gallipoli campaign was bogging down. Had the British stopped there, they would have been overextended and subject to a Turkish counterattack. As it happened, the British general in charge of the Indian army in Mesopotamia, Sir John Nixon, with the support of the British government, decided to continue moving up the Tigris River toward Baghdad. His subordinate, Major General Charles Townshend, led four brigades up the river in November 1915. At Ctesiphon, just south of Baghdad, Townshend's Indian force encountered a larger Turkish force, which they fought to a standstill. With many of his officers and troops wounded and sick, Townshend withdrew south to the town of Kut, which he fortified in preparation for a siege.

Townshend had fought before in such a situation. In 1895, as a junior officer, he successfully commanded Indian troops who were besieged at Chitral on India's Northwest Frontier. Yet Kut was different. Townshend hoped to be relieved by Indian units to the south, even though he knew that these were outnumbered. At Kut, Townshend overestimated his food supply. Indian troops were unwilling to contemplate eating cattle and horses, which would have violated religious scruples. The Ottoman force was led by professional officers, including both Turks and Germans, who engineered excellent positions in order to prevent a breakout or an attack from the outside. And the environment around Kut favored the attackers: winter rains turned the banks of the river into a sea of mud, making it difficult for armies to move. Townshend and his troops began to starve. On April 29, 1916, Townshend surrendered his force of thirteen thousand. This was the worst defeat for the British Empire since 1781, when Washington defeated Cornwallis at Yorktown. Townshend himself was treated well in captivity, living in a villa near Istanbul, but most of his soldiers were killed in forced marches that the Ottomans required them to make on their way to prison. Ottoman and German victories in the Middle East and the propaganda that went with them did not persuade many Indians to rebel against the British Empire, even as the empire's prestige suffered. And at least the oil remained secure.

WAR IN THE CAUCASUS AND THE ARMENIAN GENOCIDE

To the far north, the Ottomans were stopped by the Russians in an assault on another environmentally challenging area, the Caucasus Mountains. In the previous century, the Russians had displaced hundreds of thousands of Turks from their homes in the region. The Ottomans thought that an invasion would inspire a revolt against Russia, much as they hoped that they could inspire Indians to rise against the British. The Ottoman leadership attacked as early as possible in 1914—in December, in fact, in one of the coldest and snowiest parts of Europe. Nearly 150,000 Ottoman troops advanced against one hundred thousand Russians. As in other First World War campaigns, the defenders had significant advantages, but these were made more significant by poor Ottoman preparation to transport adequate supplies for cold-weather fighting. In December 1914 and January 1915, Russian forces inflicted significant defeats on the Ottomans, who suffered approximately eighty thousand casualties, most of them from frostbite, disease, and hunger.

The Ottoman leadership had only themselves to blame. Their grand visions of retaking Turkish territory from the Russians came up against the realities of topography and climate. Yet instead of blaming themselves, the Ottoman leadership began to fix blame on the Armenians, a minority group of several million people who lived in the Caucasus on both the Russian side and the Ottoman side. On both sides, the Armenians had suffered repression. Some Ottoman Armenians were indeed fighting for the Russians, but many were not. In any case, in the spring of 1915, when the Russian army halted its advance in the Caucasus on account of the fighting in Eastern Europe, Ottoman soldiers began to massacre Armenians. Armenian resistance did not help; the looting, raping, and killing continued. In May 1915, the Ottoman government ordered the army to force Armenians to march south to Lebanon and Syria. Armenians who resisted were ordered to be killed, while many more died on the marches. Many fled to Russian Armenia and died in transit. And those who survived the march to the south did not necessarily survive the war: they were kept in unsanitary camps that experienced severe shortages of food for the duration of the war. It is not known exactly how many Armenians lived under the Ottomans before the war or how many were killed during the war. The standard figures were calculated by a famous historian, Arnold Toynbee, who worked for the wartime British government. Toynbee made a rough estimate that six hundred thousand Armenians died, six hundred thousand migrated, and six hundred thousand survived.[6]

Historians and politicians have debated the extent of Armenian suffering. The Ottoman government called for forced migration and allowed its troops to kill hundreds of thousands. The massacres and forced migrations show the extent to which the war was continuous with the earlier era of imperialism. On both sides, in fact, the war stoked imperialist imaginations. Ottoman Turks hoped for a greater Turkey. Encouraged by the Germans, the Ottomans imagined that their troops could march far into Russian Central Asia, where Turkic languages are spoken, and from there pose a threat to British India. For their own part, the Germans began to imagine a greater Germany in the east, also taken at the expense of Russia. The Allies were just as imaginative. Not only did they take German territories in Africa, Asia, and the Pacific.

The British, French, and Russians promised Austrian land to Italians who dreamed of a "greater Italy." In March 1915, the British and French promised the Russians that, when the Ottomans were defeated, Russia could possess all of Ottoman Armenia, plus Istanbul and the waterways that connected the Black Sea to the Aegean. The next month, the British and French promised the Greeks and Italians that, in exchange for participation in the war, they could have large parts of the land along Turkey's Aegean coast.

Ottoman victories at Gallipoli and Kut did not cause the Allies to reconsider their own imperialist tendencies. In the winter of 1915 to 1916, the Russian general Nikolai Yudenich, equipping his army well for winter fighting, captured the heavily fortified city of Erzerum by maneuvering at altitudes as high as three thousand meters in the Kargapazar Mountains and outflanking the Ottoman defenders. Yudenich continued his advance through eastern Turkey, defeating a Turkish army at Erzingan by inflicting thirty-four thousand casualties. By the fall of 1916, when cold weather set in again, Russian forces occupied much of eastern Turkey.

As the Russians carved up the northern portion of the Ottoman Empire, the British and French aimed to do the same with the south. In May 1916, four months after the Allied defeat at Gallipoli and just a few weeks after the fall of Kut, a British diplomat, Sir Mark Sykes, and a French diplomat, François Picot, negotiated an agreement in which their governments divided the Ottoman Empire's Middle Eastern territories into British and French zones of "direct control" and "spheres of influence." The British would have Palestine and Iraq, while the French would have Syria and Lebanon. Both powers would work to supervise or control local Arab leaders. Never mind that, several months earlier, the chief British administrator in Egypt, Sir Henry McMahon, had promised an Arab leader, Sherif Hussein, that Arabs would govern these territories for themselves.[7] The very same imperialist thinking that had contributed to the outbreak of the war—that vast territories could be conquered in spite of the realities of geography and technology—persisted throughout the war and even helped to prolong it.

Chapter Ten

The Offensives of 1916

During the first two years of the war, soldiers and civilians on both sides suffered terribly. In 1916, it seemed that more suffering would be necessary: victory appeared to be a distant possibility. It was unlikely that colonial uprisings would destabilize the Allies. France and Britain had fought Germany to a standstill on the Western Front and stalemate prevailed on the Italian front, too. On the Eastern Front, movement was still possible, but it seemed unlikely that either Germany or Russia had the resources to knock each other out of the war.

Both sides lost hundreds of thousands of soldiers, yet, as the historian John Keegan points out, at the end of 1915 armies were bigger than ever. Russia replaced its casualties with massive numbers of conscripts. Russian industry expanded, too, providing rifles, cannons, and shells, as well as trucks, telegraphs, and airplanes, at such a pace that the army was now as well equipped as the German and French armies. In France, production rose, too, bolstered by the entry of women into the factory workforce. More Frenchmen could not be found to join the army, but the army undertook a reorganization scheme that helped it to use its manpower more efficiently. The French could rely on the British for more manpower. The British had a small regular army of eleven divisions before the war. As the war got under way, the defense secretary, Lord Kitchener, encouraged men from the same towns, industries, or ethnic groups to form their own battalions. These were called the "pals battalions" and formed the core of Kitchener's "new army" of thirty divisions. In addition, Britain could now rely on twenty-eight divisions of "territorials" or reservists, for a total of seventy divisions.[1] Additional manpower allowed political and military leaders to reconsider their strategies. The wise management of one's own population, together with the depletion of the other side's, became central to the strategies of the Allies and the Central Powers.

THE BATTLE OF VERDUN

In December 1915, representatives of all the Allied countries met in Chantilly, France, to plan the next steps in the war. The Allies were agreed on the need for attrition on the various fronts, in other words, for steady operations aimed at reducing the enemy's manpower. The strategy of attrition now played an important role in Allied warfare; so would the concept of the breakthrough. During the fighting of 1915, the British and French reached the same conclusion: that a breakthrough would be possible if only sufficient numbers of troops and resources could be concentrated at an advantageous point on the German lines. The French commander, General Joseph Joffre, proposed to his counterparts from Britain, Italy, Russia, and Serbia that in a matter of weeks they should all begin concentrated offensives aiming for a breakthrough against specific, vulnerable points in the German and Austrian lines. The Allies hesitated about the timing—the British and Russians preferred to wait for months—but all the Allies agreed on the principle of going on the offensive.

The Germans had reached the same conclusion about the need for a breakthrough operation, although their geographical situation required them to think somewhat differently than the Allies. The Allies surrounded the Central Powers. The Austrians had suffered such casualties that they could not be counted on for a major offensive contribution against Russia. The Germans, for their own part, could only launch a major offensive against either France or Russia. Russian geography required the German army to advance over vast spaces, while France was small enough that it seemed feasible, from a geographic standpoint, that it might be knocked out of the war. In some ways, this was the same logic that underlay the Schlieffen Plan. On Christmas Day 1915, Germany's lead general, Erich von Falkenhayn, recommended to Kaiser Wilhelm several measures that he hoped would end the war. He advocated a resumption of unrestricted submarine warfare, which the kaiser judged to be too dangerous from a diplomatic standpoint. The kaiser agreed to Falkenhayn's main proposal: that an offensive begin on the French positions at Verdun, an ancient fortress city near the Meuse River on the southern sector of the Western Front. Falkenhayn argued that, even though Verdun was surrounded by two rings of modern forts, they could be easily breached by heavy artillery and that they were, in addition, lightly garrisoned: after German successes against the forts in Belgium, the French removed their own forts' cannons and placed them in the field. In the event that a breakthrough did not occur, Falkenhayn hoped that the battle would "compel the French to throw in every man they have. If they do so the forces of France will bleed to death." He argued for attrition, as the historian John Keegan points out, but, as another historian, Hew Strachan, has shown, Falkenhayn's planning for the operation indicated that he hoped for a breakthrough.[2]

The chief evidence in support of Strachan's claim is that Falkenhayn endorsed new kinds of battlefield tactics that troops had developed in the trench warfare of 1915. These tactics were used in the opening weeks of the battle of Verdun. Verdun was a bulge, or salient, held by three divisions of the French Third Army, two of which were made up of reservists. They were backed up by one division stationed behind the lines. Opposite them was the German Fifth Army, commanded by the kaiser's son, Crown Prince Wilhelm, whom Falkenhayn reinforced with six regular divisions, four reserve divisions, and extra artillery. The best German troops were trained as storm troopers. Armed with grenades and flamethrowers, they aimed to attack in small units, firing, moving, and taking shelter along the battlefield. In avoiding the massed wave assaults of 1914 and 1915, the storm troopers were expected to hold advanced sections of the battlefield long enough that regular troops could arrive and consolidate the positions. These kinds of movements by the infantry complicated the role of the artillery. In a massed wave assault, the artillery fired its initial bombardment and then either stopped firing or aimed for the enemy's rear, so as not to hit the infantry. Now storm-trooper tactics made accurate observation and communication even more important. To improve observation, and to impede French observations, Falkenhayn deployed more airplanes than usual.

New tactics gave the German army certain advantages, yet the French army had advantages of a more conventional sort, in the form of terrain. A long ridge—known to geologists as a cuesta—extends from north to south along the eastern side of Verdun and the Meuse River. In order to capture Verdun, the German army would have to dislodge the French from the ridge. French commanders did not intend to make this easy. They placed Verdun's principal fortifications along the ridge. French defenders would occupy the high ground, where they could see German forces exposed below. Easy French observation made the Germans vulnerable to artillery fire, while German soldiers would have to attack uphill at many points on the French line.[3]

To make the landscape of Verdun even more challenging for the Germans, bad weather caused Falkenhayn to postpone the attack from February 12 to February 21. Even though the weather was bad, and even though Falkenhayn had hoped to achieve complete air superiority, the French commanders observed that German forces were massing for an attack. They ordered their troops to reinforce their forts, trenches, and shelters. On February 21, the Germans began a massive, nine-hour artillery bombardment, which destroyed French communications entirely and may have killed half of the French troops on the front lines. German storm troopers advanced in their small units. They encountered heavy resistance from the remaining French troops, but the Germans pushed them back. The key French fort of Douaumont fell on the 25th. At that point, it seemed that the German army was about to achieve a breakthrough and capture Verdun.

The French high command decided to reinforce Verdun, considering it to be an important symbol of French resistance. How many lives was a symbol worth? In some ways, a retreat at Verdun would have been a good thing for the French. If they had fallen back to the line of woods west of the Meuse River, they would have been able to form a straight line of trenches, instead of having to defend a salient. The French decision to stand and fight at Verdun has been criticized as impractical and unrealistic, yet symbols were important in a war that was engaging entire societies. Public opinion sustained a war effort based on sacrifice and attrition. In fact, stalemate and the prospect of long-term, total war meant that a country could lose if public opinion cracked under pressure. At Verdun, Joffre decided to supplement the Third Army with the Second Army. He placed the Second Army's general, Philippe Pétain, in command of the entire operation, because he had a reputation as a tough, fighting general.

Pétain had commanded brigades at the front during 1914 and 1915 and reached different conclusions about trench warfare than his German counterparts. Instead of using new infantry tactics to achieve breakthrough, Pétain believed that the best way to win the war was by means of "active defense." Troops should hold their positions and keep pressure on the enemy by occasional forward attacks, supported by artillery, but should never advance beyond range of artillery and communications, as had happened in several of the battles of 1915. A breakthrough would only happen when the enemy was completely worn down by active defense. In other words, Pétain depended on attrition to achieve victory. He also depended on psychological toughness. Troops had to be willing to sustain horrible losses. They also had to be willing to reoccupy the forts. Pétain analyzed the German attacks on forts during 1914 and concluded that the forts had withstood shelling reasonably well; it was the soldiers in them who had cracked. He ordered that the forts of Verdun be rearmed and instructed fort commanders to teach soldiers to maintain their composure under heavy shelling. Pétain based his artillery in and around the forts and almost immediately was able to disrupt German movements on the battlefield. He increased the number of French aircraft, to improve French observation and to impede German efforts in the air. And finally, he oversaw the construction and maintenance of roads and railways to the front, which enabled massive supplies and reinforcements to be brought forward.

Reinforcements were key in the terrible fighting, which the human psyche could not withstand for long periods. In March and April 1916, Pétain rotated forty different divisions at Verdun. The road that carried them there was called *la voie sacrée*, literally "the holy way" but perhaps best translated as "the way of sacrifice."[4]

For all of Pétain's logistics and toughness, the French were still nearly defeated. In April and May, Falkenhayn ordered attacks on a wider front that pushed French troops back to their last lines of defense. They clung tenaciously to ground that was shelled repeatedly, a muddy landscape pockmarked with huge holes. The French soldier Henri Barbusse described a devastated village near Verdun and the surrounding country in his novel *Under Fire*:

> We caught glimpses of the whitish heaps of houses and the vague spiders' webs of hanging roofs. . . . In one cellar, through a grill, on the edge of the waves of this petrified ocean, we made out the fire that the guardians of this dead place keep alight. We waded through marshy fields, we got lost in silent regions where the mud grabbed us by the feet, then we more or less managed to regain our balance on another road, the one leading from Carency to Souchez. The tall poplars lining it are broken, their trunks shredded; at one place there is a huge colonnade of shattered trees. Then, accompanying us on either side through the darkness we can see dwarf phantoms of trees, split into palms or completely wrecked into chopped wood or string, bent over on themselves, as if kneeling. From time to time potholes interrupt our march and make the column wobble unevenly; or the road becomes a pond which we cross on our heels, making a sound of splashing oars with our feet. Planks have been put down in the mud at intervals. When, slippery with mud, they veer to one side our feet slide on them, and sometimes there is enough water for them to float. Then, under a man's weight, they go "flack!" and sink. The man falls or staggers, with frenzied stream of oaths.[5]

The German attack on Verdun—and the French defense—had transformed the appearance of the landscape, and it had also made it into a malevolent force, sucking soldiers into the mud. The landscape of the trenches, lit by flare shells, took on a peculiar appearance:

> The air suddenly lights up: a flare. The scenery in which I am lost appears clearly around me. You can see the crest of our trench, jagged, disheveled, and, plastered along the forward wall, every five meters, like vertical larvae, the shadows of those on watch. A few drops of light show where their guns are beside them. The trench is shored up with sandbags; it has been enlarged everywhere and in lots of places broken by landslides. The sandbags, lying flat and disjointed on top of each other, have the appearance, in the astral light of the flare, of those vast dismantled slabs of ancient monuments in ruins. I look through the peephole. In the pale misty light spread by the flare I can see the rows of stakes and even the slender lines of barbed wire crossing over from one stake to the next. It's right in front of me, like pen-strokes scribbled and

hatching the pallid pock-marked field. Further down, in the nocturnal ocean
filling the ravine, silence and immobility gather.[6]

Natural metaphors such as larvae and oceans seem out of place in the
unnatural trenches, while the night is as enormous and encompassing as the
ocean. And in this historic region of France, even sandbags take on the
appearance of fallen monuments.

The intense destruction of the battle continued for months. In June, the
Germans pressed harder, even using a new type of gas, phosgene, to disrupt
French artillery. With casualties mounting and defeat seeming imminent,
Joffre replaced Pétain with General Robert Nivelle. Nivelle was known to be
a master coordinator of artillery, a good choice for a battle that was about
controlling and surviving artillery fire. At around the same time as Nivelle's
appointment, circumstances began to favor the French. Russian advances in
the east, together with the British and French offensive on the Somme, began
to stretch German resources to the point where offensives were difficult to
sustain.

One final offensive at Verdun, launched on July 11, still did not result in a
breakthrough. The next month, the kaiser replaced Falkenhayn with Hindenburg, the victor of Tannenberg. Under Hindenburg, major German offensives
no longer took place at Verdun, although steady fighting continued. The
initiative shifted to the French. In October, the French regained Fort Douaumont. In December, a French offensive recaptured all the territory yielded to
the Germans in the winter and spring. Ten months of fighting resulted in a
return to the status quo, at least as far as territory was concerned, although
the landscape now was unrecognizable. The landscape was not the only
resource altered by the battle. On both sides, manpower was seriously depleted. There were 337,000 German casualties, including 143,000 killed,
compared to 377,000 French casualties, with 162,000 killed. On both sides,
so many units rotated through Verdun that there was hardly a community in
France or Germany that was not touched in some way by the battle.

OFFENSIVES IN SOUTHERN AND EASTERN EUROPE

German failure at Verdun was compounded by Austrian failures against
Italy. Against Falkenhayn's advice, Austria's lead general, Conrad, planned a
breakthrough attack against Italy in the Trentino, the mountainous region to
the northwest of Venice. Falkenhayn had counseled against an Austrian offensive because the German offensive against France drew troops away from
the Eastern Front. A possible Russian attack would have to be met by Austrians as well as by Germans. If the Austrians stuck to a defensive war
against the Italians, the risk from Russia would be diminished. Yet the Austrian government was bent on revenge against Italy, the former member of

the Central Powers that had joined the Allies in the hopes of gaining Austrian territory. Austrian hopes for a symbolic victory resembled, in a way, the French decision to stand at Verdun. Public opinion mattered a great deal, and "punishing" Italy might be a way of shoring up a sense of purpose in the Austro-Hungarian Empire. Conrad prepared for what he called the Punishment Expedition by moving troops from the Russian front to form two armies near the Trentino. On May 15, 1916, he ordered a massive artillery barrage, followed by the advance of fourteen divisions along a seventy-kilometer front in the mountains. Italian units were initially outnumbered four to one, but many fought hard and executed orderly retreats to fortified rear positions. Italy's lead general, Luigi Cadorna, rushed reinforcements to the front. Meanwhile, as Austrian troops advanced through the mountainous terrain, they found it difficult to transport their artillery and maintain their communications—the factors that had limited attempts at breakthrough on the Western Front in the previous year on more favorable terrain. By June, the Italians were holding the Austrians to a gain of only twenty-five kilometers. At that point, a Russian offensive forced Conrad to shift many of his troops back east. Austrian troops on the Trentino reverted to defending their positions, pursuing a scorched-earth policy as they went. For twenty-five kilometers of mountainous territory, they had sustained eighty thousand casualties. The Italians lost 147,000. But the Italian army had increased in size, from thirty-six divisions in 1914 to sixty-five divisions in 1916. As Austrian forces were reduced in Italy, Cadorna resumed the offensive along the Isonzo River, making small but significant gains during the second half of 1916.[7]

While defending the Trentino, Cadorna pleaded for help from the Allies. The December 1915 conference at Chantilly had resulted in pledges to mount simultaneous offensives along all fronts. The German attack at Verdun and the Austrian attack on the Trentino temporarily halted Allied plans to go on the offensive. In light of the pressure on the French and the Italians, offensives by the British and the Russians appeared to be good solutions. The British hesitated to follow through on their pledge at Chantilly, citing the need to train soldiers and amass shells. The Russians were prepared to attack. They had sustained terrible casualties in 1914 and 1915, but more troops were conscripted and Russian industry was producing vast quantities of arms and equipment. The Russians had strong motivations, too. Not only were German troops close to the capital, Petrograd; Germany had conquered much of Russian Poland and the Baltic and was turning the region into a colony, complete with German settlers and a dependent economy (the Allies were not the only imperialists). To forestall further German advances and to help the French at Verdun, in March 1916 the Russian Second Army attacked the German Tenth Army in the vicinity of Lake Naroch, suffering nearly one hundred thousand casualties in a failed attack that cost the Germans twenty thousand.

Attacks against German troops in the north seemed unlikely to succeed, but the Russian general staff expected to make another massive assault after adequate preparations were made. In the meantime, a diversion was planned for the south, in Galicia, on the front that was held jointly by the Germans and Austrians. During the winter of 1915 to 1916, Austrian and German troops had constructed trenches that were the equal of the best German trenches on the Western Front. Yet one of Russia's best generals, Alexei Brusilov, commander of the Southern Front, had developed a plan for an offensive that resembled Falkenhayn's plan at Verdun, in that it incorporated new battlefield tactics in order to achieve a breakthrough. Brusilov's officers studied the Austrian and German trenches carefully, pinpointing their positions for precise bombardment. Along the front, Russian troops dug saps— trenches that extended to within one hundred meters of the Austrians and Germans—that were intended to reduce the distance that attacking soldiers would have to run. Adequate reserves were put in place to relieve the first line of attackers and press forward through the breach. The Russians attacked on June 4, taking the Austrians and Germans by surprise. Accurate artillery fire cut barbed wire and pinned Austrian troops in their trenches. Russian troops rose from their saps and leapt into the Austrian trenches. In the Austrian sectors, reserves advanced to the front lines, only to be devastated by more Russian shells.

Brusilov's tactics produced the much-anticipated breakthrough. Russian forces advanced rapidly along a front that stretched four hundred kilometers from north to south. In some southern sectors that were held by the Austrians alone, the Russian army advanced one hundred kilometers. Brusilov and his troops continued to march west throughout the summer, inflicting more than seven hundred thousand casualties on the Central Powers and capturing four hundred thousand. In the east, it appeared that the war had been completely transformed, but Russian casualties had also been high: in the vicinity of one million. It began to seem that the Russian army had advanced too far. Supply lines were stretched far enough that ammunition and supplies were short once again. It is at this point that Russian soldiers hesitated to obey orders. And while Austrian troops had retreated in panic, German troops retreated in an orderly fashion and in the summer of 1916 formed the backbone of successful resistance to the Russians. The Germans now became the senior partners in the alliance. Conrad stepped down, and the German general staff, led by Hindenburg, took overall command.

The first success of the reorganized command in the east came at the expense of Romania. The Romanian government maintained neutrality during the first two years of the war but in the summer of 1916 declared war against the Central Powers. It seemed an auspicious time to do so. The Brusilov offensive appeared to be pushing the Austrians and Germans back, while the Austrian offensive in the Trentino and the German offensive at

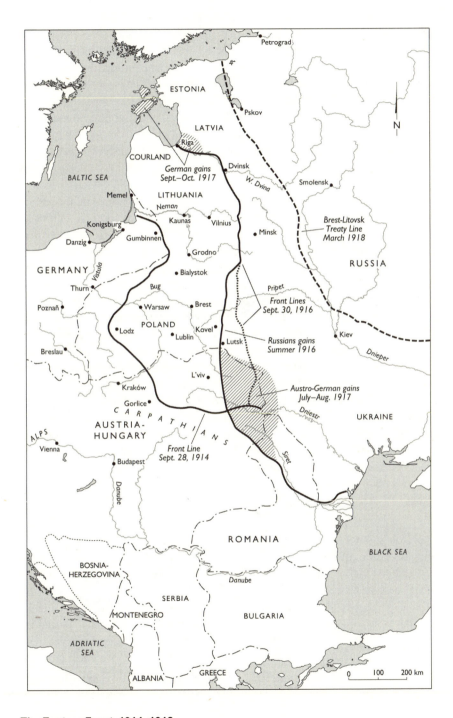

The Eastern Front, 1914–1918

Verdun were stalemated. Romania had a sizable army of 564,000, with experience fighting in the Balkan wars that preceded the First World War. The Romanian government hoped to take Transylvania from the Austro-Hungarian Empire. Romanian territorial ambitions were encouraged by the Allies, who promised support from the Russian armies to the north and from the British and French army at Salonika, on the Aegean.

Romanian greed came up against the realities of geography, manpower, and technology. Romania was in fact surrounded by the Central Powers, with Austria-Hungary to the northeast and Bulgaria to the south. The Allied armies in the east were fully occupied already and were unlikely to be of much help. In fact, on August 17, 1916, when France and Russia promised Romania parts of the Austro-Hungarian Empire, including Transylvania, they secretly agreed to go back on their word once the war was over. And finally, Romanian confidence in their army was misplaced. They lacked the most modern training and technology and also lacked the fighting experience that the Germans, Austrians, and Bulgarians now had. During the last week of August, Romania launched an offensive into Transylvania, initially capturing the eastern half of the mountainous territory. Austrian and German armies, led by the former chief of staff, Falkenhayn, counterattacked from the west, pushing the Romanians out of Austro-Hungarian Transylvania during September. In October, the Romanians made a stand in their own part of Transylvania, blocking the mountain passes and preventing Falkenhayn from advancing on the capital, Bucharest. That was not enough. At the same time, combined Bulgarian, German, and Turkish forces led by the German general August von Mackensen crossed the Danube River, Romania's southern border, and pressed northward. Little help came from the Allies. Bucharest surrendered on December 6, 1916. The Romanian army, having experienced 350,000 casualties, escaped across the border to Russian Moldavia.

THE BATTLE OF THE SOMME

The Romanian campaign illustrated, once again, that it was one thing to imagine the conquest of a new territory, but another thing to carry it out. It is best understood as a sequel to the Brusilov offensive, which, begun in June 1916, demonstrated that a breakthrough was possible. Shortly after the launch of the Brusilov offensive, the war's most famous attempt at breakthrough was launched in the north of France, where the British, assisted by the French, attacked the Germans in the vicinity of the Somme River. The Somme offensive was first conceived after the Chantilly conference. German failure to break through at Verdun, combined with the initial success of the Brusilov offensive, raised the possibility that with one more "big push" the Allies might defeat the Central Powers. Yet British planning for this big push was not carried out as well as the planning for the Brusilov offensive, or even as well as Falkenhayn's attack on Verdun.

British generals on the Western Front were reaching the same conclusions as the generals of the other Allied countries and the Central Powers: that assaults should be made on broad fronts with limited objectives, the principal limits being the range of artillery and communications. Breakthroughs would be achieved by gradually biting away at enemy positions. This position was most persuasively advocated by the commander of the British Fourth Army, Sir Henry Rawlinson. The supreme commander of the British Expeditionary Force (BEF), Sir Douglas Haig, disagreed. Haig acknowledged the force of Rawlinson's argument, but, as the historian Hew Strachan has shown, Haig believed that Verdun was wearing down the German army to such an extent that a major breakthrough was possible. Haig prevailed: he ordered a massive weeklong artillery bombardment starting on June 24, followed by a massed infantry assault on July 1. The initial assault was designed to push deep past German lines and was to be followed up by the rapid advance of a reserve force of infantry and cavalry. Strachan points out that either Haig's approach or Rawlinson's approach might have worked. What actually happened was that Rawlinson, charged with the detailed planning, incorporated enough of his own ideas into Haig's scheme that what resulted was a compromise. As the compromise plan unfolded on the battlefield, it spelled failure for the massive Allied effort.[8]

Manpower issues played an important part in Haig and Rawlinson's calculations as they built up the seventeen divisions of the British Fourth Army, who, together with three divisions from the Third Army, were charged with the assault on the Somme. Four were regular divisions that were experienced but that had also suffered extensive casualties since the start of the war. Four were "territorial" divisions, mostly made up of reservists, some of whom had combat experience. The remaining twelve divisions were from the "new army" of volunteers, including many "pals" battalions. Their infantry and artillery had no experience and had undergone rapid training. They were still included in the plan for breaking through. This was very much unlike the Germans at Verdun and the Russians in Galicia: both planned their breakthrough attempts by taking advantage of the skills of veteran artillerymen and infantrymen who were assigned precise, complex tasks related to fire and movement. At the Somme, only the British veterans could be counted on to execute these kinds of tactics, and they were in the minority. The British veterans were supplemented by five divisions of French veterans positioned on the southern flank of the planned assault, but their experience still did not outweigh the inexperience of the newly recruited British divisions.

The British Fourth Army faced a formidable barrier. The Somme had been a quiet sector of the Western Front, which allowed the German divisions stationed there to spend the better part of a year preparing fortifications.

Trenches were protected by thick barbed wire and well-hidden machine-gun posts, while the trenches themselves were built solidly. They included shelters dug ten meters under the ground, deep enough to protect troops during a heavy bombardment.

The British bombardment began on June 24, 1916. Fifteen hundred British cannons, supported by seven hundred French cannons to the south, positioned along a forty-kilometer front, fired 1.5 million shells. The heavy artillery aimed to destroy trenches while the light artillery aimed for barbed wire. Then, in the hour before the attack began on July 1, more than two hundred thousand shells were fired and ten enormous mines—tunnels dug under the German trenches and filled with explosives—were detonated. With the explosion, nineteen divisions of British troops, aided by the five French divisions to their south, began to advance across no-man's-land. Their artillery supported them with a "creeping barrage"—a wall of shellfire synchronized to move ahead of them.

The results of the shelling were disappointing. In most parts of the line, German soldiers waited until the shellfire stopped, then climbed out of their deep dugouts to engage the attackers. There were several instances in which British troops advanced standing up, walking across no-man's-land in row upon row, weighted down by heavy packs of equipment. Some British officers thought that inexperienced troops could not be taught the complex small-unit tactics of fire and movement. This image—of battalion after battalion marching across no-man's-land in waves—has been presented by many historians as evidence of the incompetence of the British generals. Yet recently historians have shown that, on the first day at the Somme, British units used variable tactics. Some units did walk across, following a creeping barrage, and were massacred by fire from German artillery, machine guns, and rifles. Some of the British units that took this approach survived and fought hard. But most British units at the Somme moved forward during the night without a creeping barrage. These units had varying degrees of success as well. What is certain, though, is that the first day at the Somme—July 1, 1916—was the worst day in the history of the British army. In one day, the Germans killed twenty thousand and wounded forty thousand more. Along the northern British part of the front, few significant gains were made.[9] By contrast, on the first day at the Somme, the five French divisions to the south did make significant gains. The French laid down a heavier artillery barrage than the British, while overall their units appear to have fought better. At the end of the first day, the French possessed the first line of German trenches. After ten days, the French had advanced as much as ten kilometers. They paused to wait for the British.

The French generals preferred to make large attacks, then recover and prepare for the next large attack. British generals preferred to follow up on the disastrous first day at the Somme with small attacks on different parts of the front. In two weeks, British troops captured twenty square miles at a cost of twenty-five thousand casualties. These were significant gains at a significant cost. A larger effort was made on July 14, when British and French troops were able to exploit gains in the central and southern parts of the front and capture the second line of the German trenches. German losses became heavy, too. Falkenhayn, still the chief of the general staff, dispatched Germany's leading specialist on defensive warfare, Colonel Fritz von Lossberg, to rearrange the defenses at the Somme. Instead of placing most troops in the frontline trenches, Lossberg positioned more in the second and third lines, to slow any possible breakthrough. German reinforcements poured to the front, too. In the following weeks and months of brutal fighting, British and French troops made numerous assaults. The farthest dent in the German lines was made in the center, at Delville Wood, occupied for six days by a brigade of South Africans at a cost of two-thirds of their men. Not to be outdone by their fellow colonials, the First and Second Australian divisions, including many veterans of Gallipoli, captured and held Pozières, at a cost of eleven thousand casualties.

On September 15, 1916, more colonial troops—this time two divisions from Canada and one from New Zealand—were involved in a larger assault that included forty-eight tanks, the first time this technology was used in battle. The tanks surprised the Germans, but the ungainly machines experienced numerous mechanical problems and became bogged down in the treacherous terrain. Only four were able to follow British troops all the way forward to the German trenches. Like previous attacks on the Somme, the operations of September 15 gained little ground—two thousand meters—at a high cost in casualties—twenty-nine thousand. The same types of results characterized the final major assaults of the battle, which took place in mid-November, before the winter set in fully. With these assaults, the battle finally ended. In five months of fighting, Allied forces advanced eleven kilometers. British forces experienced 420,000 casualties, while the French had 195,000. Only from the standpoint of attrition could the battle be considered a draw. The German casualty figures are disputed, but estimates range from 450,000 to 680,000.

Heavy losses at the Somme and Verdun made Hindenburg and the other senior German generals even more acutely aware of the management of their key resource: men. They concluded that, along the Western Front, they needed to consolidate their positions by eliminating salients, such as the bulge at the Somme. During the winter of 1916–1917, the German army constructed a rear line of trenches that stretched in a fairly straight line from Arras to Malmaison, as much as sixty kilometers behind the largest salient south of the Somme. In mid-March, the Germans retreated quietly, concealing their movements. On March 25, 1917, the Allied leadership detected the retreat. Allied troops advanced through the eerily quiet German sector, to find that it had been wrecked and booby-trapped. In some ways, the attrition at the battle of the Somme might be credited with pushing the Germans back in the winter of 1916–1917. But now they occupied even better positions that could be defended with less manpower. Hindenburg reversed Falkenhayn's plan of 1916. After Verdun and the Somme, the Western Front seemed too strong for a German breakthrough, while in the east there were signs that Russia could be knocked out of the war.

Chapter Eleven

Naval War and the U.S. Entry, 1916–1917

The results of the 1916 offensives were decidedly mixed. The battles of Verdun and the Somme put considerable strain on France as well as on Germany. In the south, Italian resilience challenged Austria, especially after the successes of Russia's Brusilov offensive in the east. The combined effects of the Trentino, Isonzo, and Brusilov campaigns put a serious strain on Austria. In the east, Germany emerged as the senior partner of the Central Powers, taking leadership of the war against Romania and Russia. Russian success in the Brusilov offensive overextended the tsar's resources nearly to the breaking point, although Russian success over the Ottomans compared favorably to the failed British efforts at Gallipoli and Kut. With France, Russia, Austria, and Turkey under terrible pressure by 1916, and with Italy playing a purely regional role, Britain and Germany emerged as the dominant powers in the world war. Before the war, Britain had the greatest power at sea while Germany had the greatest power on land. Both countries were financial and industrial powerhouses. From 1914 to 1916, the British built their army into a significant power on land, thanks to the recruitment of volunteers at home and in the colonies. Could Germany threaten Britain at sea?

THE BATTLE OF JUTLAND

The start of 1916 found the battleships and battlecruisers of the British and German fleets in their ports. The British battleships of the Grand Fleet, commanded by Admiral Sir John Jellicoe, were based at Scapa Flow, in the Orkney Islands, north of Scotland. The Grand Fleet's Battlecruiser Squadron, commanded by Vice Admiral Sir David Beatty, was stationed at Rosyth, near Edinburgh. In stationing the two fleets in Scotland, the British were able to enforce a blockade of the northern passages of the North Sea, while leaving the coast of England vulnerable to attack. This vulnerability was offset by good British naval intelligence. Unbeknownst to the Germans, the British had cracked the German navy's principal codes. When German naval radio transmissions indicated an impending attack on England, the Grand Fleet could be sent south. This was a case in which a clever response to a new technology did produce a significant result.

The German High Seas Fleet, commanded by Admiral Reinhard Scheer, was smaller than Britain's Grand Fleet. At the start of 1916, the Germans had fewer battleships and battlecruisers than the British—twenty-seven to thirty-seven—but the Germans enjoyed certain advantages. Their ships had better armor, and their crews had better gunners. Their ammunition was better, and it was stored more safely. Even so, the kaiser and his government doubted that the German navy could defeat the British at sea. The German navy was best kept intact, in port at Wilhelmshaven, as a defensive measure. Admiral Scheer and most of his officers disliked such passivity. They believed that they could not only raid the coast of England but, in doing so, draw smaller units of the Grand Fleet into battle and destroy them, piece by piece. When Scheer took command in February 1916, he persuaded the kaiser to allow him to engage in more aggressive raiding and patrolling. In the next three months, German squadrons made six ventures into the North Sea, at one point shelling the small English port of Lowestoft.

In making their sorties, the Germans were willing to sacrifice radio silence for speed and maneuverability. British naval intelligence's coastal radio stations picked up German signals in the last week of May 1916 that indicated that Scheer and his fleet were going to steam up toward the Skaggerak, the waters between Norway and the part of Denmark called Jutland. Jellicoe's battleships and Beatty's battlecruisers left Scapa Flow and Rosyth even before Scheer left Wilhelmshaven on May 30. By the morning of May 31, more than 250 British and German ships of all types were all headed toward the Skaggerak.

Never before had so many ships of such tremendous tonnage gone into battle at once. Beatty's battlecruisers, joined now by the four fastest British battleships, had the greatest speed and encountered the Germans first, at 3:20 p.m. As it happened, the British battlecruisers found the German battlecruisers, which led Beatty on a chase, hoping to draw him toward the more heavily armed German battleships. The ships exchanged fire, and the Germans sank two British battlecruisers—they exploded when their ammunition storage chambers were hit by shells. Beatty then ran up against the main body of the German fleet and fled north, toward Jellicoe's battleships. At 6:17 p.m., the British battleships opened fire on the Germans. The Germans responded with their own massed gunfire, and the battle raged back and forth, with ships maneuvering and firing, covered, increasingly, by smokescreens and darkness. At 7:20, Scheer launched a torpedo attack by a squadron of destroyers. The British fleet took evasive action, effectively ending the battle. That night the German fleet steamed back to Wilhelmshaven and the British ships returned to their ports, too. The Germans lost one old pre-*Dreadnought* battleship and one battlecruiser, plus nine smaller ships, with a total loss of 2,551 sailors. The British lost three battlecruisers and twelve smaller ships, with a total loss of 6,094 sailors.

Based on the number of ships sunk and the number of sailors killed, it can be argued that the German navy won the battle of Jutland. This is true in an operational sense. Looking at broader issues of strategy, it appears that the British won. After Jutland, the German navy remained, for the most part, in port at Wilhelmshaven. German ships left in force just two times. Their battleships fought the British battlecruisers again at Heligoland in November 1917, and in April 1918 the fleet steamed to Norway and back again without fighting. The main outcome of Jutland, though, was that the British fleet remained intact and was still able to enforce the blockade.

THE WIDENING OF THE WAR

While the British blockaded Germany, the Allies came to depend extensively on war materials from the United States. It is often thought that the war ended sooner because of American intervention, and that prior to 1917 the United States leaned strongly in favor of the Allies. Yet the declaration of war by the United States was not inevitable. In fact, the Allies were not favored by all Americans all the time. Considerable segments of the population disliked the Allies for a variety of reasons. The Allied blockade of the Central Powers had resulted in annoying searches of American ships plus the blacklisting of firms that did business with Germany. Irish Americans held a grudge of long standing against the British and were particularly concerned by the violent way Britain's rulers in Ireland suppressed the Easter Rebellion of 1916. Many Americans also hesitated to support the Russians, whose autocratic government did not share their political values. Russia's persecution of the Jews before and during the war did not win the tsar many friends. Finally, the United States had a substantial population of German Americans. German culture had influenced American culture quite substantially, ranging from education, music, and philosophy to frankfurters, hamburgers, and lager beers.

Yet there were significant reasons for Americans to support the Allies. The British and French shared political values with Americans. Wilson was a proponent of democratic national self-determination, which resonated with the political cultures of Britain and France, even if these countries and the United States held colonial possessions. Besides, the invasion of Belgium and France made Germany appear to be the aggressor nation in the eyes of many Americans. And submarine warfare, particularly the sinking of the *Lusitania* in 1915, showed Germany in a particularly bad light. President Wilson protested the sinking of the *Lusitania* and other ships. His threats persuaded Chancellor Theobald von Bethmann-Hollweg and the kaiser to end unrestricted submarine warfare. Once again, in order to sink a merchant ship, submarines were to abide by "cruiser rules": they would have to surface, verify the ship's nationality, and allow the crew to abandon ship.

In some ways, the ending of unrestricted submarine warfare worked for both Germany and the United States. Throughout 1916, most Americans preferred to remain neutral. It was an election year, and both candidates, the Democrat Woodrow Wilson and the Republican Charles Evans Hughes, made a show of opposing U.S. intervention in the war. Wilson, the winner, believed that he could mediate a settlement between the Allies and the Central Powers. He looked forward to a day when all international disputes could be resolved by a League of Nations, where all nations would gather to discuss and work out their differences peacefully. Wilson spent much of 1916 working with the German government to persuade them to clarify their war aims as a prelude to negotiations. Yet fewer and fewer leaders in Germany (or in Britain and France) considered the possibility of a negotiated end to the war, and many in the German navy and the German government did not like fighting a deadlocked war with one arm tied behind its back. In the winter of 1916–1917, the British blockade began to have perceptible effects on civilians, at least in part because the 1916 potato crop failed and it proved impossible to make up the shortage with imports. Better U-boats were being delivered to the German navy and were succeeding in sinking Allied shipping, even under cruiser rules. A resumption of unrestricted submarine warfare could sink enough ships bound for Britain—and scare enough away—that Britain might begin to starve.

Britain's defeat might come quickly, argued the proponents of resuming unrestricted submarine warfare. The downside of resuming unrestricted submarine warfare was that it practically guaranteed the entry of the United States on the side of the Allies. The United States had vast, untapped human and material resources that could stack the odds heavily in favor of the Allies. These concerns were downplayed in Germany as domestic politics began a shift to the right and leading generals such as Hindenburg and Ludendorff achieved more influence. The generals, along with the new German foreign secretary, Arthur Zimmerman, took the position that unrestricted submarine warfare was likely to push Britain out of the war before the United States could send large numbers of troops to Europe. The decision to resume unrestricted submarine warfare in a "war zone" surrounding the British Isles was announced on February 1, 1917. It was a gamble second only to the implementation of the Schlieffen Plan in 1914.

Initially, it appeared that the gamble might work. President Wilson was outraged that Germany would violate its pledges to restrict submarines, but members of the U.S. Congress were not quite ready to declare war. Two months of unrestricted submarine warfare started to persuade many Americans that war was necessary. In the end, it was a diplomatic blunder by Germany that made entry into the war inevitable. In January 1917, while the kaiser, Hindenburg, and Ludendorff were considering whether or not to resume unrestricted submarine warfare, Arthur Zimmerman began to explore ways to neutralize the United States should it choose to intervene. Mexico was the logical place to look for trouble. Since 1910, Mexico had been in a state of revolutionary turmoil. U.S. troops had intervened twice. Once, in 1914–1915, Wilson had stationed troops at Veracruz in order to support one presidential contender over another. And then, in 1916, U.S. troops pursued the revolutionary Pancho Villa into Mexico and managed to run afoul of Villa's enemy, the president, Venustiano Carranza. U.S. troops did not perform especially well in Mexico and left a certain degree of resentment in their wake.

The German government judged correctly that some in Mexico might be willing to fight a war against the United States. Today this idea seems ridiculous, but in 1916 it was not an improbable proposition. At that time, the U.S. army was still quite small. In January 1917, Zimmerman sent a telegram to his ambassadors in Washington and Mexico City requesting that they propose an alliance between Germany and Mexico. The terms of the proposed alliance were stated clearly. If the United States entered the war against Germany, Germany would help Mexico to regain the territories that it lost to the Republic of Texas and the United States during the 1830s and 1840s. Zimmerman made the further suggestion that the Mexicans should try to persuade the Japanese to leave the Allies for the Central Powers.

Zimmerman's note was transmitted by telegram from Berlin to Washington over three separate lines. All were intercepted and decoded by British intelligence. The British presented the telegram to the U.S. government in late February 1917, hoping it would push them toward joining the Allies. It did. President Wilson was infuriated by the German government's aggressiveness. He released the telegram to the press on March 1, and the telegram itself was confirmed shortly thereafter by Zimmerman, who may have hoped to use the threat of a German-Mexican alliance to keep the United States out of the war. If this was his strategy, it backfired. The Mexican government was not interested in an alliance with Germany. And Zimmerman's note persuaded most Americans that war with Germany was worthwhile and unavoidable. On April 2, Wilson asked Congress to declare war. He reviewed the German government's actions against U.S. citizens and made the case that a state of neutrality no longer existed. It was in the national interest of the United States to go to war.

Besides discussing the U.S. national interest, Wilson also made several points that were more idealistic. He was careful to state that "we have no quarrel with the German people," claiming that the war started in Europe without governments consulting their peoples. To prevent future wars, Wilson announced that "the world must be made safe for democracy." He promised that the United States did not seek to conquer any territory. On April 6, the Congress voted to declare war by an overwhelming majority. The war would only be fought against Germany, not against the other Central Powers, which had not attacked the United States. The United States would fight as an "associate" of Britain, France, and Russia, not as a full ally. This meant that Wilson intended for the United States to retain a degree of independence on the battlefield and at the peace negotiations.

The entry of the United States increased the global scope of the war. Now both Canada and the United States were fighting on the side of the Allies. Mexico rejected the Central Powers. Other countries in the Americas chose the side of the Allies, either by declaring war or by severing diplomatic relations with Germany. There were few risks in doing so at a time when the Allies controlled the world's oceans. Economic benefits could be had from joining the Allies—even if few Latin American soldiers and sailors saw action in the war.

By the end of 1917, other countries fell in line with the Allies, too. Since the start of the war, Greece had wavered between the Allies, the Central Powers, and neutrality. The Greek king, Constantine, was the kaiser's brother-in-law, while the Allied invasion of the Dardanelles inspired Greek nationalists who sought territorial gains against the Ottomans. In October 1915, the French and British began to land 75,000 soldiers at Salonika, in the northeast corner of Greece, in order to put pressure on Bulgaria, which was fighting on the side of the Central Powers. The Salonika campaign became a stalemate, but the French and British presence did persuade Greek nationalist politicians, led by the prime minister, Eleutherios Venizelos, to form a rival, pro-Allied government based in Salonika. The intervention of the French army and navy in Greek politics resulted in King Constantine's abdication in June 1917, clearing the way for an official Greek declaration of war against Germany.

German connections were strong in Brazil, too. In fact, the foreign minister of Brazil, Lauro Mueller, was originally a German citizen. Many German immigrants lived in Brazil, just like in the United States. Few Brazilians wanted to be involved in the war, but when German submarines began to sink Brazilian ships in the same way that they were sinking U.S. ships, popular opinion turned against Germany. Brazil declared war in October

1917. From that point until the war's end in the following year, the Brazilian navy made significant contributions to Allied patrols in the South Atlantic.

On the other side of the globe, a Chinese declaration of war had been sought by Britain and France, which hoped to recruit Chinese workers for the war effort. Even so, a Chinese declaration of war was resisted by Japan, which did not want China to participate in future peace negotiations. To allay Japanese concerns, Britain and France secretly offered Japan possession of all German territory in China. China was in the midst of revolutionary turmoil and would have trouble resisting such encroachments. The government in Beijing was controlled by northern warlords who hoped to join the Allies and nominally fight against Germany in order to gain loans and military equipment that could be turned against the nationalist movement, which controlled south China. In China, as in other countries, there was a close relationship between domestic politics and the war.

Ultimately, the involvement of China, Brazil, and Greece on the Allied side did little to change the war's outcome. The entry of the United States was a different story. The German government gambled that their army could knock the Allies out of the war before the Americans could tip the balance. In the end, Germany came close to winning. American forces did help the Allies, while Wilson's idealism set the stage for the peace conference.

Chapter Twelve

The Strains of Total War

Jutland, Somme, Verdun. Brusilov, Trentino, Isonzo. For good reason, 1916 has been called the "Year of Battles." In each of these big battles, one of the sides attempted to break through the stalemate and failed. There were also countless smaller battles that took place that year. Every shot fired was financed and produced by civilians, who were beginning to feel the strain of the war by the winter of 1916–1917. This was a "total war," in the sense that it required the massive mobilization of material resources and human efforts. Victories made the efforts seem worthwhile, but defeat and stalemate ran the risk of persuading people at home to give up.

THE EXPERIENCE OF TOTAL WAR

In all countries, civilians were enrolled in the war effort. Even with many working men absent at the front, production of war materials increased drastically, as did production of underlying necessities such as coal, oil, and steel. Most governments put into effect measures to boost production. Limits were placed on the numbers of skilled workers allowed to join the military. Workers' rights to strike were curtailed while health and safety standards were allowed to lapse. Workforces, like armies, had their manpower issues, too. Numbers of workers were increased by recruiting and training women, who, like civilian men, also suffered from poor working conditions. Hours were longer than in the prewar days, while it was now commonplace to be exposed to explosives, which posed short-term dangers from explosions and also long-term dangers to health. One female factory worker in England, M. Hall, recalled that "after each day when we got home we had a lovely good wash. And believe me the water was blood-red and our skin was perfectly yellow, right down through the body, legs, and toenails even, perfectly yellow. In some people it caused a rash and a very nasty rash all round the chin. . . . The hair, if it was fair or brown it went a beautiful gold, but if it was any grey, it went grass-green."[1] Workplace contamination caused respiratory and reproductive problems; yet many women also reported that working in a factory, together with other women, gave them a sense of pride and camaraderie.

This was not necessarily the first time that women worked outside of their homes—many of the young women who found work on farms and in factories had already worked as domestic servants—but it was their first time to be part of large groups of women outside of the home. One of the largest groups of women working outside of the home was nurses. On both sides of the war, tens of thousands of nurses served in a variety of positions, some at home, some overseas. Typically, they were recruited from the middle and upper classes. Most armies prohibited nurses from serving at the front, but nurses in mobile field hospitals were subject to terrifying bombing and shelling, while they also witnessed the war's terrible toll on human bodies. Katherine Hodges North was a British nurse who served in the Red Cross on the Western and Eastern Fronts. After the war, she recalled one particularly trying moment in Galicia:

> I had never fainted in my life, but I came nearest to it one morning in the dressing room. I was working with E. on a patient and at the other end of the room a man who had a dreadful head wound was being dressed. The top of his head was split open and his brain was bulging out, suddenly he began to scream, a scream that I soon began to know only too well. I hope I may never have to hear it again. His voice went up into a high, thin piercing shrill note, it was inhuman, it was frightful. One realized that it was the sound produced from a human being in a state of agony, which eliminated reason. It was so appallingly dreadful that for a minute or two the room was black and swaying in front of me. I shoved my head down and prayed for control, and thank goodness in a few moments was all right, but I was dripping with perspiration from head to foot.[2]

Such wounds were well beyond the ability of the nurses and doctors of 1914 to 1918 to provide effective treatments. A Russian nurse, Lidiya Zakharova, recalled similarly harrowing moments near the front lines. She described one experience, in which she followed Russian soldiers after they overran a German trench. What she saw in the trench reminded her of one of nature's most powerful forces, and her account is filled with thoughts about the natural world:

> It was a gruesome spectacle. A city of the dead, its inhabitants frozen in the most unlikely positions, as if a raging, deadly hurricane had just swept past. Some were lying on their backs, others face down. They were all intertwined, so you could not tell whose arms and legs were whose. Many were sitting in poses that made them seem alive, leaning on the parapet or the back wall of the

trench. But most terrible were those who had not fallen, but stood shoulder to shoulder, still holding their rifles, eyes open and glazed with the tranquility of non-existence, as if they were listening to the ominous cries of the crows flying overhead. There is a limit, by the way, beyond which the human mind can perceive no more horrors, as a saturated sponge can soak up no more water.[3]

Zakharova became keenly aware of the ways the intense technological warfare of the First World War pushed the human body and the human mind to its limits.

Some nurses, like doctors, resorted to alcohol and opiates to ease their own suffering. A Swiss nurse in the Austrian army, Maria Naepflin, recalled:

Already in Serbia I had realized that several doctors were morphine addicts, and even one of the most competent had that reputation. . . . When I came back to Vienna from Serbia ill, crushed, and broken, I recovered physically during my month's leave, but my mental depression remained. . . . I was overcome by the desire to try morphine. . . . After a brief period of use, I was satisfied with my progress and especially with my improved state of mind. My heavy thoughts seemed blown away. But now I could not stop. . . . With that, my morphine addiction was sealed. There was no going back.[4]

Women who served as nurses experienced the traumas of the front lines and responded in much the same ways as men. A handful of women even fought in combat, although, with the exception of a female battalion organized by the Russian army at the end of the war, such instances were few and far between. Some women served as spies, while others worked as prostitutes, many unwillingly. Women experienced the war in a variety of ways, not only as soldiers, nurses, and laborers. Women who stayed at home to take care of families also experienced significant differences during wartime. The major powers all granted allowances to women whose husbands were fighting. This made military recruitment easier, while giving many women increased financial independence—no longer did they have to ask working husbands for a share of their paychecks.[5]

The nations at war needed manpower and womanpower at all costs while striving to maintain basic social needs at home. In addition to recruiting women workers and paying women who stayed at home, France also recruited workers from its colonies as well as from China, Portugal, and Spain in order to keep domestic production at high levels. Britain came to rely heavily on imported human resources from Australia, Canada, and the United States. Canada and the United States also increased the production of grain, meat, and munitions, selling both to buyers from Britain. Australia sold meat and grain to Britain, too, while supplying wool for the British army's uniforms. By the end of the war, Canada was producing between one-fourth and one-third of all British shells, while the United States was providing Britain with

80 percent of its meats and fats. As a result of higher production, farmers and manufacturers in North America experienced labor shortages and also borrowed more money. More land was put under crops and more coal and oil were burned, adding to the environmental impacts of agriculture and industry. By the end of the war, these countries were contributing large contingents of men to the war effort, too, which, together with the supply of materials, gave them great influence over Allied decision-making.[6]

By contrast, the blockade made it difficult for Germany to acquire goods from overseas, particularly nitrates, which were mined in Chile and used in the manufacture of explosives. German chemical engineers developed a process for extracting nitrates from the air, but shortages persisted throughout the war as Germany, like other countries, produced massive amounts of munitions.

WARTIME FINANCE

Producing munitions and other materials for the war effort was terribly expensive. The war's cost has been estimated at $82,400,000,000 in 1913 dollars. It is difficult for historians to translate old currency figures into new ones, but let us try. One way to convert the figures is to use the Consumer Price Index, which has tracked the price of consumer goods and services since 1913. According to this way of measuring, the First World War cost $1,946,612,610,000 in 2013 dollars. It was easier for some countries to pay the cost than it was for others. Britain and Germany had extensive financial, industrial, and natural resources, and comparatively little fighting occurred within their national boundaries. France also had plenty of resources, but the German conquest of northeastern France deprived it of a substantial portion of its factories and mines, many of which were damaged or destroyed. The other major combatants (Austria-Hungary, Italy, the Ottoman Empire, and Russia) were all endowed with significant natural resources but did not yet have advanced industrial economies and were highly susceptible to the social and economic problems associated with the costs of the war.

How was all this spending paid for? Today history students usually guess that people paid for the cost of war in taxes, including income taxes, business taxes, and customs duties, but that was not the case. In Britain, only one-fourth of the cost of the war was paid through taxes. This does not seem very high—and Britain relied on taxes more than any other country. Instead of taxes, most countries paid for the war in two ways: (1) by manipulating the supply of money and (2) by borrowing.

Manipulating the money supply can be a tricky exercise. Before the war, all the Central and Entente Powers linked their currencies to the gold standard. Each country held large reserves of gold to back the currency. Theoretically, money could be exchanged for gold, and the value of money was related to the value of gold. In 1914, all countries dropped the gold standard. Now money was related to more abstract concepts, such as the value of labor and commodities. Governments acquired more money to pay for the war simply by printing it—a lot of it. Western European countries increased the supply of currency between five and ten times. Printing more money led to a decline in the value of the currency. More money "chased" the same amount of goods and services, which causes prices to rise—inflation. Inflation demoralizes consumers and savers and affects the middle classes especially hard. For this reason, creating inflation is a dangerous strategy in a total war, when the efforts of every person are needed. What is interesting about the First World War is that, in most countries, fivefold and tenfold increases in the money supply did not result in fivefold and tenfold increases in the rate of inflation. Instead, prices merely doubled in Britain and Germany, tripled in France, and quadrupled in Italy.[7]

These were the four most modern countries fighting the war. They prevented inflation from rising higher by asking citizens to buy war bonds, which had the effect of lessening the amount of money that citizens would spend on goods and services, a check on inflation. Germany issued new war bonds every six months starting in September 1914. They were so popular that they financed two-thirds of Germany's wartime spending. There were two reasons for their popularity. In the first place, they offered a good profit: they could be redeemed in ten years at 5 percent interest. In the second place, they supported a war effort that many German people believed in, at least until the end of 1916. German failures at Verdun caused many ordinary Germans to wonder about the credit of their government. Declining enthusiasm for war bonds helped to increase inflation. The French government faced questions about its war effort, too. After all, in 1914 the French army had lost substantial portions of France to the Germans, and by 1916 had still not driven away the invaders. The French government allayed fears about France's long-term success by issuing short-term bonds. Some could be redeemed in three months. Other countries took different approaches. In Russia, there were not that many ordinary citizens who could invest money in bonds, so the government paid for the war by printing money, in effect taxing its population through inflation. A similar situation prevailed in the Austro-Hungarian Empire. The war was paid for by placing hard strains on civilians.[8]

Germany was prosperous enough that it could sustain itself and the other Central Powers for a time. The Central Powers were also able to borrow and trade with the Netherlands, Denmark, Norway, and Sweden—buying much on credit—although access and credit became increasingly difficult over the course of the war. The Central Powers were cut off from most other sources of money and imports, which was not the case with the Allies. Britain,

France, and Russia all bought supplies and borrowed money from each other and from the United States. The United States had tremendous natural resources and industrial capacity, plus New York was beginning to replace London as the center of world finance.

Allied finances have been characterized by the historian David Stevenson as a "web of interdependence." Russia borrowed heavily from Britain and France while Italy borrowed mainly from Britain. In fact, Italian participation on the side of the Allies had been bought, in part, by the British government offering loans for the Italians to buy military supplies as well as petroleum and food. France borrowed most heavily from Britain—to the tune of 7.8 billion francs between 1914 and 1916—but also borrowed 3.4 billion francs from the United States. The Americans came to play a significant role in Allied finances. The French borrowed a significant amount of money from the Americans. The Russians could not, partly because they had poor credit, partly because Russia's treatment of the Jews incensed Jewish American financiers. American reluctance to lend money to the Russians was counterbalanced by British desire to keep Russia in the war—the British financed Russian purchases in the United States, and many Italian purchases, too.[9]

Britain lent money to its allies and also borrowed heavily from the Americans in order to purchase American goods. The British did everything they could to make this process work efficiently, appointing J. P. Morgan's bank to act as their agent in the United States. But even Morgan's clout could not remove the basic underlying problem of the war's strain. By the end of 1916, the British were buying 40 percent of their supplies in the United States, which cost approximately $200 million every month. The situation was made more difficult by the declining value of the British pound against the dollar. Put simply, as the war dragged on and the British printed more money, every pound bought less in the United States. In order to find more dollars, the British government ordered any citizens owning investments in the United States to sell them to the British government, which would use them to pay for goods bought in the United States. Even that strategy only reduced the strain temporarily. By the end of 1916, President Woodrow Wilson, disappointed that the Allies were not negotiating an end to the war, warned American investors about the risks of buying Allied bonds.[10]

British creditworthiness declined to dangerous levels by April 1917, at which point the United States entered the war on the side of the Allies. One of the curiosities of borrowing and lending is that the more a lender lends to a borrower, the more of a stake that the lender has in the success of a borrower. The United States entered the war for reasons that were, on the surface, unrelated to finance, but if the Allies had lost the war the United States would have faced an economic crisis.

The Central Powers faced a different sort of economic crisis. In 1916, Austrian and German civilians began to experience shortages of key consumer goods. An English woman, Evelyn Blücher, was married to a German and lived in Berlin. She reported in March 1916 that her neighbor was complaining about a shopping trip. "She looks quite unhappy and says that England is really succeeding, as food is getting so dreadfully scarce. Her butcher told her that he is seriously thinking of closing down. She could get no potatoes, no sugar even. The shopkeepers told her that the soldiers don't get meat more than three times a week now, and even vegetables are scarce!"[11] By the summer of 1916, fights and even riots were breaking out in shops and markets. In response, the German government instituted food rationing. Unfortunately, that year's harvest produced less than previous years. The German staples of bread and potatoes disappeared from markets, and people started to subsist on turnips. The winter of 1916–1917 was known as "the turnip winter." The food situation improved somewhat at the end of 1917 but plunged again in mid-1918. The German people frequently went hungry. They also experienced shortages of clothing, coal, and soap. People were often dirty and cold. They lost weight. But at the end of the war, there were not many reports of starvation. The war may have ended for Germany just in time.[12]

DOMESTIC POLITICS IN WARTIME

There is a tendency to think of wartime as a special time when domestic policymaking lies suspended and the focus shifts to battles and diplomacy. Yet it is important to consider the ways domestic social life and politics carry on and change during wartime. The First World War shaped, and was shaped by, the politics of the home front. As the war dragged on and it seemed that victory on the battlefield would be elusive, both sides increasingly hoped to damage each other enough that people on the home front would grow weary and demand surrender. At the start of 1917, domestic problems were prominent in some countries, not so prominent in others.

The two most cohesive countries before the war, France and Germany, remained solidly supportive of the war effort, even when both were severely strained in 1917 and 1918. At the start of the war, people in both countries decided to put aside their political differences for the sake of unity. The war was supported by all political parties as well as by trade unions and religious leaders. Even as the French army sustained high casualties, the French people remained largely supportive of the war. French territory had been invaded, including France's most important industrial region, which gave many French people a burning sense of purpose. As a result, the French government did not feel as strong a need to censor publications and correspondence, at least not as much as other countries.

By contrast, the German government engaged in heavy censorship, never allowing defeats or the extent of casualties to be acknowledged. This was not so much a reflection of German regrets about the aggression of 1914 as it was of a political culture that was less representative and more authoritarian. German unity began to break down with the poor harvests of late 1916 and the harsh winter of 1916–1917. Food prices rose faster than wages, which provoked disgruntlement. In 1916 and 1917, complaints were made more vociferously by socialists and trade unionists. The government responded to their appeals for more democracy by leaning more to the right. Increasingly, the generals Hindenburg and Ludendorff had more of a say in the day-to-day operations of the government at home.

In Italy, the government of Antonio Salandra leaned to the right, too. Factories were put under military control and the press and politics were censored. This was a response of the state to a certain lack of consensus about the war. Italy had entered the war as part of a bargain struck between the Italian government and the Allies as a way of gaining more territory. Italy had not been invaded or threatened in any way. The opportunism of the Italian government did not translate into long-lasting popular support. Socialists gave their implied support by not speaking out against the war, but they tended not to speak out in favor of the war either. By 1916, Italian casualties against Austria and Germany, combined with falling living standards and shortages of food, provided the pretext for demonstrations in a number of Italian cities.

Like Italy, Germany, and France, Britain began the war with unprecedented unity across the lines of class, politics, and religion. In Britain, there was unity, but there was also robust debate about certain aspects of the war. The British government walked the fine line between repression and democracy. Democratic tendencies were noteworthy in May 1915, when the British public was scandalized by newspaper accusations that British troops in France were not supplied with sufficient quantities of shells. At the same time, the failure of the Gallipoli campaign was becoming evident. Critics forced the Liberal prime minister Herbert Asquith to form a coalition government with conservatives and to interfere less with the generals and admirals in planning operations. Continued failure to make progress on the Western Front made it possible for a more right-leaning Liberal, David Lloyd George, to replace Asquith as prime minister in December 1916.

In Britain, censorship and repression increased, most famously in Ireland. All of Ireland was considered to be part of the United Kingdom, together with Scotland, Wales, and England, yet most Irish people believed they had significant cultural and religious differences with the dominant English people. These beliefs had been reinforced during periods of repression over the previous centuries. Before the war, Ireland was close to a civil war between nationalists, who wanted varying degrees of Irish independence, and unionists, who wanted to remain part of the United Kingdom. In 1914, the British parliament granted the Irish the right to elect their own parliament, promising that implementation would happen as soon as the war ended. Most Irish remained loyal to the United Kingdom during the war. British expectations were low: when Britain began to draft its citizens into the army in January 1916, the Irish were exempted, although some suspected this would change.

Militant nationalists remained active. One nationalist group, the Irish Volunteers, had more than ten thousand members. They smuggled weapons from Germany and drilled surreptitiously. On Easter in 1916, a group of more than a thousand armed Irish nationalists seized the main post office in Dublin along with several other buildings, hoping to spark a wider insurrection. The insurrection did not occur, as most Irish remained loyal. In a matter of days, the nationalists found themselves surrounded by twenty thousand British troops who pummeled them with artillery. With much of central Dublin ruined, the rebels surrendered. The British court-martialed and shot the leaders, a harsh punishment that caused many Irish people—and many people of Irish ancestry in Australia, Canada, and the United States—to turn against Britain's war effort, although most people in the British Empire continued to identify the war as a noble cause.

High-mindedness characterized the American approach to the war. A majority of the population came to the conclusion that it was just to fight to preserve national interests at sea, while many people also shared Wilson's desire to spread democracy and mediation throughout the world. Yet Wilson's appeals for freedom abroad did not translate into more freedoms at home. On the contrary, in the years before the war the United States had been struggling to bring more order to its rapidly changing society. Regional separatism and racism remained strong in the South. In the North, immigrants were changing the meaning of national identity. All through the country, elected officials struggled with ways of regulating the booming capitalist economy, while a socialist party was beginning to play a major role in domestic politics. When the United States entered the war in 1917, Wilson used the government to regulate American society more closely. Following the examples of economic mobilization in other countries, a War Industries Board controlled prices and production. A Committee on Public Information disseminated information about the war and enforced "voluntary" censorship on the press. Free speech was restricted by the Espionage Act of 1917 and the Sedition Act of 1918, which made it difficult to criticize the war effort. Socialists and immigrants—especially German immigrants—found themselves silenced, even attacked or jailed.

Questions of national identity played a more prominent role in the war efforts of Austria-Hungary and the Ottoman Empire. In fact, competing national identities played a large role in the disintegration of the two empires. Subjects of the Austro-Hungarian emperor, Franz-Joseph, experienced authoritarian rule and censorship that was similar to Germany's, although the Austrian half of the empire was more repressive than the Hungarian half. Members of the core German-speaking and Hungarian-speaking nationalities remained loyal, as did other groups that stood to benefit from clear association with the Central Powers. Austria's Poles preferred Franz-Joseph to Tsar Nicholas, while Hungary's Croatians stood to lose much of their territory to the Italians. As the war continued, though, the support of these groups dwindled, especially as it seemed that they were fighting only for an emperor and not for some larger principle. Among other groups, especially the Czech speakers and the Italian speakers, there was never much loyalty to begin with.[13] In the Ottoman Empire, the core Turkish people remained strongly nationalist and supportive of the war effort, while the rest of the empire began to fragment. With the exception of the Armenians, it cannot be said that the many component groups of the Ottoman Empire were nationalist in the same sense as Czechs, Hungarians, and Poles. The Arabs and Kurds who lived under the Ottoman Empire were semiautonomous and did not think of themselves as Arabs and Kurds so much as they thought of themselves as devoted Muslims who spoke different languages and resisted central authority. The war presented them with opportunities to make inroads against central authority.[14]

THE RUSSIAN REVOLUTION

During 1917 and 1918, problems of identity, combined with military failures, pressed the Ottoman Empire and the Austro-Hungarian Empire to the breaking point. The breaking point was reached earlier by the Russian Empire. Tsar Nicholas called the parliament to session only once during the war, in the summer of 1915. When it met, liberals demanded more say in the government, but Nicholas refused the request. He and his officials ran the country's war effort directly, and the tsar even took personal command of the army in September 1915. This had several consequences. Nicholas was not competent to command an army. He tended to be blamed for the Russian army's defeats, while its victories were attributed to successful generals like Brusilov.

While the tsar was away at headquarters in Mogilev, domestic matters worsened. The tsar's wife, Alexandra, played an important role in domestic policy. She was deeply unpopular, partly on account of her German ancestry, partly on account of the way she allowed herself to be influenced by Grigorii Rasputin, the mystic and healer who apparently had the ability to alleviate the hemophilia of Nicholas and Alexandra's only son, Alexei. That a faith healer could take part in the highest level of government incensed progressives, liberals, and even a few young, forward-thinking aristocrats, who invited Rasputin to a party in December 1916. Believing that Rasputin had supernatural powers, the aristocrats poisoned him, shot him, and threw him into a freezing river, just to make sure of it.

Rasputin's assassination exposed only the tip of the iceberg. In the decade before the war, Russian industrial production had boomed, with many people migrating to the cities in search of work. The war years only accelerated these changes. Working conditions were often terrible. On top of that, working men resented being drafted for the tsar's army, while city dwellers resented shortages of food and supplies. Even as overall productivity rose, individual productivity began to fall as more men left for the front and as the remaining workers suffered from cold and hunger. The tsar's government repressed strikes and dissent, but this did not stop the spread of industrial unrest in 1916. Socialists began to organize factory workers, townspeople, soldiers, and sailors with increasing success. On February 25, 1917, women factory workers in Petrograd struck, demonstrating for more bread and better working conditions while also demanding an end to tsarism. Within a few days, several hundred thousand workers joined them. When Tsar Nicholas ordered Petrograd's troops to disperse the crowds, some units followed his orders and some did not. The disobedient troops—some of them members of elite guards units—instead killed their officers and defended the protesters. Members of parliament gathered and called on Nicholas to step down from the throne.

Members of parliament quickly formed what was called the Provisional Government, intending to rule until a new constitution was put in place. The government was headed by a prime minister, Prince Georgy Yevgenyevich Lvov, whose moderate socialism and easy manner appealed to many sides but whose leadership was ineffective. The Provisional Government's authority was contested by a new type of authority, the soviet, which means "council" in Russian. Throughout Russia, local soviets of workers and educated people, including soldiers and sailors, met together and began to pass and enforce laws, superseding the authority of local governments as well as the central government. These laws extended from mundane matters to matters of national importance. The Petrograd Soviet had enough military and naval force under its control to intimidate the Provisional Government. The only reason that the Petrograd Soviet did not exercise total control was that it remained divided over its long-term political objectives. The body was dominated by socialists, who were divided into several camps. The dominant Mensheviks were urban revolutionaries who supported gradual change—and the war effort—and preferred to work with the Provisional Government. The minority Bolsheviks were urban revolutionaries who supported rapid change, including the overthrow of the Provisional Government and the ending of the war. The Socialist Revolutionaries, or SRs, were rural revolutionaries who mainly sought land redistribution.

While these divisions were the subject of debate, the members of the Petrograd Soviet did agree on several short-term goals, one of which was to take control of the army and navy before the Provisional Government could. Majorities in the Provisional Government and the Petrograd Soviet supported the war effort, but, on March 1, 1917, the Petrograd Soviet issued "Army Order Number One," which stated that the soviet could contradict orders given to the army by the Provisional Government. The order also encouraged soldiers to form committees that would control equipment, including weapons, and that would advise senior officers. Soldiers, like the rest of Russia's citizens, were given freedom to express their opinions. In the military, as in Russia, the old order was swept aside, while a new dual form of authority took shape. The Provisional Government, its officials, and its officers ran things, but the soviets oversaw their actions and plausibly threatened to undermine them. By this point, Tsar Nicholas and the idea of tsarism itself had become irrelevant. Nicholas accepted the advice of his generals and abdicated on March 2, 1917. He asked his brother Michael to take his place, but Michael refused. He understood that the Russian monarchy was finished.

Authority was now divided between the Provisional Government, the local soviets, and the Petrograd Soviet. The soviets and the government had their reasons for remaining committed to the war. Members of the Provisional Government subscribed to a wide range of political views from the right, center, and left, but nearly all were strongly nationalist and disliked the idea of Russia being dominated by Austria and Germany. Members of the soviets were nearly all hoping for an international socialist revolution, yet they, too, feared that a German victory might jeopardize their gains. Russian officers and soldiers supported nationalism or revolution well enough for the Russian army to remain potent for several months. During this time, one leader, Alexander Kerensky, was able to unify the country behind the war effort. Kerensky was a young lawyer and moderate socialist who served as a member of parliament and also served as a member of the Petrograd Soviet. Deriving authority from both bodies, he served first as the Provisional Government's minister of justice and then, in May, he became the minister of war. He used his authority to fire generals whom he considered incompetent. Kerensky promoted Brusilov to the position of chief of staff, and together they began to plan a new offensive against the Austrians in the south. Meanwhile, at home, inflation was spiraling, food was scarce, and labor was restless. In July, the Bolsheviks decided that the time was ripe to seize power in Petrograd, but Kerensky was able to find enough loyal troops to stop them.

Kerensky became prime minister, but his good relations with his troops were not enough to defeat the Austrians and Germans. Kerensky and Brusilov launched their offensive in July and found that troops who declared their loyalty to Russia were not necessarily interested in taking the offensive against the Central Powers. Some Russian units remained intact and pushed successfully along a three-hundred-kilometer front in Galicia. Even so, Russian officers were so undermined by soldiers' soviets that many of them struggled to keep their units together. An Austrian and German counterattack devastated the Russians, who fell back more than a hundred kilometers.

The Central Powers followed up their victory by aiming a deathblow at Russia's capital. In the first week of September, Germany launched an offensive against what had been Russia's strongest defenses, in the Baltic region just to the west of Petrograd. In the vicinity of Riga, Latvia, the German Eighth Army attacked the Russian Twelfth Army using new battlefield tactics that improved upon the use of storm troopers at Verdun. At Riga, the Germans began battle with a short bombardment with regular shells and gas shells. Storm troopers attacked, bypassing the strongest fortifications and aiming to disrupt communications with the rear. Second-line units were then given the job of eliminating the soldiers in enemy strongpoints. These tactics devastated the Russian Twelfth Army, which retreated in disarray toward Petrograd. The Germans followed up their success by moving troops eastward into good positions for attacking Petrograd. Kerensky's authority was challenged by Brusilov's replacement as chief of staff, Lavr Kornilov, a right-winger who now plotted to overthrow the government. The coup failed because only a handful of troops were willing to follow him.

Fearing coups and German advances, Kerensky and the Provisional Government retreated to Moscow, but their rule was effectively finished. The Bolsheviks, led by Vladimir Ilyich Lenin and Leon Trotsky, staged a successful coup in Petrograd on October 24–25, 1917. They had few followers, but the low morale of their opponents and the atmosphere of defeatism in the army and navy made it possible for their Red Guards to seize control of key centers of communication and transportation. On October 26, Lenin announced that a new government was forming that would redistribute land and make peace. The Bolsheviks declared a three-month truce that the Germans accepted. During that time, the two sides negotiated the terms of surrender at Brest-Litovsk, a fortress town in the formerly Russian part of Poland. Trotsky and his fellow Bolsheviks stalled the negotiations, hoping that revolution would break out in Germany. German negotiators lost patience, and in February 1918 their government accepted their recommendation to renew the attack on Russia. In a matter of weeks, the German army advanced several hundred more kilometers along the front. Under severe pressure, on March 3, 1918, the Bolsheviks signed the Treaty of Brest-Litovsk, ending the war between Russia and the Central Powers. According to the terms of the agreement, Russia handed over an enormous area, to include, from north to south, Finland, the Baltic countries, Poland, Belorussia, Ukraine, and the Caucasus. The Bolsheviks turned their attention to internal problems and began to form a Red Army to defend their territory against their opponents in a looming civil war. With Russia out of the war, Austria and Germany could now concentrate on the Italian Front and the Western Front.

Chapter Thirteen

The Offensives of 1917

Russia's elimination weakened the Allies considerably, even with the entry of the United States into the war. At the end of 1916, Russia had an army with more than seven million men. The American contribution was never expected to be that substantial. In April 1917, the U.S. army had 107,000 regular troops available, plus 132,000 members of the part-time militia, the National Guard. The navy was substantial and could deploy its 15,000 marines to supplement the army. All told, the United States had 254,000 troops available, half as many as Romania. To make matters worse, with the exception of several units of soldiers and marines, plus a handful of veterans of the U.S. war against Spain in 1898, the United States forces did not have combat experience. Neither did they have the experience of the European armies in logistics and operations.

The Americans made small contributions to the Allies during 1917. The Allies knew that they had to rely on their own efforts. France, Britain, and Italy were all pressed hard at home and at the front. The Allies were helped by contributions of manpower from the colonies, which had increased substantially, while munitions production in the Allied countries had increased to massive, sufficient levels. The initial collapse of the tsar's government in February 1917 was thought, by some, to bring clarity to the war's aims—at least now the British, French, and Italians were not associated with an autocratic emperor. But as the Russian army collapsed over the course of 1917, the Allies were faced with a new manpower problem: the need to defeat the Germans before they could transfer enough troops from east to west to tip the balance on the Western and Italian Fronts.

The Allies planned great offensives during a second conference at Chantilly, in November 1916, but by the spring of 1917 the situation had changed. Not only was Russia collapsing and the United States entering the war, but unrestricted submarine warfare was taking a toll on Allied shipping, while the German positions, moved back during the winter to the fortified Hindenburg Line, were even more formidable than before. Their trenches were well constructed according to the new theory of "defense in depth"—the front-line positions contained trenches and machine-gun posts that were intended to be manned lightly, while the rear trenches and communication trenches were dug to accommodate large forces that would respond rapidly to Allied attacks. In addition, the German withdrawal made it possible for them to choose the most favorable ground for their artillery, on commanding heights with excellent views. The German army translated its knowledge of geography, manpower, and weapons into the construction of formidable positions. The strong fortifications, combined with the victory over Russia, boosted morale in the aftermath of Verdun.

Believing that the German army was at its breaking point, British and French commanders made plans for more offensive operations. Nivelle, who had emerged from the battle of Verdun as France's most respected general, now replaced Joffre as supreme French commander. His plans for a breakthrough offensive received the support of both the French and British governments. The British government even decided to make the BEF subordinate to Nivelle's command, although Britain's commanding general, Sir Douglas Haig, had deep reservations about Nivelle's plan. Haig had hoped to attack again at the Somme and also along the Belgian coast. But Nivelle's plan required the British to mount a diversionary attack in Arras, north of the Somme battlefield, while a larger French attack would occur to the south along the Aisne River, near a ridge called the Chemin des Dames. With the Germans reacting to the north and to the south, a third Allied force would drive through the center and win the war. Haig went along with Nivelle's plan reluctantly, extracting as many concessions as he could from the French commander.

THE NIVELLE OFFENSIVE AND THE FRENCH MUTINY

According to the Allied plan, the British were to attack first and divert German resources to the north. Haig amassed eighteen British, Canadian, and Australian divisions, with heavy artillery support, to the west of Arras. Haig's attack, while reluctant, at least demonstrated some of the ways the British army had refined its fighting methods. From April 4 to 9, a massive artillery bombardment, using better shells than the ones used at the Somme, did significant damage to the German barbed wire and fortifications. At the Somme in 1916, British shells had a fuse that exploded after the shell buried itself in the ground, limiting the possible damage to barbed wire. To make matters worse, many shells fired at the Somme did not detonate. Now British shells were built to explode at the very moment of impact and nearly every shell exploded. Improved gas shells were fired at German artillery positions, killing many of their horses and making it difficult for them to shift positions.

After the slaughter at the Somme, the British army also began to use improved tactics. Smaller units were given smaller objectives. When they reached them, they held the ground and allowed a small reserve unit to bypass them and seize the next enemy position. Holding ground was made easier by equipping the troops with greater numbers of light, portable Lewis machine guns than had been done in the past. Using these weapons and tactics, British, Canadian, and Australian troops advanced on April 9, some of them moving in tunnels toward the German lines. Even though the artillery bombardment gave the Germans advanced knowledge of the impending attack, and even though they moved reserve troops in position, the new shells and tactics succeeded. On the first day of the battle, the Allies succeeded in breaking through, most spectacularly at Vimy Ridge, a heavily fortified hill that was captured by four Canadian divisions. The assault slowed as Canadians, Australians, and British came up against German reserves. After several days, casualties began to rise and the weather became horrible, with sleet and snow blanketing the early spring mud. The weather slowed the advance, and, by the last week of April, enough German reinforcements were in place for the classic Western Front battle of attrition to resume. A month after the offensive began, the British, Canadians, and Australians counted more than a hundred thousand casualties.

The large diversionary offensive in Arras exacerbated the Allied manpower problem, as Haig had predicted. The only glimmer of success had been the capture of Vimy Ridge. To the south, the main assault by the French resulted in significantly worse problems for the Allies. In mid-March, the Allies discovered that the Germans had withdrawn to the Hindenburg Line, but Nivelle did not change his plans to take into account the fact that the Germans were now in substantially better positions. On April 16, 1917, Nivelle's twenty divisions advanced on German positions between Rheims and Soissons. Nivelle's carefully designed artillery barrage moved ahead of the troops too quickly, which resulted in many of them being killed by German soldiers who had sheltered safely in well-built trenches and machine-gun posts. German aircraft drove French aircraft out of the skies, hindering French artillery spotting while helping the German artillery. German artillery succeeded in destroying or disabling all of the nearly two hundred French tanks that attempted to breach the Hindenburg Line. After a week, the assault was plainly failing. There were more than a hundred thousand French casualties, including thirty thousand killed.

Faced with such horrible losses, French troops began to refuse orders to attack. As the historian John Keegan has pointed out, they did not mutiny so much as go on strike. (There was, in fact, an outbreak of strikes on the

French home front at this time, too, and some French socialists were starting to advocate peace.) The French army, like the other armies of the First World War, was of necessity an army of civilians, many of whom had peacetime experience with strikes. There were a few instances of officers being confronted or killed by their men, but the situation was not as bad as the Russian army's, where discipline was breaking down completely. Instead of killing officers, French troops voiced complaints not only about Nivelle's wasteful offensive, but also about food, housing, and leave policies. The soldiers remained committed to defending against any further German attacks, but they indicated that they were no longer willing to go on the offensive.

The French army and the French government responded to the citizen army's strike mainly through negotiation and reforms. The management of the army was changed. Nivelle was replaced by Philippe Pétain, another hero of Verdun who was best known as an advocate of defensive warfare. Pétain spoke with soldiers and officers and introduced reforms. He adopted the German tactic of defense in depth, placing fewer troops in the front lines and more in the rear. Troops in the rear underwent extensive training in weapons and tactics and also received political education about the war effort. Leaves were extended to longer periods of time, helping soldiers to reconnect with their civilian lives. Pétain also insisted that soldiers who were guilty of overtly mutinous activities be court-martialed. Units were required to turn in their own mutineers for trial. There were more than three thousand trials and six hundred convictions. Of those, four dozen were shot. The French army remained cohesive, yet it was now clear that it would be some time before it could be used again in an offensive.[1]

THE BRITISH OFFENSIVE IN FLANDERS

By May 1917, with the French army no longer willing to push forward, the Allies were in trouble. The British nearly achieved a breakthrough beyond Vimy Ridge, but they were stopped by German reinforcements and bad weather. The U.S. army was still hopelessly small. The Russian army was holding together, but the Petrograd Soviet's Order Number One was undermining discipline and morale. There was a glimmer of hope for the Allies in Italy. On May 10, following an artillery bombardment, the Italian army sent thirty-eight divisions into action along a forty-kilometer front beside the Isonzo. In what came to be known as the Tenth Battle of the Isonzo, the Italian army advanced deep into Austrian territory, nearing the city of Trieste. Initially, the Austrians had only fourteen divisions to oppose the Italians, but Austrian reinforcements came just in time to turn back the Italians. By the end of the first week of June 1917, the Italians had retreated to their original positions along the Isonzo, having suffered more than 150,000 casualties, with 36,000 killed. By contrast, the Austrians lost 7,300. On June 10, the Italians made a related attack on Austrian positions in the Trentino—fortified after 1916's failed Punishment Expedition. The Austrians survived an Italian barrage by hiding in deep bunkers, carved into the stone. The Italian attack became a disaster, resulting in a further 25,000 casualties.[2]

With the Italian, French, Russian, and American armies unable to make an offensive contribution, British politicians and generals considered their poor options. Britain had to maintain pressure on Germany, otherwise German forces could be used to knock out the Russians and the Italians before turning to the west and knocking out the French. Britain now had significantly larger forces on the Western Front, thanks to contributions from its colonies. Weapons, training, and tactics had improved considerably, as had been demonstrated at Vimy Ridge. Haig, still in command of the BEF, had wanted to launch an offensive in Belgium since 1915. The northern part of the Western Front lay closer to British supplies and communications, while the capture of the Belgian coastline, especially the German submarine base at Ostend, would help the British navy. Haig had not been able to launch a Belgian offensive because his commitments to the French had drawn British forces south, where they fought the Germans at the Somme. But now with the French army on the defensive, Haig had more freedom to pursue his plans.

Haig entrusted a limited offensive to the British Second Army, composed of British, Irish, Australian, and New Zealand divisions and commanded by General Sir Hubert Plumer. Plumer had a reputation for thorough planning and thoughtful consideration of the needs of his troops. He planned thoroughly for an assault on the heavily fortified German trenches to the south of the Ypres salient, aiming to advance three kilometers and capture the ridge at Messines, just beyond the town of Wytschaete. To attain this goal, Plumer trained his troops in the same tactics as were used at Vimy Ridge. An artillery barrage with better shells would be a prelude to an infantry advance in which small units leapfrogged each other. In one of the most innovative tactics of the war, Plumer's engineers dug nineteen mines under the German positions, using silent pumps to remove water and to circulate air. The tunnels were packed with half a million kilograms of explosives. After seventeen days of artillery bombardment, the mines were detonated early in the morning of June 7, 1917. The explosion was so loud that it could be heard in southeastern England. The Second Army rushed toward their objectives and by the middle of the afternoon the British, Irish, Australians, and New Zealanders had captured Messines Ridge. They dug in quickly and held their positions against a German counterattack. Plumer proved that, by using good tactics, small bites could be taken out of the German line and favorable positions could be captured. The British lost seventeen thousand casualties, a large number of soldiers that was still, by the standards of First World War generals, a moderate loss.

Haig interpreted moderate losses at Messines to indicate that a major breakthrough was still possible. His superiors were skeptical. The British prime minister, Lloyd George, was appalled by the casualties incurred by Britain during the war—up to this point 250,000 Britons had lost their lives. Lloyd George doubted that progress on the Western Front was worth the cost and began considering other theaters of operations for success. But Haig had the reluctant support of the British chief of staff, Field Marshal Lord Robertson. Robertson did not believe that a breakthrough was possible, given the rough equality between the British and German forces in Belgium. Robertson did believe that victory could come from attrition, and so was inclined to authorize Haig to attack. Haig presented his plans to a meeting of Britain's inner cabinet responsible for the direction of the war, which included Lord Curzon, the former governor of India; Lord Milner, the former governor of South Africa; and J. C. Smuts, the South African general and politician—an illustration of how the experience of imperialism could shape the experience of war. In the meetings, Lloyd George grilled Haig on his plans and on the prospects for success and grudgingly acquiesced. His coalition government of liberals and conservatives might break down if conservatives suspected him of meddling too much in military affairs.

Haig chose to launch his offensive from the Ypres salient. The main assault would be made by the British Fifth Army, commanded by the cavalry general, Sir Hubert Gough. To the north, the Fifth Army was supported by the French First Army. To the south, it was supported by Plumer's Second Army. All told, the Allies had eighteen divisions against ten German divisions, giving them an advantage in manpower that was not sufficient by the standards of the Western Front. The Germans prepared their positions well, with nine lines of defenses, including barbed wire, machine-gun bunkers, and small forts called pillboxes.

The Third Battle of Ypres became noteworthy for its exceptionally challenging environmental conditions. The defenders enjoyed a special advantage in the terrain. The land around Ypres is low-lying and waterlogged. In the centuries before the war, Belgian farmers and engineers had dug canals and ditches to drain the land. In 1914 and 1915, during the First and Second Battles of Ypres, shellfire ruined the drainage system. The muddy terrain made it difficult for armies to move, a condition that favored defenders heavily over attackers. Haig planned to shell the Germans, then advance, then move the artillery, then start shelling and advancing again, at each stage taking another bite out of the German defenses until they reached the relatively high ground centered at Gheluvelt and Passchendaele.

Haig wanted to attack but had to do so before the fall rains made the Ypres salient impassable for men, horses, and artillery. He began the third

Ypres offensive with a massive artillery bombardment that lasted for fifteen days. On July 31, 1917, Allied troops advanced eastward from the Ypres salient. They made rapid progress through the first German lines, but by the late afternoon communications had broken down between the infantry at the front and the artillery and commanding officers in the rear. At that point, the German artillery and infantry made a forceful counterattack. Many British troops fell back, consolidating their positions. At the same time, it began to rain in a torrent that lasted for days. The battlefield became a sea of mud so deep that men and horses became stuck in it up to their waists. Many drowned. The landscape became completely impassable for artillery and supplies. On August 4, Haig halted the attack. The British had gained two kilometers at a cost of eight thousand lives, an appalling result that only looked good by comparison to the first day at the Somme.

Haig persisted in making his assault in spite of the environmental conditions and the stout German resistance. Two weeks of steady rain did not deter him from launching another major assault along the front on August 16, 1917. Again, one or two kilometers were gained. Again, dogged German resistance and terrible mud made any further advance impossible. Now the total Allied casualties were eighteen thousand killed and fifty thousand wounded. Lloyd George called Haig to London to discuss the battle, and once again the generals persuaded him to allow Haig to continue. Haig relied on Plumer's guidance to plan the rest of the attacks. The Allies would attack in "small bites" after massive artillery bombardments. During the late summer and early fall, Allied forces made several successful attacks across the muddy fields of Ypres. The Germans, holding their reserves in the rear, counterattacked, pushing them back some, but not all, of the distance. The Germans also began to fire shells loaded with a new gas, mustard gas, which killed by burning the skin and mucous membranes.

The result of this bitter, seesaw warfare was that by the second week of October 1917 the Allies possessed the ridge to the east of Ypres that they had hoped to attain. Britain's best divisions were exhausted, but Haig believed that the breakthrough might still be imminent. He aimed his next blow at German positions around the ruined village of Passchendaele, ten kilometers east of the starting line of July 31. With British forces exhausted, Haig was forced to rely completely on colonial forces. First he turned to the New Zealand Division and the Second Australian Division, which had been kept in reserve. In October, with the rains continuing at record levels during the second week of October, he ordered them to advance on Passchendaele. Thousands of New Zealanders and Australians died in the assault, with hundreds of them drowning in the mud. No ground was gained, and both Gough and Plumer pressed Haig to end the campaign.

Instead of stopping the battle of Passchendaele, Haig turned to the Canadians, whose commanding general, Sir Arthur Currie, hesitated to sacrifice his troops. This was a serious matter because the governments of Canada and the other "dominions" of the British Empire, including Australia, New Zealand, and South Africa, reserved rights over the disposition of their troops. Currie weighed asking his government to intervene but did not, mainly because he supported Haig's overall approach to war on the Western Front. Currie informed Haig that he believed the battle should be brought to an end, then ordered his troops to carry out Haig's orders. In the final week of October 1917, the Third and Fourth Canadian Divisions pressed forward, capturing half a kilometer of ground with heavy casualties. They were relieved by the First and Second Canadian Divisions, who captured the village of Passchendaele and consolidated their positions in the first week of November. From August to November, during the Third Battle of Ypres (also known as the Battle of Passchendaele), British and colonial forces lost 70,000 killed and 170,000 wounded. They gained ten kilometers.[3]

THE CENTRAL POWERS' OFFENSIVE IN ITALY

Passchendaele was a victory that was not worth the cost. With Allied manpower weakened further, it would have been an ideal moment for Germany to move its troops from Russia and attempt to win on the Western Front. Instead, in late 1917, after the collapse of the Russian war effort, German and Austrian leaders decided that their next strategic objective was to knock Italy out of the war. Some troops still needed to be stationed in the east, but most eastern troops could now be deployed south against Italy. The Germans made this decision in order to keep their Austrian allies in the war. The Austrian effort in Italy had bogged down into a demoralizing defensive war reminiscent of the Western Front, but whereas German morale remained strong, Austrian morale was fading. German officers visiting the Italian front noted Austrian weakness and recommended to their government that German troops, who were more numerous, better trained, and better equipped, be sent to help the Austrians move forward. Germany sent seven divisions, all trained in the infiltration tactics used at Riga, to work side by side with eight Austrian divisions.

The armies of the Central Powers nearly won a major breakthrough victory in Italy. On October 24, 1917, the joint Austrian and German force attacked the Italians along the northern sector of the Isonzo River on a long front centered near the town of Caporetto. The attack began in the early morning, with a massive artillery bombardment together with the release of phosgene gas from projector tubes. Italian troops were positioned on the heights, but German storm troopers, armed with light machine guns and light artillery, drove through the valleys, bypassing Italian strongholds, and cut off Italian communications. Many of the Italian defenders had recently been drafted from industrial areas, such as Turin, where there were increasing numbers of strikes. Tens of thousands of Italian troops began to surrender. The Italian commanding general, Luigi Cadorna, ordered a retreat to the Tagliamento River, to the southwest, but the Germans and Austrians broke through the line. Cadorna moved his troops back again, to the Piave River, just to the northeast of Venice. By this point, nearly three hundred thousand Italian soldiers had surrendered, along with much of their army's artillery, but enough soldiers remained to hold the line at the Piave.

The Italian government took steps to improve the situation. The dictatorial Cadorna was replaced by the more considerate General Armando Diaz. In early November, Britain and France sent nine divisions to bolster the Italian army. Morale recovered somewhat, and the Germans and Austrians were prevented from capturing Venice. This was due, at least in part, to the trouble that the Central Powers had in supplying and reinforcing their armies over the long distance between the Isonzo and the Piave. The Italian army began to restore itself, although, like the French army, for the foreseeable future it could only contemplate defensive warfare.

TECHNOLOGY AND BREAKTHROUGHS

The Germans had nearly achieved a breakthrough by using advanced tactics and technologies. British weapons and tactics had improved considerably, too. Haig and his colleagues continued to believe in breakthrough, in spite of the contradictions at Passchendaele. Shortly after the capture of Passchendaele, the commander of the British Third Army, General Sir Julian Byng, devised a plan for tanks, supported by artillery, cavalry, infantry, and aircraft, to break through at Cambrai, to the south of Arras and Vimy Ridge. The tanks were supported by new artillery tactics. Before the big bombardment that commonly preceded big offensives, artillery officers checked the accuracy of their guns by "registering" them, in other words, firing a preliminary shot at a target, observing its fall, and calibrating the gun accordingly. Second and third shots were then fired to pinpoint accuracy. This way of registering artillery was risky because the other side might be able to detect the location of the gun and fire on it, either destroying it or forcing its soldiers to move it and have to register it again. Shot registration also reduced the element of surprise, although it must be said that, before a big offensive, shot registration was followed by massive weeklong bombardments, which completely eliminated the possibility of surprise. In 1917, British artillery officers began to experiment with "silent" registration, a technique that combined mathematics, new technologies, and the extensive experience of First World War artillerymen with their weapons. German targets were noted and mapped as well as possible by observers on the ground and in the air. Microphones placed along the front lines were used to listen to German artillery fire and then to triangulate the exact positions of German guns. Knowing these exact positions, British officers created mathematical formulas for aiming cannons that allowed them to factor in weather conditions as well as the wear and tear on the inside of a gun's barrel. In this way, British artillery prepared to hit German targets on the first shot, without having to fire registration shots.

The application of these new techniques to the Western Front resulted in measured success for the British. The battle of Cambrai began on November 20, 1917, with a sudden, intensive British bombardment of the German Second Army's positions along a ten-kilometer front. Silent registration worked. Pinpoint artillery fire surprised the German troops, who abandoned their posts. Then three hundred British tanks advanced with the troops of the Third Army, assisted by fourteen squadrons of airplanes. Some British tanks broke down, others were hit by German shells, but by noon the most advanced line of tanks had pressed ten kilometers into the German positions. At this point, the British began to deploy their cavalry for the much-anticipated breakthrough. The German commander, General Georg von der Marwitz, ordered a counterattack by his reserves. The German troops stopped the British advance; then ten days later, enough German reserves had arrived at Cambrai for them to begin a massive counteroffensive. The Germans used the storm trooper tactics that they had employed on the Eastern and Italian Fronts to push the British back. By the end of November, both sides were more or less where they were at the beginning of the battle. Both sides had more than forty-five thousand casualties. Cambrai was the most innovative battle of the war from a technological perspective. Its combined use of technologies and tactics foreshadowed the battles of the Second World War. But still there was not a lasting breakthrough.

Both sides believed that new tactics and new weapons promised to help break the other side. Instead, they tended only to exacerbate the conflict. Such was the case with the German U-boat campaign of 1917, which pitted 120 submarines against Allied and neutral shipping in the zone of unrestricted submarine warfare declared around the British Isles. Initially, Allied and neutral losses were quite high. In February 1917, the German U-boats sank 540,006 tons of shipping, including 313,486 tons that were British. In April 1917, 881,207 tons went to the bottom, 545,282 tons of it British. British ships had only a one-in-four chance of surviving a round-trip between Britain and the United States. Merchant vessels steamed out into the North Atlantic, alone and unprotected. It was difficult for the U-boats to find them in the open waters of the Atlantic but rather easy to pick them off as they entered the western approaches to British ports. Naval leaders were wedded to offensive warfare and preferred to use their ships to sweep for submarines—a low-yielding tactic—rather than to guard merchant ships.

The sinkings of early 1917 caused the governments on both sides of the Atlantic to force their navies to reconsider. In May 1917, the British and U.S. navies began to provide destroyer escorts for convoys of twenty ships that set sail almost every day. Convoys worked because they concentrated ships together in one place. When ships were spread about the sea by themselves, the U-boats were more likely to find them. In addition, naval vessels could communicate by radio with naval intelligence, which would often decode the positions of U-boats. U-boats that attacked convoys also could not rise to the surface, lest they be fired upon by destroyers, thus decreasing the overall accuracy of torpedo fire. As convoys were implemented, fewer ships sank. In November and December 1917, 289,212 tons and 399,111 tons were sunk, an improvement over the early months of the year. After March 1918, the Allies never lost more than three hundred thousand tons per month. And starting in the final months of 1917, the Allies were sinking about eight U-boats per month, either by direct fire from destroyers or by laying mines. Eight U-boats were built every month, on average, so the size of the U-boat fleet remained somewhat constant, although it was difficult to replace the experienced crews that were lost at sea. By contrast, the Allies were able to build new merchant ships faster than they lost them. The German navy shifted its submarine operations to British coastal waters, where the Allies began to use aircraft in antisubmarine patrols. Antisubmarine efforts were substantial enough that U-boats were never able to scare merchant shipping off the seas, as Germany's admirals had promised the kaiser. Yet submarines still sank quite a few ships, adding significantly to Allied war losses. At sea, as on land, neither side could claim a victory.[4]

By contrast to the proponents of new technologies on land and at sea, in the air, the airplane had few promoters who believed it would win the war. Nevertheless, by 1917 aircraft manufacturing and flying skills had improved to such an extent that the airplane did begin to have a significant impact on the battlefield as well as on the broader strategy of the war. In 1914, the Allies and the Central Powers had a total of about seven hundred aircraft. The airplanes were unarmed and were used mainly for purposes of observation, although radio communication with the ground was still in the most rudimentary stages. Airplane pilots played a key role in the opening battles on the Eastern and Western Fronts. Aviators on both sides relayed observations of opponents' movements to commanding officers, who factored aerial intelligence into their decision-making.

As the war became stalemated on the Western Front, aerial observation became important for planning artillery and infantry attacks, especially since new camera technologies allowed images to be wider and more focused. In order to deprive their enemies of aerial intelligence, both sides began to emphasize the development of aircraft that could be used in combat against other aircraft, what came to be known as fighter planes. In 1914, when opposing aircraft encountered each other, pilots and observers fired pistols, shotguns, and rifles and even threw bricks and grenades at each other. The introduction of machine guns to airplanes changed air-to-air combat and aircraft design. At the start of the war, there were many airplanes in service with push-propellers, facing backward, as well as airplanes with pull-propellers (tractor-propellers) facing forward. When machine guns were first mounted on airplanes, they had to fire away from the propeller. These were most easily mounted on airplanes with push-propellers, but pilots were beginning to prefer pull-propellers. The push-propeller allows unimpeded views and can easily mount forward-firing machine guns, but the pull-propeller engine gives pilots more protection in a crash. If a machine gun is mounted to fire forward in a pull-propeller plane, it will obviously blow the propeller to splinters. Designers were forced to mount machine guns to fire over the propeller or to the rear, taking care to make it impossible for the gunner to destroy the tail.

One airplane manufacturer who worked closely with German pilots, the Dutchman Anton Fokker, was aware that, before the war, French designers had experimented with a gear called an interrupter that connected an airplane's engine to a machine gun. It allowed a machine gun to fire through a propeller without hitting the blades, an innovation that allowed machine guns to be mounted on the forward part of the airplane, between the propeller and the pilot, making it easier to coordinate aim and flying direction. The French had never perfected the design: French pilots had used it with some success, but the propellers still got hit regularly enough that they had to be covered by metal deflector shields. Fokker installed a version of the interrupter in a German airplane. The trials went so well that German fighters, armed with interrupters, began to drive Allied fighters and observers out of the skies.

With the development and refinement of the interrupter, pull-propeller fighter planes became the most common aircraft of the war. They were produced by the thousands. By 1917, there were tens of thousands of fighters in the skies. Combat shifted from one-on-one "dogfights" to group actions in which "squadrons" of aircraft tried to drive each other out of the skies over the battlefield. In this way, the other side would be denied aerial observation for artillery fire. The war in the air became just as industrialized as the war on the ground. Pilots were depicted as glamorous "knights of the air," even though their combat depended on their skills with industrialized equipment flying in mass formations. Their casualty rates were high, while the stress of flying trapped in rickety machines while enduring cold temperatures as well as fire from the air and the ground caused many to suffer from anxiety and depression.

Increasingly, aircraft were used for the unglamorous work of attacking soldiers on the ground. In 1914, small airplanes dropped grenades, gasoline bombs, and even darts on top of infantry and cavalry units. By 1917 and

1918, improved fighter aircraft were capable of dropping small bombs and of using their machine guns to fire on troops. Attacking soldiers in this way was highly dangerous. Airplanes were still relatively slow and were shot down by fire from cannons, machine guns, and rifles. Airplanes may have been glamorous to some, but many observers sensed that they had become simply one more means of dealing death on the battlefield. At the Battle of the Somme in 1916, Philip Gibbs conveyed this thought with a striking natural metaphor. He wrote that "over my head came a flight of six aeroplanes, led by a single monoplane, which steered steadily towards the enemy. The sky was deeply blue above them, and when the sun caught their wings they were as beautiful and delicate as butterflies. But they were carrying death with them, and were out to bomb the enemy's batteries and to drop their explosives into masses of men behind the German lines."[5]

The history of the air war has been so overshadowed by accounts of fighter pilots that few people realize that bombers were important, too. French bombers were among the most innovative. France relied on the well-built Voisin single-engine light bomber, which remained a reliable design for several years. It was one of the first airplanes built of steel, and it used one of the first optical bomb sights. As early as 1915, French pilots were using it to practice raiding in massed formations, one of the key tactics to emerge out of the war in the air. In 1917, they replaced their Voisins with the Breguet, one of the fastest aircraft of the war, partly because it was built from a new, innovative material: duralumin, an early form of aluminum that German engineers had formulated in the years before the war.

The French were innovators in the design of single-engine light bombers, but the overall trend in bomber construction was toward multiple-engine, heavy bombers. One of the pioneers of heavy bomber design was the Russian Igor Sikorsky (who became famous after the war as a designer of helicopters). In 1913, Sikorsky built the first four-engine biplane, the "Il'ya Murometz," as a civilian passenger plane—complete with a heated cabin for sixteen and a toilet. By 1915, the Murometz was armed with between four and eight machine guns and converted to bombing and reconnaissance. It had the capacity to carry eight hundred kilograms of bombs at a range of five hundred kilometers. Alternatively, if it carried extra gasoline instead of bombs, it could stay in the air on reconnaissance missions for eight hours. Only seventy-five of the Il'ya Murometz were produced, owing to its complicated construction and Russia's limited industrial capabilities, but only one was ever shot down.

Germany, Britain, and Italy also developed their own heavy bombers. The Italians used a heavy bomber, the Caproni, that had two pull-propellers and one push-propeller, giving it great reliability. The Italians used the Caproni in massed attacks with dozens of planes against Austrian troops during the Tenth and Eleventh Battles of the Isonzo. Massed bombing raids against

Austrian positions continued until the end of the war. The Italians also used heavy bombers against Austrian shipyards and industrial facilities near Trieste. The British unveiled their first heavy bomber, the twin-engine Handley-Page, relatively late in the war, in 1916. The British used it in much the same way as the Italians used the Caproni—for raids on enemy trenches and for bombing industrial targets. In the final months of 1917, the British used the Handley-Page and other, smaller aircraft for raids on German cities. These were aimed mainly at industrial targets and continued throughout the war, even though German artillery and fighter planes shot down many of the British planes.

In part, the purpose of the British campaign was psychological—to demonstrate that Britain could retaliate against German raids on England. During the early years of the war, Germany launched zeppelins against Britain. Zeppelins were long, cigar-shaped blimps armed with machine guns and bombs. They flew at high altitudes where they could not be attacked by fighters and artillery, yet their altitude impeded their accuracy. Intrepid fighter pilots who wished to shoot them down sometimes followed them to their bases, where they would have to descend and be vulnerable. To replace the questionable zeppelins, Germany deployed two high-altitude bombers: the twin-engine Gotha in the spring of 1917 and the enormous Giant four-engine bomber in the fall. For the rest of the war, they raided London and southeastern England, causing significant damage and inflicting hundreds of casualties. These losses from long-range bombing were not high compared to the losses experienced during the Second World War, but they did cause high levels of concern on home fronts that were already under considerable strain.

Chapter Fourteen

Allied Empire-Building, 1916–1918

Many historians believe that the First World War was the modern world's watershed, in which stable political, economic, and social orders broke down under the strains of total war. Modern weaponry in the hands of land-hungry nationalists produced unprecedented dislocations, including forced mass migrations and famines. On the battlefields, industrialized slaughter caused many people to abandon faith in progress. Yet in much of Africa and the Middle East, the war did not produce such great transformations. The same transformations had already begun to occur in the nineteenth century. Land-hungry European nationalists had already caused Africans and Middle Easterners to experience total wars that produced the breakdown of old orders as well as famines, migrations, and massacres. When Europeans caused and prolonged the First World War on their own territory, Europeans essentially did to themselves what they had already done to others. They made themselves subject to the worst aspects of modernity by launching imperialist wars of aggression and conquest on their own continent. Meanwhile, in Africa and the Middle East, where these things had been happening for several decades already, the First World War did not introduce significantly new historical trends. The war only accelerated the effects of European capitalism, imperialism, and nationalism.

WAR IN AFRICA, 1916–1918

One of the greatest aviation exploits of the First World War involved the Zeppelin L.59. In the spring of 1917, the Germans expanded its size and outfitted it with medical and military supplies. They dispatched it first to Bulgaria and then in May sent it across the Aegean and Mediterranean Seas, on a mission to fly over Egypt and Sudan and then continue southward, where it would deliver the supplies to Paul von Lettow-Vorbeck, the German officer commanding in Tanzania. The zeppelin traveled as far south as the central Sudan when mechanical difficulties persuaded its captain to change course and head back to Bulgaria. It reached Bulgaria in late November.

The mission of the L.59 failed, although it did highlight German concerns about Tanzania. In the early years of the war, an African force commanded by Lettow-Vorbeck defeated British and Indian forces in Tanzania. Lettow-Vorbeck withdrew to the north, near Mount Kilimanjaro, where his force posed a threat to the British colony of Kenya. At the start of 1916, the British appointed Jan C. Smuts, a leading South African politician who had led a band of guerrillas against the British during the Boer War, to command British forces in eastern Africa. Smuts did not have training as a professional soldier. He was familiar with the long-standing method of Boer warfare: the "commando." Horsemen rode to the scene of battle, dismounted, fired, re-mounted, and maneuvered. This tactic was particularly well suited to the terrain and the subtropical climate of South Africa. But Smuts's decision to rely on mounted Europeans for the campaign against Lettow-Vorbeck's African soldiers was disastrous, for reasons that have much to do with the environment of Tanzania. Two diseases are prevalent in Tanzania and the other countries of central and eastern Africa: malaria and trypanosomiasis, or sleeping sickness. The first debilitates and kills people; the second debilitates and kills people and their animals, including horses and cattle. Children in malarial regions die in great numbers, but those who survive and who contin-ue to be exposed to the mosquitoes that spread the disease develop immunity. Lettow-Vorbeck's African soldiers had this immunity, while the Europeans under Smuts did not. Smuts was sufficiently wedded to ideas about the superiority of Europeans that he did not initially consider the use of African troops himself.[1]

Conditions in eastern Africa brought manpower issues to the forefront. At the start of his 1916 campaign, Smuts had available to him seventy thousand soldiers, including units from the Belgian Congo, Portuguese Mozambique, and British Kenya as well as South Africa. Lettow-Vorbeck commanded sixteen thousand troops, most of them African. In 1916, as Smuts advanced from Kenya, Lettow-Vorbeck retreated south along the coast, destroying bridges and railroad tracks. His troops evaded the British force, using guerril-la tactics that Lettow-Vorbeck, a professional soldier, actually disliked. Meanwhile, Smuts, who was experienced in waging a guerrilla war, began to lose men and horses to disease. During 1916, Smuts lost 100 percent of his horses every month. Several dozen men died from malaria, but more than ten thousand had malarial symptoms: fever, anemia, and fatigue all hindered Smuts's efforts. Both sides resolved manpower issues by forcing tens of thousands of African men to serve as porters, a policy that did not exactly win them over to the cause of European empire-building. Problems of supplying food and water resulted in malnutrition and dysentery, disabling and killing porters and troops alike.

The problems of supply also led both armies to live off the land, plundering settlements as they marched. One of the British officers, Richard Meinertzhagen, recalled the way his troops took control of a village:

> There were three huts. The people were turned out by the village chief and within two to four hours we made a new large village of huts and tents for 240–250 men. . . . Even when we let some people stay behind in a village, we still get to keep everything, even if there isn't much that we like (because the ever-growing demand for food cannot be satisfied). In this sense, the war is an endurance test for this [imperialist] system of governing and, judging by my experience here, I would say that it is a success. But it is dreadful how the amount of baggage increases. It took me an entire day to reduce it to three loads, and yet there is still so much I think I will need ten porters! Looting is one of the necessary evils of the war in Africa. We have managed to teach our Askaris [African soldiers] to behave more humanely, but not to desist from looting *per se*. All the troops, including the whites, have been directly dependent on plunder for munitions, clothing and food. All the blacks are mad on looting, whether it is the Askaris or the porters, man, woman, or child. It is also difficult to stop the blacks from raping women, because they see them as property, like cows or huts. The women who come along with us usually don't want to go back to their husbands, having tasted the freedom of the soldiering life.[2]

To Meinertzhagen, rape produced freedom, while looting, a necessary evil, was part of the success story of imperialism. Meinertzhagen appeared not to have a sense of irony. The contradictions of wartime imperialism were sensed more keenly by one of his opponents, Ludwig Deppe, who served as Lettow-Vorbeck's medical officer. After the war, Deppe wrote that "behind us we have left destroyed fields, ransacked magazines, and, for the immediate future, starvation. We were no longer the agents of culture; our track was marked by death, plundering and evacuated villages."[3] Environmental destruction was not only a side effect of the campaign; it was part of the strategy of both sides. Destroying the sources of food and supplies would deprive the enemy. That destruction would also harm the people of eastern Africa was a mere afterthought. Such thinking was consistent with the imperialist sentiment of the late nineteenth century. The well-being of African people came second to the satisfaction of Europe's desire for geographic expansion and raw materials.

The environmental destruction and human misery of the East African campaign look bad from hindsight. Even so, both commanders can still be admired for some of their military accomplishments. Lettow-Vorbeck could claim victory mainly by preserving the viability of his forces and by pinning down large numbers of his enemies. Smuts could claim victory because, by the end of 1916, he had captured most of the coastline, including the important port of Dar es Salaam. Smuts had accomplished much, from a superficial perspective. He was promoted to sit on the Imperial War Cabinet in London. Command passed to other officers, who continued the arduous campaign throughout 1917 and 1918, pursuing Lettow-Vorbeck and his force through the interior of eastern Africa. The Allies kept European troops, Indian troops, and their African porters in the field and in 1917 began to supplement them with African troops from Kenya and West Africa, where adults were likely to have immunity to malaria. These troops helped the Allies drive Lettow-Vorbeck out of Tanzania. After several sharp battles in July, September, and October 1917, Lettow-Vorbeck retreated across the southern border into Portuguese Mozambique with only two thousand soldiers. The small force eluded the Allies as it engaged in hit-and-run warfare in Mozambique and then in Northern Rhodesia (Zambia) throughout 1918. At the end of the war, Lettow-Vorbeck and his troops were still a small danger.[4]

The fighting in Tanzania was associated with destruction and conscription. Recruitment for the Allied war effort spread much farther throughout Africa. In French Africa, men were recruited for fighting as well as for labor. In the years before the war, the French army began to recruit and train large numbers of men in West Africa, thinking that, in the event of a war in Europe, French troops would no longer be able to man colonial garrisons. When war broke out, not only did French troops return to France, but many African recruits went with them. Over the course of 1914 to 1919, 171,000 soldiers from West Africa fought in France, with more than eighty thousand of them becoming casualties. Other French colonies sent laborers and troops as well, including forty-five thousand from Madagascar.

For some years, the French were inclined to let colonized people assimilate to French political culture, which was not the case in Britain, where racial beliefs persuaded most policymakers to keep Africans at arm's length. Britain did not use African troops in combat in Europe for a variety of reasons, ranging from beliefs that Africans were inferior to fears that exposing Africans to warfare in Europe might diminish their respect for Europeans. Even so, some British troops from Africa saw action against Lettow-Vorbeck and also against the Turks in the Middle East. The British government did use Africans extensively in labor battalions that worked directly behind the lines.

Labor recruitment ensured that the impact of the war on Africa was quite significant. Porters were recruited—and mistreated—in every colonial campaign. It is estimated that, for the East African campaign, German East Africa (Tanzania) and British Nyasaland (Malawi) each provided two hundred thousand porters, most of them recruited by various means of coercion. It is likely that, in East Africa alone, one hundred thousand porters died while on campaign. In other parts of Africa, recruitment was heavy, too, but treatment was better. In Namibia, the South African forces employed thirty-five thousand laborers, while in Sinai the British recruited three hundred thousand. Algeria provided ninety thousand laborers for France. The figures are impressive. What has to be remembered as well is that each of these men was absent from a household that depended on his labor to produce crops or that depended on his earnings as a migrant worker.

The war created social patterns in Africa that were familiar to people in Europe, too. Basic production was done increasingly by women as well as by children and the elderly. Local self-sufficiency increased, too, as Africans took over jobs vacated by Europeans who returned home. Cities expanded as wartime job opportunities arose. Prices rose, which fostered unrest and even strikes and rebellions in some places. Many Africans hoped that enduring wartime circumstances might bring them benefits when the war was over, in the form of greater freedoms under colonial rule. In general, these hopes were not satisfied.[5]

WAR IN THE MIDDLE EAST, 1916–1918

In the Middle East, too, many people—Arabs, Armenians, Jews, Kurds, and others—hoped to be free from British, French, Ottoman, or Russian domination, yet hopes for freedom were often frustrated. After the Ottoman victories at Gallipoli and Kut, their war effort began to falter. And although Britain and France planned to divide the Middle East between them, the French focused on defending their homeland while the British, drawing on troops from India, Australia, and other parts of their empire, took on a much larger role in the Middle East. The new British prime minister, David Lloyd George, was an avid empire builder. He also believed that widening the war was an acceptable way to defeat the Central Powers. Lloyd George was skeptical of Haig and the British chief of staff, General Sir William Robertson, who sought to concentrate British efforts on the Western Front.

In the Middle East, British forces made significant advances. The Mesopotamia Campaign resumed in December 1916, when a British and Indian army under General Sir Frederick Stanley Maude began to advance up the Tigris and Euphrates again. Maude's British and Indian forces now seriously outnumbered the Ottomans—five infantry and two cavalry divisions to forces equivalent to one and a half divisions—and Maude paid more careful attention to issues of supply than his predecessors in Iraq. Under Maude's command, British gunboats advanced slowly up the Tigris while railroads were constructed to carry supplies forward. British and Indian soldiers advanced gradually while the Ottomans retreated, destroying supplies and towns along the way. By March 1917, the British flag was flying over Baghdad.

Instead of continuing the advance during the hot summer, Maude decided to wait until the fall, when weather conditions were more favorable. In September and October, Maude's forces consolidated their hold on central Iraq. When Maude died of cholera in November 1917, the British advance stopped, just short of the oil fields of northern Iraq. In spite of the lure of this target, the British held back their force until the very last weeks of the war. The Western Front required the resources. In Palestine, Lloyd George hoped for British forces to capture Jerusalem by Christmas 1917, but here, too, the manpower problems of the Western Front often took precedence. The Allies had already had one victory in the Sinai Desert, between Egypt and Palestine. In the first week of February 1915, an Ottoman army of twenty thousand had actually attempted an invasion of Egypt by marching across the Sinai Desert, one of the most hostile, arid environments on the planet. Ottoman troops transported several weeks' supply of drinking water as well as pontoons made in Germany to help cross the Suez Canal and enter Egypt. British and Indian soldiers, supported by Allied naval vessels, defended the canal successfully, inflicting thousands of casualties on the Ottomans. Once again, modern weapons tended to favor defenders over attackers, even attackers who were well led and well equipped. Nevertheless, it was not until 1917 that the British decided to follow up their victory with a drive into Palestine.

The British appointed a commander from the Western Front, General Sir Edmund Allenby, placing him in charge of a force of Australian, British, and Indian soldiers. During his 1917 and 1918 campaigns in Palestine and Syria, he often had to compete with the needs of the Western Front. Allenby adopted the same technique as Maude, building up supplies and transport carefully and advancing slowly. Allenby built a railroad running from Egypt to supply his troops, and he even built a pipeline across the Sinai Desert so that Egyptian water could supply troops in Palestine. He attacked Ottoman forces at Beersheba and Gaza in October and November 1917, respectively, and captured Jerusalem in early December. Turkish forces, commanded by German generals—first by Falkenhayn and then by Liman von Sanders— held a line on the coast at Haifa. Allenby's advance to central Palestine left his troops exhausted and stretched their supply lines to the limit. The British government, pressed for manpower on the Western Front, began to withdraw British troops from the Middle East. They were replaced by recruits from India, who needed to be trained. Allenby had to pause for several months. [6]

As much as Allenby's advance had led to exhaustion and to a need to regroup, it also inspired both Arabs and Jews. The Allied governments had received support and finance from Jews, many of whom, in turn, were associated with Zionism, the movement that sought the creation of a Jewish homeland. Zionism was supported by many Jews in Allied countries, particularly in Russia, where the tsars had oppressed the Jews terribly, and also in the United States, where many Russian Jews had fled. Jews were not exactly embraced by the British ruling classes, whose members had a long history of anti-Semitism, but as the war dragged on, the influence of British and American Zionists became greater. Lloyd George found them sympathetic. As Allenby's forces converged on Jerusalem, Lloyd George's foreign secretary, Lord Arthur Balfour, wrote a public letter to the prominent Zionist banker Lord Rothschild promising that a Jewish homeland would be created in Palestine.[7]

The Balfour Declaration, as it is known, has proven controversial. In many ways, it reflects imperialism: far away in London, a British statesman divided the territory of a distant land. In other ways, the declaration was good, in that it sought to help a historically repressed minority. In the letter, Balfour indicated that this promise should not be taken to mean that the British government favored Jews over Arabs, but he must have realized that the declaration was not likely to be received well by Arabs. In fact, the declaration was at odds with the participation of Arab soldiers on the side of the British. In 1917, approximately ten thousand Arab men, organized in several groups and financed and supplied by the British, were fighting against the Ottomans. One British officer, T. E. Lawrence, famously acted as military adviser to two of these groups. One, under Feisal, son of the Sharif of Mecca, raided Turkish outposts and disrupted the Ottoman railway to the Hijaz, the Red Sea coast of Arabia, while another, under a Bedouin sheik named Auda, captured the port of Aqaba.

During 1917 and 1918, Arab cavalry (and camelry) played an important role in British operations, especially in the final campaign of the war in Palestine. During the first eight months of 1918, British forces in Palestine regrouped, for the same reasons they did in Mesopotamia: experienced troops were needed for the Western Front; new troops in the Middle East needed to be trained; and Ottoman forces were basically in a defensive posture. The Ottoman army was losing thousands of troops to desertion, even as the Ottomans were able to end their war with the Russians. In September 1918, Allenby renewed his advance up the Mediterranean coast of Palestine, defeating Turkish forces by the combined use of infantry, cavalry, and airplanes. Allenby's troops, together with Arab cavalry and camelry, captured all of Palestine and at the very end of the war were occupying Damascus in Syria.

The Arabs, led by Feisal, were in a good position to bargain for a measure of freedom from the Allies. They knew that the Allies would have to be pushed: after the Bolsheviks seized power in Russia, they discovered the Allies' secret agreements dividing the Middle East. The Bolsheviks published the documents—much to the consternation of the Allies—as part of their effort to stir up a worldwide communist revolution. The Arabs then knew that the British and French were inclined to expand their empires in the

Middle East, in spite of the promises they had made in support of Arab independence.

In the Middle East, as in Africa, the Allies acted to expand their empires, much in the same way that Germany sought to expand its territories in Eastern Europe. The U.S. entry into the war raised awkward questions about imperialism. President Wilson had given public support to democracy and self-determination. After the U.S. entry into the war, Wilson was dismayed to learn from the British government that secret agreements had been reached among the Allies about how best to divide the spoils. To be sure, President Wilson's support for national self-determination must be taken with a grain of salt. Wilson supported racial segregation at home, while he had also sanctioned U.S. intervention in Mexico. Yet his rhetoric inspired many people who lived under colonial domination. The Bolshevik revelations, combined with pressure at home from anti-imperialists, forced Wilson to clarify U.S. war aims. [8] The new war aims, stated in his "Fourteen Points" speech, sought a greater degree of idealism in international relations.

Chapter Fifteen

The War's End, 1918

By the start of 1918, the world was starting to look like a very different place. The old Austrian, Ottoman, and Russian empires were unraveling. Various peoples around the world were making claims to sovereign nationhood. Meanwhile, the British, French, Germans, and Japanese hoped to expand their empires. Europeans (in and out of uniform) grew weary of the war. The Bolsheviks awaited a worldwide communist revolution.

Germany began 1918 with several distinct advantages. Russia was knocked out of the war, while the French and British were showing signs of war-weariness. In the spring of 1918, a hard German push on the Western Front nearly knocked the Allies out of the war before American troops could arrive in significant numbers. The Germans failed—and the Allies succeeded—because American manpower, coupled with Allied productivity and innovation, outdid a Germany that had reached the limit of what its population and resources could sustain. Allied victory owed as much to German exhaustion as it did to any other factor.

PRESIDENT WILSON AND ALLIED WAR OBJECTIVES

In the midst of international turmoil, the U.S. president, Woodrow Wilson, made a further push to clarify Allied war aims. On January 8, 1918, he gave a speech in which he announced that the days of secret treaties, "aggrandizement," and "conquest" were finished. The world order would be based on Wilson's ideals, condensed into his famous Fourteen Points.

A careful reading of the Fourteen Points indicates that Wilson was balancing between idealism and the practical need to cooperate with his allies. The First Point denounced secret diplomacy, yet realistically it seems that it would be rather difficult for all diplomacy to be public. The Second Point supported freedom of navigation, a rhetorical blow struck against Germany's unrestricted submarine warfare, yet he supported "international action for the enforcement of international covenants," a way of allowing for the Allied blockade of Germany. By the time of the speech, the U.S. navy was cooperating fully with Allied convoy and blockade efforts in the Atlantic and the North Sea.

Some of the Fourteen Points have the veneer of idealism yet were written in such a way as to be comfortable for cautious Americans. The Third Point gave qualified support for free trade, by demanding "the removal, so far as possible, of all economic barriers" and the "equality of trade conditions." This, Wilson argued, would lend itself to peace among nations, but his language also allowed for continuing the high tariffs that the United States placed on many imports. The Fourth Point advocated arms reductions, but only "to the lowest point consistent with domestic safety."

Several more of the Fourteen Points advocated national self-determination, but only to a degree. The Fifth Point is worth quoting at length:

> A free, open-minded, and absolutely impartial adjustment of all colonial claims, based upon a strict observance of the principle that in determining all such questions of sovereignty the interests of the populations concerned must have equal weight with the equitable claims of the government whose title is to be determined.

In the past, Wilson had spoken in favor of national self-determination, but in the Fifth Point he merely asks that the interests of the subject peoples be considered equally with the interest of their government. This phrase was basically empty—the Americans, British, and French already claimed to rule for the benefit of their colonial subjects.

Wilson next moved on to a discussion of particular territories that were involved in Allied war aims. Invaded parts of Belgium, France, and Russia would be evacuated by the Germans, while the various nationalities of Eastern Europe and the Middle East should have self-determination. Yet there were limits. In the Twelfth Point, he supported the right of Turks to have their own nation-state in Anatolia but undermined Turkey by advocating the transformation of the Dardanelles into an international waterway, a disguised plea to persuade the Russians to rejoin the Allied war effort.

Wilson concluded his speech by returning to a point of abstract principle, the creation of a League of Nations, where disputes would be settled peaceably. This was Wilson's most cherished international idea: a League of Nations, which he had proposed for several years by the time he made his speech. The Allies were inclined to accept Wilson's proposal—the British and French parliaments voted their support for the idea in mid-1917.

Around Europe there was a mixed response to Wilson's Fourteen Points. While the Allies believed that the League of Nations was a tolerably good idea, the British and French governments were not inclined to accept many of Wilson's more specific points about territorial changes. Wilson's allies in London, Paris, and Rome did not institute major changes in policy on account of the Fourteen Points. Many of the points were already on the Allied agenda for discussion at the war's conclusion. Interestingly the governments of the Central Powers came to have a greater appreciation for the Fourteen Points. To them, the speech was significant for some of the things that Wilson did not say. Wilson did not advocate unconditional surrender and a division of the spoils, which would have entailed a fight to the finish. Instead, Wilson emphasized negotiation. This meant that the final months of the war, in the fall of 1918, would resemble maneuvering for position at the peace conference more than anything else. Before that happened, though, in the spring of 1918, the Germans made a final push on the Western Front, hoping to knock out the Allies in a massive blow before U.S. forces could arrive in significant numbers. The final battles on the Western Front determined who would win the First World War.

GERMANY'S SPRING OFFENSIVES OF 1918

At the start of 1918, the key issue facing strategists on both sides was manpower. The German victory over the Russians paved the way for massive transfers of troops from the east to the west. The Germans left forty divisions of reservists to police their newly conquered territories in Eastern Europe and transferred the rest of their soldiers to France and Belgium. This gave the Germans a total of 192 divisions to deploy on the Western Front, against 178 Allied divisions. For the first time since 1914, German forces on the Western Front outnumbered the Allies. Moving beyond arithmetic, it is important to note that the German units from the east had high morale. Most units had tasted victory in battle from Tannenberg in 1914 to Riga in 1917. Many were trained in the new storm-trooper tactics. Their arrival on the Western Front gave a significant boost to the German soldiers who were already there. With superiority in morale and numbers, it now seemed possible to Germany's lead general, Erich Ludendorff, for Germany to knock the Allies out of the war. Yet he had to do so with the forces at hand. The German population could not sustain much more military recruitment.

The Germans had numerical superiority on the Western Front, but the Allies were still formidable. The French army was recovering from the mutinies (or strikes) of 1917 thanks to the reforms of Philippe Pétain. The British and colonial troops who had fought at Passchendaele were weakened, but the rest of the British army had good morale and had done much to improve its tactics on the battlefield. Even the small Belgian army, positioned at the north end of the Western Front, remained cohesive after three years of combat. And the Allies were finally beginning to receive substantial reinforcements from the United States. The historian John Keegan points out that the 318,000 American soldiers who arrived by March 1918, supplemented by a million more over the course of the next five months, were perceived to be a "disequilibrating force," in other words, a force that could tip the balance. American troops arriving in France had plenty of spirit. They lacked experience, but in order to learn about the battlefield conditions on the Western Front they trained with French and British advisers.[1]

With the arrival of the Americans, the question of Allied command structure was raised again. The British and French pressed for American units to be absorbed into British and French units. The U.S. commander, General John Pershing, together with President Wilson, recognized that this would diminish American influence over the peace negotiations and so they fought to preserve an independent American army. The French army remained the largest of the Allied armies, so it seemed logical to place a French general, Ferdinand Foch, in the position of supreme commander of all Allied forces. The British government found continued French command to be convenient. The prime minister, Lloyd George, was appalled by the loss of life caused by Haig's determination to break through on the Western Front. Lloyd George would have fired Haig if Haig had not been so popular with generals, politicians, and the public. Lloyd George agreed to place his lead general under the command of Foch, ironically in order to have more influence over him.

Foch's German counterpart was Erich Ludendorff, who realized that if the Germans were going to win the war, they had to attack before the Americans arrived in force. Ludendorff planned a series of several major operations at different locations on the Western Front. The first assault, Operation Michael, occurred on March 21, when seventy-six top German divisions attacked twenty-eight British divisions along a hundred-kilometer front. The Germans unleashed a surprise bombardment with explosives and gas, and then attacked with storm troopers. The main brunt of the assault fell on the divisions of Britain's Fifth Army, commanded by Gough, who was disliked by many of his officers for his lack of attention to planning. His troops were still recovering from Passchendaele, too, while they occupied positions that were not yet fully constructed, thanks to the German pullback of 1917. For all these reasons, on the first day of Operation Michael, many British troops of the Fifth Army fled and twenty thousand prisoners were taken. Only a handful of small units, such as the South African Brigade, fought well enough to hold their ground.

Operation Michael was costing the Germans tens of thousands of casualties, but their troops appeared to be making a breakthrough. After two days of advances, German commanders imagined that they might be able to drive

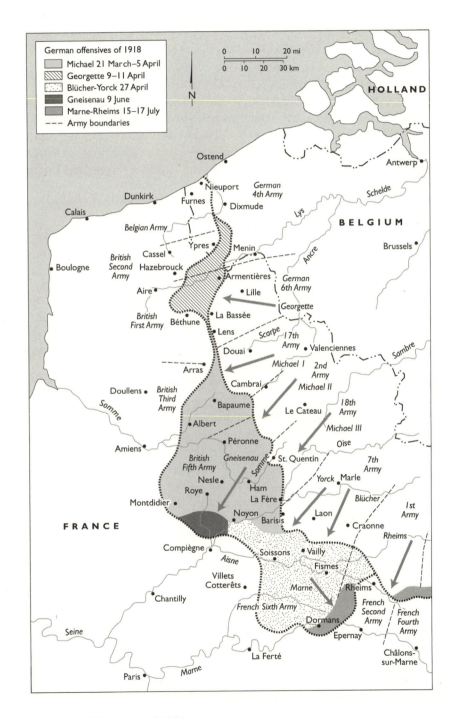

The German Offensives of 1918

a wedge between British forces in the northern sector of the Western Front and the French to the south. Ludendorff poured more men into the breach, but they were slowed down by the rough terrain of the old Somme battlefield. German soldiers were hungry, too, after years of blockade-induced privations. When German troops overran Allied supply bases, they stopped to plunder and gorge themselves. One German soldier, Paul Hub, wrote home to his fiancée, Maria Thumm, that "it's great to take part in this kind of war of movement. When we move on we always come across civilians. That's when we find booty. The English tins of meat are fantastic compared to ours. And English sugar tastes so good! Unfortunately, we've finished the English cigarettes and biscuits." The troops foraged for consumer goods, and they hunted, too. "The first few days we went pigeon-hunting. I shot some too. They taste delicious. There were many sheep here, but the Prussians ate them all. Some of our infantrymen said that dog tastes just as good and brought one in. Of course it's all a matter of taste." He even sent things back home, where he suspected that basic consumer goods were lacking. "One of my men found a pound of soap today. I have put three large pieces of soap and a bundle of string in a parcel for you. I don't know when I'll get to send it. But you do need this kind of thing, don't you?"[2]

As German units looted the countryside and otherwise recovered from their marching, Allied reserves were able to stop the Germans. Operation Michael ended in the first week of April. By that time, Ludendorff was ready with another stroke at the British, this time in Flanders, along a hundred-kilometer front between Ypres and Béthune. In Operation Georgette, as it was called, another huge shelling with gas and explosives was followed by a massed assault using storm troopers. Haig issued famous orders not to retreat: "With our backs to the wall . . . Every position must be held to the last man. There must be no retirement." The British commanders of the First and Second armies, Horne and Plumer, observed the spirit of Haig's command rather than the letter. They staged an orderly retreat, helped by the Belgian army under King Albert. Taking up positions to the rear, the Allied troops held back the Germans and prevented the capture of Ypres. After three weeks of fighting, Ludendorff broke off the action.

Ludendorff, Hindenburg, and the German government pondered the next move. Victory remained elusive, but the generals and the kaiser remained committed to war. The Allied forces were proving resilient in the north, for the most part, so Ludendorff decided to commit his remaining soldiers to Operation Blücher-Yorck, an attack on the Allied center that aimed directly at Paris. On May 27, after another massive bombardment along another hundred-kilometer front, forty German divisions advanced against eleven French, three British, and two American divisions. The Germans, using storm-trooper tactics again, pushed a large bulge in the French lines, forcing the French to withdraw forty kilometers.

When it began to seem that the Germans might be able to capture the roads to Paris, the Allied forces rallied. The American Second and Third divisions halted the German advance in the vicinity of Chateau-Thierry. A brigade of U.S. Marines held a key railway junction at Belleau Wood. One of their officers, Captain Lloyd Williams, was encouraged to retreat by a group of French soldiers. He replied, "Hell, we just got here!" The Americans, British, and French sensed that Paris was vulnerable and fought with spirit, once again demonstrating that the issue of manpower was closely related to the issue of morale. On June 9, the Germans launched a follow-up offensive, code-named "Gneisenau," near the Marne River. German forces were stopped by the French and Americans, who counterattacked and pushed the Germans back. Some German officers and politicians began to question Ludendorff's leadership and started to express interest in peace negotiations.

The tide had turned against the Germans. Ludendorff mounted one more offensive near the Marne, Operation Marne-Rheims, against the French and Americans. French intelligence learned of the offensive in advance, and the Allies planned not only a defense but also a counteroffensive. On July 15, fifty-two German divisions attacked, and by July 17 they had advanced into the Allied positions but were bogged down. The next day, the French and Americans counterattacked successfully in what was called the Second Battle of the Marne. By this point, Ludendorff's spring offensives had cost the German army hundreds of thousands of soldiers killed, wounded, or captured. Even more soldiers were weakened by malnutrition and disease. The Germans could no longer replace their casualties. Their manpower was spent. By contrast, the Americans were delivering between two and three hundred thousand soldiers to France every month. American manpower was an important element of Allied success in the summer of 1918. So was the contribution of colonial forces to the British and French armies. Manpower was the key factor in a war of attrition.

In the spring of 1918, manpower problems on both sides were made worse by an environmental disaster, an especially potent worldwide influenza epidemic. Typically, the "flu" causes aches, fevers, and respiratory symptoms that otherwise healthy people can overcome. Usually, the only people who die from influenza are young, sick, or old. But every influenza outbreak involves new mutations of the virus, and the virus of 1918 was the worst ever. In the spring of 1918, the flu struck especially heavily against adults between the ages of twenty and forty, precisely the age of most soldiers and sailors—as well as doctors and nurses. To make matters worse, influenza is spread by the blowing, coughing, and sneezing associated with respiratory symptoms, which are particularly easy to spread in the confines of ships, trenches, and barracks. During the spring of 1918, hundreds of thousands of soldiers and sailors on both sides came down with the flu and were temporarily incapacitated. Typically, severe symptoms lasted for three days, followed by one or two weeks of weakness. Ludendorff actually blamed the failure of his spring offensives on influenza, stating that "It was a grievous business having to listen every morning to the chiefs of staff's recital of the number of influenza cases, and their complaints about the weakness of their troops."[3]

ALLIED VICTORY

In August 1918, the Allies took to the offensive against the weakening German army. On August 8, the British Fourth Army and the French First Army attacked along the old Somme battlefields. During the assault, the British relied heavily on technologies that had improved considerably during the war. British artillery batteries used the preregistration techniques developed in 1917 to identify and immobilize almost every German battery. The Allies flew almost two thousand aircraft against the Germans, achieving complete superiority in the air. Allied aircraft attacked ground troops and also relayed information to the Allied artillery, which now dominated the battlefield. The noise of so many airplanes also had the effect of concealing the sound of five hundred British tanks launched against the Germans. The tanks worked in support of mainly Australian and Canadian infantrymen, now considered to be the best troops in the British Expeditionary Force. To the south, the French attacked simultaneously, using approximately seventy tanks and several hundred airplanes.

Airplanes and tanks demonstrated that not only were the Allies winning the war with American and colonial manpower, they were also winning with superior technologies. All along the front, the Germans withdrew. Approximately twenty thousand German troops surrendered, indicating that the German army was now demoralized from its failure to win during the spring. For this reason, Ludendorff called August 8 the "black day of the German army." Yet that day—and the following weeks—were not entirely black. Once again the initial Allied breakthrough staggered to a halt because of high casualties and also because commanders had difficulty communicating with and supplying advancing troops. To make matters more complicated, the British, Canadian, and Australian soldiers had to advance across the old Somme battlefield, which was nearly impassable from all the old trenches, barbed wire, shell holes, and debris of previous battles. As the advance slowed, the British launched attacks by their own First Army and Third Army on German positions in the north. Again, the Germans retreated, but the big breakthrough did not occur. By the end of August 1918, it appeared that the German army was in trouble, but it still had the ability to hold its ground and inflict terrible casualties on the Allies.

It was in August, September, and October that the manpower situation of both sides was made worse by another outbreak of influenza. In the spring, most soldiers recovered from influenza. In the fall, the disease was much more severe: it appears that over the summer the influenza virus mutated. It continued to affect a disproportionate number of people between the ages of twenty and forty. This time, respiratory symptoms were so severe that many died. Severe symptoms came on so quickly that soldiers were reported to fall off their horses dead. The disease spread rapidly, too, affecting people on every continent. People who lived in close proximity to other people were the most likely to contract and spread the disease. This included people who lived in cities, as well as sailors and soldiers. Around the world, it is estimated that thirty million people died. On the Western Front, the fall influenza killed tens of thousands of soldiers and incapacitated even more. The Allies suffered twenty thousand deaths, and possibly five times that many soldiers were incapacitated temporarily. German records are not complete, but it is known that German soldiers were dying from influenza, too. Veterans who had been exposed to the spring influenza appeared to suffer less. The troops who were the most severely affected included the new arrivals from the United States.[4]

Even with the influenza epidemic, the Americans, led by General John J. Pershing, still had a tremendous advantage in manpower. During the spring, American troops had fought as part of larger British and French operations defending against Ludendorff's offensives. Now the Americans had five hundred thousand troops in France, enough to constitute a separate army. From then on, every month the Americans expected 250,000 more troops to arrive in France. Pershing and Wilson persistently advocated a separate American force, in order to maximize American strength at the peace negotiations. The French and British granted their wish. On September 12, the First American Army, with heavy support from Allied aircraft and artillery, attacked German positions at St. Mihiel, a salient to the south of Verdun. By coincidence, the German forces were already in the process of making a strategic withdrawal when the massive attack began. Still, they were taken by surprise and beaten badly by the Americans. Pershing lost seven thousand casualties, but the Americans captured more than fifteen thousand Germans, once again demonstrating that the German army was suffering morale problems.

In late September, Pershing followed up his success at St. Mihiel by pushing north between the Aisne and Meuse rivers, in the vicinity of the Argonne Forest. The Americans now had nearly one million troops. They divided into the First and Second American armies and were supported on their eastern flank by the French Fourth Army, comprising French and colonial troops. The French and American armies advanced slowly in the Meuse-Argonne campaign, facing German resistance that was more determined. Casualties were heavy, with the Americans losing eighteen thousand killed and ninety thousand wounded, many from poison gas, while seventy thousand were sick with the flu. German casualties are not known.

Slowly, the Germans gave ground. It seemed not to matter that American logistics were often inefficient and American tactics often ineffective. American inexperience was compensated for by American manpower and resources. This situation was remarked upon by the German veteran Erich Maria Remarque in his novel *All Quiet on the Western Front*. At this point in the war, he wrote:

> There are so many airmen here, and they are so sure of themselves that they give chase to single individuals, just as though they were hares. For every one German plane there come at least five English and American. For one hungry, wretched German soldier come five of the enemy, fresh and fit. For one German army loaf there are fifty tins of canned beef over there. We are not beaten, for as soldiers we are better and more experienced; we are simply crushed and driven back by overwhelming superior forces. [5]

At the end of October, the French and American force recaptured the town of Sédan, on the Meuse River near the southern corner of Belgium. Meanwhile, in Belgium, the British and Belgian armies managed to advance steadily westward during October. The Allies were now in a good position to strike into Germany. German soldiers appear to have recognized this. The closer the Allies got to Germany, the better the German soldiers fought.

Despite the best efforts of German soldiers, the kaiser and his advisers began to recognize that their position was hopeless. Some generals disagreed: Ludendorff was demoralized by the defeats of August and September 1918, but in October, as the German army recovered, he expected to be able to continue the fight. Hindenburg sided with Ludendorff, but they were overruled by the kaiser, who attempted to open peace negotiations with the Americans. The kaiser and his principal advisers were concerned by the military situation, but they were also worried by domestic developments. The blockade was starving Germany, and significant numbers of sailors, soldiers, and workers were leaning toward communism, influenced by the revolution in Russia. On October 4, the kaiser announced that Germany accepted Wilson's Fourteen Points as the basis of a peace settlement. Germany asked for an armistice—a halt in the fighting.

Chapter Sixteen

The Peace Settlements

The German decision for peace was influenced not only by the situation in Germany and on the Western Front but also by events elsewhere. British forces—including many soldiers from India, Australia, and other colonies—had defeated the Ottomans in Palestine and Iraq. On October 30, the Ottoman government negotiated an armistice on a British battleship near the port of Mudros, off the island of Lemnos. The terms of the Mudros armistice were harsh, but the Ottoman government was in a relatively weak position. The Ottomans were required to disband their army and surrender all territories outside of Turkey. Inside Turkey, they were forced to allow the Allies access to all ports and railways. The Allies gained control of the Dardanelles, while the Allies reserved the right to control Armenia, too.

More bad news came for the Central Powers. In September, Serbian, British, and French armies based in Salonika pressed north into Bulgaria. Bulgaria—which had joined the Central Powers in 1915—surrendered to the Allies. An Allied advance to liberate Romania was now possible. This alarmed Ludendorff and the German leadership because Romania supplied most of Germany's petroleum products, including lubricating oils and aircraft fuel.

The Allies did not immediately invade Romania, but they did press a large attack on the Central Powers in Italy. More than fifty Italian divisions, supported by British and French divisions, attacked an equivalent number of Austrian divisions spread for fifty kilometers along the Piave River. The fighting was fierce, but in the final days of October 1918, the Allies broke through. The Austro-Hungarian emperor, Karl, asked the Allies for an armistice. Shortly thereafter, the Austrian army—and the Austrian Empire—began to collapse. In the first week of November, Allied soldiers pressed north and east, toward the Alps, while Allied ships took control of Trieste, the port that was one of Italy's main war objectives. By this point Emperor Karl, lacking an army and a navy and leaning toward acceptance of the Fourteen Points, did not take steps to suppress nationalist movements that were taking power in Croatia, Czechoslovakia, Hungary, Poland, and other parts of the old Austrian Empire. In Austria itself, Karl was overthrown during the last week of October, when a provisional republican government took power.

While the Central Powers were being divided by imperialists and nationalists, President Wilson made it clear that he would not negotiate with the German government as it was currently constituted. Under pressure, Kaiser Wilhelm renounced power and declared himself to be a constitutional monarch, along the lines of the British monarchy. He allowed a center-left coalition government to form in the Reichstag, or parliament, headed by Prince Max of Baden, who became Germany's new chancellor. During October, Prince Max exchanged messages with Wilson, with the result that the new German government accepted the Fourteen Points. The Fourteen Points were, however, open to interpretation, and the Germans tended to think that their own ideas about the points would prevail. Wilson angered the British and French by negotiating directly with the Germans, yet in October the two powers accepted the Fourteen Points as the basis of negotiations. They, too, had their own self-serving interpretations of the points, and these differed from the views of the Germans. Not everybody in Germany was ready for peace. Ludendorff believed that, if only the war could be continued, the fighting would die down during the winter, which would allow the German army to regroup. His belief in continuing the war was not shared by a majority of the generals or the members of the Reichstag. He was dismissed by the kaiser in late October.

It was becoming evident that, after years of hardship, most Germans were turning against the war. A few shared Ludendorff's views but were stifled. German sailors stationed in the port of Kiel received word that their officers were planning a suicidal mission against the British navy. On October 27, crew members of several battleships refused to obey orders. By November 4, an all-out mutiny was taking place, with sailors taking charge of ships and weapons and defying the German government. Revolutionary sailors took control of other ports, too, and even went inland to promote revolution. Meanwhile, leftist factory workers took to the streets throughout Germany and took control of most of Germany's provincial capitals. It was also becoming clear that the German government's peace overtures were persuading many German soldiers that it was pointless to continue fighting.

Prince Max's center-left coalition was not able to run the country for long. On November 9, he announced that he was handing over the chancellorship to a moderate socialist, Friedrich Ebert. Ebert sought to contain the revolution by supporting the authority of army officers and by concluding a cease-fire quickly with the Allies, so the German army could be maintained as a counterrevolutionary force. The kaiser abdicated and fled to Holland, opening the way for Ebert's socialist government to conclude the armistice negotiations with the Allies. At 11 o'clock on November 11—the eleventh hour of the eleventh day of the eleventh month—the guns fell silent.

THE IMPACT OF WAR

The First World War was special and the First World War was not special. It was not special in that it was a continuation of previous trends such as imperialism, industrialization, and nationalism. It was special in that it sped up and intensified all those historical processes. This ensured that the world of 1919 would be quite different from the world of 1914.

The most notable changes were geographical. Boundaries in Africa, Europe, and the Middle East changed drastically, as some empires were broken up into nation-states and other empires exchanged colonies. In many places, significant environmental damage had occurred. On the battlefields of Eastern and Southern Europe, as well as in Africa and the Middle East, large stretches of territory had been burned and pillaged. Surviving residents returned in many cases and within several years were typically able to rehabilitate the land. On the Western Front, a relatively small area had seen four years of intensive fighting. Near the battlefields of Ypres, the Somme, and Verdun, the landscape was completely devastated, to the point where it was unrecognizable.

The war had a significant impact on landscapes and boundaries around the world. It also had an impact on the way people imagined the land. The war was inspired, in part, by German officers like Schlieffen who imagined that they could move millions of soldiers against France and then turn them around and move them against Russia, in spite of the limitations of terrain and transport. After years of frustrated movements on the Western Front, generals on both sides drew on their experiences to envision ways of combining manpower and technologies in order to achieve movement again. Meanwhile, this heavily industrial war accelerated skepticism about industrialization among ordinary soldiers who experienced combat firsthand. They revealed their views of technology, environment, and war in the art, fiction, and memoirs that came out during and after the war. They provided soldiers and readers with a way of processing new ideas about the environment and technology as well as a way of coping with the enormous scale of the war's losses.

The war took a terrible toll in human lives. The precise figure cannot be known because many deaths went unrecorded and also because many wartime records were destroyed. Yet there is some consensus among historians that between eight and nine million soldiers died during the war. The estimates in table 16.1 by the historian Niall Ferguson are consistent with the estimates of most other scholars.

Ferguson notes that, even though the Allies won, in doing so they lost more soldiers than the Central Powers. He makes the further suggestion that the Central Powers were more efficient at killing. In order to make this macabre calculation, Ferguson draws on the war expenditures calculated by another historian, Gerd Hardach, who has shown that the Allies spent $57,000,000,000 on their war effort (measured in 1913 dollars), while the Central Powers spent $24,700,000,000. In other words, the Allies spent twice as much money to achieve almost one million fewer deaths. [1]

The war did not just cost the lives of soldiers. The historian David Stevenson estimates that, between 1914 and 1921, the total population loss in Europe alone due to the war included fifty million more. These losses are attributable to war-related causes, such as bombing, famine, and invasion. They also include European deaths from the influenza epidemic, which was hastened by wartime conditions, as well as children who would have been conceived had their fathers not been absent, wounded, or killed. [2]

The growth and decline of populations, as well as the allocation of manpower and other resources by states, are among the central concerns of an environmental history, and therefore have been a central focus of this book. It is also important to pay some attention to the application of medicine to diseases and injuries. In addition to these population losses, many came home from the war disabled. Advances in wartime medical treatments made it more likely that wounded soldiers would survive than, say, the soldiers wounded in midcentury wars such as the American Civil War and the Wars of German and Italian Unification. Hospitals near the front lines implemented the new system of triage, in which patients were sorted and then treated

Table 16.1.

Country	Soldiers' Deaths
Germany	2,037,000
Austria-Hungary	1,100,000
Bulgaria and Ottoman Empire	892,000
Total Central Powers	*4,029,000*
Russia	1,811,000
France	1,398,000
Britain	723,000
British Empire	198,000
United States	114,000
Other Allied countries	599,000
Total Allied	*4,843,000*
TOTAL SOLDIERS' DEATHS	**8,872,000**

according to the severity of their wounds. Doctors and nurses were now aware of the germ theory of disease, developed by Louis Pasteur, Robert Koch, and Joseph Lister during the late nineteenth century. They were careful to wash hands and equipment while treating patients, thereby limiting the spread of infections. Blood transfusions began during the First World War, too, as doctors began to understand the role of blood typing. Blood losses from wounds and from surgery could now be made up, to an extent, by transferring blood to patients from unwounded soldiers. Surgeons also experimented with plastic and reconstructive surgery, to help soldiers who had lost limbs or who had been disfigured. Early psychology began to offer insights about mental illnesses developed by soldiers. In one noteworthy breakthrough, the English psychiatrist W. H. Rivers demonstrated that traumatized soldiers displayed symptoms of mental illness because they repressed their bad experiences. Uncovering and discussing these experiences could often help them to recover. Still, many remained traumatized by the war, not only by direct experiences of fighting, but also by losses of family and friends. In understanding the impact of the war from a material perspective, it is important to note that wartime trauma pushed the human mind to its natural limits. Some minds survived intact; others did not.

Soldiers and civilians suffered trauma in all participating countries. Soldiers had traumatic experiences while civilians in occupied areas experienced trauma, too. The German occupation of Belgium and northwestern France was noted for its harshness. Food remained scarce, while men were often used as forced labor. In Eastern Europe, where the fighting shifted back and forth over vast expanses of territory, overrun civilian areas were subject to murder, rape, and theft. Both sides persecuted Jews. In the Middle East, the Ottoman army persecuted the Armenians, while in Africa, the British, French, and Germans all forced men to work as porters, which resulted in the deaths of thousands. Civilians and soldiers experienced trauma in many different ways. Unfortunately, all this trauma did not persuade most people to abandon violence. On the contrary, the historians Stéphane Audoin-Rouzeau and Annette Becker argue in their book, *14–18: Understanding the Great War*, that before and during the war many civilians and soldiers embraced a culture of violence; that during the war, brutal behavior became normal; and that after the war, violence remained routine and accepted. Another historian, Joanna Bourke, explains the normalization of violence in wartime in her book *An Intimate History of Killing* by showing that soldiers found it thrilling to kill their enemies. The normalization of trauma and violence helps explain the rise of totalitarian regimes in the 1920s and 1930s.

As violence became normal, mourning became widespread. Nearly every community in the combatant countries lost members in the war. With the news of each death, friends and relatives processed the absence of loved ones, typically without the bodies of the dead, which were either lost or interred near the battlefield. Mourners turned to religion and even to séances and spiritualism to mitigate their grief.

Wartime losses were often described as senseless by the historians, novelists, and poets who wrote about the war in the following decades. The war's senselessness was thought to find its typical expression in modern art and literature, in which traditional forms were rejected in favor of the experimental. But as Jay Winter points out in *Sites of Memory, Sites of Mourning*, modernism preceded the war as an alternative art form, while most people processed the grief of the war in architecture, art, and literature that looked to the traditional forms of the eighteenth and nineteenth centuries for solace. Much of the war's art and literature employs traditional methods in order to communicate wartime suffering clearly to the audience, while the tens of thousands of war memorials built in the 1920s and 1930s tended to have features that were classic and easily understood. In particular, the buildings and landscapes that commemorate the war in national cemeteries are very traditional, with neoclassical forms and lists of dead soldiers' names. The inscriptions on the monuments often took on a tone that was not nationalistic but that was still righteous, claiming that the soldiers made noble sacrifices for just causes. The memorialization of dead soldiers in this way, and the extensive efforts made to identify and bury their remains, stands in marked contrast to earlier practices that were less mindful. Only a century earlier, the dead soldiers of the Napoleonic Wars were heaved into mass graves.

THE PEACE SETTLEMENTS

The pervasiveness of mourning and the acceptance of violence help to explain the harsh terms of the peace settlement that the Allies imposed on the Central Powers. The Central Powers ought to have been pitied, but the war had been so bad that in Britain and France most soldiers and civilians sought revenge. At the end of the war, elections confirmed that British and French voters wanted a harsh settlement. The Germans had signed the armistice thinking that a better settlement might be available, along the lines of Wilson's Fourteen Points, but this was not to happen. Wilson's idealism was moderated by Lloyd George's and Clemenceau's vengefulness, and also by a lack of support in the United States itself. In the congressional elections of November 1918, Wilson's Democrats lost heavily to the Republicans, who now controlled Congress.

Making peace became an exercise in historical interpretation. Historical questions underlay the peace negotiations: How bad was the damage? How much did the war cost? Whose fault was it? Interpretations of the war varied. The British and French had a realistic view of the war. It was a continuation of past policies in which these states maximized their own interests. To the

British and French, victory provided several opportunities: to seize territory, to neutralize Germany, and to repay debts. Many Americans held a realistic view of the war, too: now that the threat from Germany was eliminated, it was time to withdraw again across the Atlantic and to embrace isolation. Yet to Wilson the victory presented opportunities that were more idealistic: to put international relations on a more peaceful footing. This did not happen.

The central question faced by the peacemakers was: what was to be done about Germany? The German government had sacrificed two million men in a failed cause. The human cost of the war had been high for Germany, and so had the economic cost. The German homeland was undamaged—in sharp contrast to France and Belgium—but the German economy was still subject to the British blockade and the German people had suffered great deprivations. (Technically, the war had not ended. An armistice was a mere pause in the war. The Allies continued the blockade in order to pressure the Germans into signing a peace treaty.) Inflation continued to spiral, and socialists threatened to stage a revolution like the one that was occurring in Russia. In the spring of 1919, the Allies began to allow shipments of food to Germany, but only after the Germans surrendered their merchant fleet and paid for the food in gold. All throughout Germany, veterans—including thousands who had been wounded—were returning to civilian life. Many were traumatized by combat, and quite a few had grown accustomed to using violence as a means to resolve conflicts.

The peace treaty was negotiated at the Palace of Versailles on the outskirts of Paris. All nations that had participated in the war were represented, although the most influential were the principal Allies: Britain, France, Italy, Japan, and the United States. All were motivated by greed. The Americans wanted their loans to be repaid. The British and French sought reparations from Germany (in part to pay off loans from the United States) and also hoped to expand their colonial empires in Africa at the expense of Germany. The Japanese hoped to secure German ports in China. The Italians hoped to gain territory from Austria. In the end, the Italians got less than they wanted, and their delegation left the peace talks early. The Japanese were content with their gains in China yet were disappointed by the Allies' unwillingness to include a statement opposing racial discrimination in the League of Nations' covenant. All the Allies treated the German delegation with contempt. The Germans were not included in the negotiations—the Allies negotiated the terms among themselves and then on May 7, 1919, presented them to the German diplomats, who were housed behind barbed wire.

The treaty blamed the Germans for the outbreak of the war. As a consequence, the terms of the treaty were quite harsh:

• Germany had to return Alsace and Lorraine to France.

- Germany lost all its colonial possessions, which were given to the League of Nations and then administered by the Allies.
- Germany had to give up numerous eastern territories so that a new Polish nation could be created. This included a strip of territory near the Baltic port of Gdansk that gave Poland access to the sea but that severed the German territory of East Prussia from the rest of the country.
- Germany had to allow the French to occupy several of its western territories, including the Saar industrial region, for fifteen years. The Allies were permitted to remove iron and coal from the region.
- The German army could no longer have more than one hundred thousand soldiers.
- The German navy was limited to twelve ships. None of these could be bigger than a light cruiser (ten thousand tons).
- Germany had to give up all submarines, tanks, and military aircraft.
- Germany had to surrender most of its merchant ships and one-fourth of its fishing ships.
- Germany had to pay war reparations to the Allies. The armistice agreement said that Germany had to pay for damage to occupied territory, but now the treaty said that Germany had to repay the Allies for the full cost of the war, which would be determined by a postwar commission.

Germany's representatives at Versailles found the terms of the treaty humiliating. The German delegation rejected the notion that Germany was responsible for the war. They recognized that Germany had lost the war and would have to surrender some territory, but they found the notion of paying the entire cost of the war to be preposterous. In Germany, government officials and the general public debated for several weeks whether they should sign the treaty. In mid-June, the Allies became impatient and threatened to resume the war. Under pressure, Germany signed the treaty, with the majority of German leaders agreeing that an Allied invasion and occupation might lead to a treaty that was even worse. In 1921, the reparations commission determined that Germany had to pay 132,000,000,000 gold marks, equivalent to $33,000,000. This sum is equivalent to about $400,000,000,000 in today's money. It was impossible for the German government to raise this kind of money through taxes. Instead, the government resorted to inflation, which hurt the economy even more. During the 1920s, the reparations were renegotiated. First, they were reduced and American loans were provided to support the payments. They were reduced further in the late 1920s and then cancelled in 1931 when the Great Depression was in full swing. That still left many terms of the treaty that were resented in Germany. Hitler's rise to power in 1933 was based in part on the popularity of his appeals to the German people to reject the Versailles Treaty. Under Hitler's leadership, Germany scrapped all of the treaty's terms.

Germany was treated harshly at Versailles. The other treaties signed between the Allies and the Central Powers recognized the dissolution of empires and redrew the maps of Eastern Europe and the Middle East. The Ottoman Empire's territories were divided between France, Britain, and Greece by the 1920 Treaty of Sèvres. The Ottoman Empire's Arab territories were placed under the supervision of the League of Nations, to be governed temporarily, as "mandates," by France and Britain. Britain received what are today the countries of Iraq, Jordan, and Palestine, while France received Syria and Lebanon. The division of the Middle East came as no surprise to the Turks, the dominant ethnic group in the empire.

Wilson's statements about self-determination implied that Turks would no longer rule Arabs. The same logic led most Turks to believe that they would govern themselves on the Anatolian peninsula, a Turkish-speaking homeland with a significant Greek-speaking minority. Yet the peninsula was divided by the Allies. Istanbul remained Ottoman but was occupied indefinitely by the Allies, who limited the Ottoman army to fifty thousand men. The Ottomans also retained the central, northern part of Anatolia, but the Greeks were awarded western Anatolia. And the French and Italians awarded themselves southern Anatolia, while eastern Anatolia was likely to become part of the new nation of Armenia. The treaty offended most Turks' sense of nationhood. The Ottoman government signed the treaty, but nationalist resistance broke out almost immediately, coalescing around the war's most suc-

Postwar Europe

cessful Ottoman general, Mustafa Kemal. Kemal took control of the government from the sultan and his ministers while leading armed resistance against
the Allies. The French and Italians decided that it was not worth fighting to
keep their Turkish colonies, but the Greeks fought a bitter two-year war
against Kemal's nationalist forces. Kemal's Turks defeated the Greeks, and
the final peace settlement of 1923 stipulated that all one million Greeks
living in western Anatolia would be removed to Greece. Meanwhile, several
hundred thousand Turks were sent from Greece to the new nation of Turkey.

Turkey became one of many new nations that grew out of the aftermath of
the First World War. The 1919 Treaty of Neuilly awarded parts of Bulgaria
to Greece and the new Yugoslavia. That country was one of many to be
recognized by the 1919 Treaty of Saint Germain-en-Laye and by the 1920
Treaty of Trianon, which together divided the Austro-Hungarian Empire into
many of its ethnic components: Austria, Czechoslovakia, Hungary, Poland,
and Yugoslavia. Italy and Romania received parts of the old empire, and
Austria was treated like Germany. Along with Germany, Austria and Hungary were forced to admit that they were guilty of starting the war, and, like
Germany, Austrian and Hungarian rearmament was prohibited. Both countries were limited to small armies of thirty thousand and thirty-five thousand
men, respectively. Austria became the only German-speaking remnant of the
old empire, yet it was prohibited from joining Germany. German-speaking
minorities lived in nearly every new Eastern European country, where their
discontent simmered throughout the 1920s and 1930s. During that time, nearly every Eastern European country slid from democracy to dictatorship.

Wilson's vision of postwar Europe had been one of democratic nation-
states successfully resisting communism. Communist parties played a role in
all European countries, yet nowhere did they establish a long-term influence.
It even might be said that, in the years 1919 to 1921, communist control of
Russia appeared to be fragile. Along Russia's borders, national groups
started to break away. Finland became independent, and for a time so did the
republics in the Caucasus and Caspian region. The Bolsheviks retained control of Russian Central Asia, despite the intervention of forces from Turkey
and British India. The Allies intervened in Russia's civil war, too, with
American, British, French, and Japanese forces taking temporary control of
port cities. Even so, the Russian Civil War was fought mainly between the
Bolsheviks, or Reds, and all other political parties, under the name of the
"Whites." These included parties ranging from monarchists to moderate
communists. The Bolsheviks were more homogeneous, and they had the
further advantage of controlling Petrograd, Moscow, and the central part of
Russia, including Russia's main rail and telegraph networks. After several
years of fighting, the Red Army, led by Leon Trotsky, defeated the White
forces.

The economic policies of the Bolsheviks, called "war communism," were disastrous. The Bolsheviks moved to abolish private property and to control markets, true to communist thinking. Industrial and agricultural production for the market ground to a halt, and millions of people starved to death. Lenin reversed this policy in 1921, at which point, under a ruthless communist dictatorship, Russia—now called the Soviet Union—began to take steps toward economic recovery.

The building of communism in Russia further undermined Wilson's vision of a peaceful world in which democratic and capitalist nation-states participated in a League of Nations. Yet it was on the home front that Wilson suffered his most difficult loss. In a cruel irony, the Republican majority in the U.S. Senate blocked ratification of the Versailles Treaty, on the grounds that participation in a League of Nations would require the United States to intervene in overseas conflicts, when it was the constitutional prerogative of the Congress to declare war. Wilson campaigned hard for ratification. Stress and exhaustion probably helped to cause Wilson to suffer a stroke, from which he never fully recovered. Meanwhile, the United States slid toward isolation from world events. The next president, the Republican Warren Harding, concluded separate peace treaties with the Central Powers. American isolationism, combined with Russian Bolshevism, French and British mean-spiritedness, and resentful nationalism in Germany, Italy, and Japan, all contributed to the advent of totalitarianism and war in the 1930s. Resentment spread to Europe's colonies, too, when loyalty was not repaid with liberty. For all these reasons, it is not surprising that some historians argue that the First World War, the Second World War, the Cold War—and the wars associated with decolonization—were one continuous conflict.

Chapter Seventeen

Understanding and Remembering the War

This book has narrated the history of the First World War while highlighting elements that pertain to technology and the environment. Geographical visions of conquest, together with technological capabilities for war, inspired plans to attack and divide other countries. Technologies such as aircraft, artillery observation, poison gas, and submarines all predated the war, while during the war designers and manufacturers improved them significantly. Even so, these improving technologies did not do as much as classic environmental factors, such as the supply of food and manpower, to change the course of the war. During the war, these environmental factors were closely bound up with victory and defeat. Meanwhile, we have considered evidence to suggest that people's views of the environment and technology changed. Modern technologies were now more likely to be treated with a mixture of appreciation and horror, while the participants in the war began to see the landscape as foreboding.

ENVIRONMENT, TECHNOLOGY, AND CHANGE

The experiences of the First World War changed many lives, but in some ways the war had a limited impact on the global environment, insofar as it can be measured. Around the world, crop production and industrial production rose, but increases can be seen in light of broader trends. In the decades before the war, industrialization and population growth were already having an impact on the environment, while production tended to decline during the disruptions of the 1920s and the Great Depression. For example, the historian Richard Tucker examined worldwide timber production during the world wars. He found that, during the First World War, there was increased production of forest products in Europe, North America, and the tropical colonies. Some areas were subject to ruinous overlogging, but generally speaking forests recovered during the 1920s. [1]

There were a number of regions where battles were fought, ranging from Eastern Europe to the Atlantic Ocean, which saw temporary but not lasting damage. The main area of environmental devastation—the main environmental sacrifice zone of the war—was concentrated in eastern France and Belgium, an area roughly the size of the U.S. state of Massachusetts. In this zone, the landscape was completely ruined. Trenches and craters scarred the land. Woodlands were destroyed, drainage systems were damaged, and unexploded shells and decomposed corpses lay under the ground. Even so, heavy postwar investment by the French government in restoration efforts resulted in substantial progress by the outbreak of the Second World War, during which much of the same land was damaged again. It is correct that the Second World War set back the recovery. It is also true that farmers are still occasionally plowing up soldiers' skeletons and unexploded shells, but on the whole the Western Front has recovered.

During the war, there were not revolutionary changes to the environment. The same might be said about technology. Most of the important weapons of the war, such as small arms and artillery, had been developed before the war and were only modified during the war. The same could be said about the main technologies of transportation and communication, such as the automobile, the steamship, and the telephone. In fact, the armies of the First World War relied most heavily on horses. For example, in mid-1917 the British army owned 591,000 horses; 213,000 mules; 47,000 camels; and 11,000 oxen. Many of the horses and mules had been bought in the United States and shipped to the Western Front, where they were used mainly for transporting supplies. New technologies did appear, such as the tank, but these were in such a rudimentary stage of development that they had only a limited usefulness. The airplane developed very rapidly during the war, and so did a few other weapons, such as poison gas. Still, we must remember that most casualties during the war may be attributed to artillery, machine guns, and rifles, as well as illness from influenza and other infectious diseases.

Old technologies remained important during the war, while people made few changes to the environment that were irrevocable, even with increasingly destructive military technologies. The greatest changes associated with the environment and technology concerned people's experiences and memories. The experience of trench warfare and massive bombardments changed the way people saw technologies and the landscape.

HUMANISTIC REPRESENTATIONS OF THE WAR

Before the war, there were certainly intellectuals like Leo Tolstoy, John Ruskin, and Mahatma Gandhi who denounced modern technology, but for the most part people associated new technologies with progress. The human experience of industrialized war from 1914 to 1918 changed that view. The leading French cubist painter of the war, Fernand Léger, famously painted abstract representations of wrecked airplanes, prewar symbols of technological progress brought low and destroyed in war. He had served as a stretcher-bearer, so he was particularly sensitive to destruction and dismemberment. His most famous painting of the war, "The Card Party," shows abstract, shining, metallic French soldiers playing cards with their dismembered limbs. The Russian artist Marc Chagall also experimented with cubism during the war. His sketch "The Wounded Soldier" portrays a Russian soldier, his head bandaged and cockeyed, glaring maniacally at the viewer.

Cubism's antirealism seems appropriate for a war that shattered the lives of many soldiers and civilians. In the disillusioned years after the war, cubism remained a key form of representation. Another artistic movement from the prewar years that was quite similar to cubism—futurism—became discredited. The founders of futurism, the poet Filippo Marinetti and the artist Umberto Boccioni, worshipped the new technologies of transportation and communication that figured so prominently in the first two decades of the twentieth century. They preached that technology, coupled with violence, could transcend the human condition. The artists who followed them resembled the cubists, in that they painted abstract, two-dimensional, and seemingly disjointed images. The futurists differed from the cubists in their choice of subject: the cubists tended to prefer portraits and still lifes, while the futurists attempted to capture motion.

One young prewar futurist, the British artist C. R. W. Nevinson, became one of the most interesting painters of the war. While serving as an ambulance driver in 1915, Nevinson painted futuristic scenes of war. In one painting, "The Machine-Gun," Nevinson shows a French machine-gun crew firing from a trench. An angular, two-dimensional soldier pulls the trigger, seemingly at one with the technology, while another shouts down the trench. In another famous painting, "A Bursting Shell," Nevinson abandons the human subject altogether and shows the rays of light and darkness thrown off by a shell as it explodes in the sky. The technology of war is certainly not elevated in Nevinson's works of 1914 to 1916, but neither is it criticized.

Nevinson's wartime experiences changed the nature of his painting. He began the war with a futuristic appreciation of technology, but he ended the war by shifting to more realistic portraits of human suffering, abandoning futurism's abstraction and its worship of technology. By the end of the war, he was working as an official government war artist. His most famous paintings are realistic portraits of dead soldiers on a devastated landscape. In "Paths of Glory," painted in 1917, the bodies of dead British soldiers lie in the mud near barbed wire, seemingly being sucked into the ground. Nevinson's "Harvest of Battle," painted just after the war ended in 1919, shows realistic British and German soldiers rising from the dead on a scarred battlefield and walking off together. In both paintings, the dead (and resurrecting) soldiers are part of the landscape, which is shown to be completely devastated.

This bizarre realism was also the preferred form of the German soldier-artist Otto Dix, although Dix's paintings, such as "The Flare" of 1917, convey raw and powerful emotions, whereas Nevinson's approach was more distant and ironic. Dix's wartime paintings, and postwar representations, are very much in the style of the expressionists, a form of art that is particularly associated with Germany and Scandinavia. The expressionists typically used bizarre realism in the depiction of subjective feelings, often feelings of dread and loneliness. Dix's approach is shared partly with Max Beckmann, another German soldier who painted and made engravings in the expressionist style. In the early years of the war he created a realistic yet tortured self-portrait while also depicting the dead and wounded bodies that he observed while working as a nurse. Many of his paintings use religious themes to highlight war's cruelty. One of his most famous paintings, "Resurrection" of 1918, shows realistic, ordinary people in the foreground of an imaginary, devastated landscape while, in the background, an apocalypse is lifting tortured bodies to the sky. The expressionists captured the war's cruelty and the defiled landscape with their bizarre realism.[2]

Many of the artistic and literary representations of the war that are already cited in this book reflect that view, but probably the most important work in shaping the memory of the war has been *All Quiet on the Western Front*, a novel based on the personal experiences of the author, Erich Maria Remarque, as a German soldier in France. In the novel, a group of German soldiers endures the terrors of industrialized warfare on the front, hiding in a dugout during a bombardment. The shelling presses them to the limits of psychological endurance:

> We sit as if in our graves waiting only to be closed in. Suddenly it howls and flashes terrifically, the dug-out cracks in all its joints under a direct hit, fortunately only a light one that the concrete blocks are able to withstand. It rings metallically, the walls reel, rifles, helmets, earth, mud, and dust fly everywhere. Sulphur flames pour in. If we were in one of those light dug-outs they have been building lately instead of this deeper one, none of us would be alive. But the effect is bad enough even so. The recruit starts to rave again and two others follow suit. One jumps up and rushes out, we have trouble with the other two. I start after one who escapes and wonder whether to shoot him in the leg— then it shrieks again, I fling myself down and when I stand up the

wall of the trench is plastered with smoking splinters, lumps of flesh, and bits of uniform. I scramble back.[3]

On the battlefield, going under the ground provides shelter, even though that leads to some soldiers coming down with claustrophobia. The landscape above, in the trenches and in no-man's-land, is filled with danger, and is described as such throughout the novel. Only the earth can save them, an earth that is described in mystical terms.

> From the earth, from the air, sustaining forces pour into us—mostly from the earth. To no man does the earth mean so much as to the soldier. When he presses himself down upon her long and powerfully, when he buries his face and his limbs deep in her from the fear of death by shell-fire, then she is his only friend, his brother, his mother; he stifles his terror and his cries in her silence and her security; she shelters him and releases him for ten seconds to live, to run, ten seconds of life; receives him again and often for ever. Earth!—Earth!—Earth! Earth with thy folds, and hollows, and holes, into which a man may fling himself and crouch down. In the spasm of terror, under the hailing of annihilation, in the bellowing death of the explosions, O Earth, thou grantest us the great resisting surge of new-won life. Our being, almost utterly carried away by the fury of the storm, streams back through our hands from thee, and we, thy redeemed ones, bury ourselves in thee, and through the long minutes in a mute agony of hope bite into thee with our lips![4]

In *All Quiet on the Western Front*, the natural world is seen as sustaining, even in combat, while industrialized warfare is terrifying. The novel is remembered mainly for its critique of nationalism and for showing that the war was senseless. In that critique, Remarque deploys natural metaphors. In one scene, the soldiers are discussing the war's origins. One soldier wonders how the war got started:

> "Mostly by one country badly offending another," answers Albert with a slight air of superiority.
> Then Tjaden pretends to be obtuse. "A country? I don't follow. A mountain in Germany cannot offend a mountain in France. Or a river, or a wood, or a field of wheat."[5]

But in many ways the war transformed the participants' views of nature. As the literary critic Paul Fussell points out, poet-soldiers later in the war had even come to view the sunrise itself as hostile, an inversion of the traditionally welcome view of the sunrise that derived, in the First World War, from the anticipation of attacks at dawn, when soldiers waited, ready, in the posture of "stand-to." One famous example of an ominous sunrise comes from Wilfred Owen's poem "Exposure":

> The poignant misery of dawn begins to grow . . .

> We only know war lasts, rain soaks, and clouds sag stormy.
> Dawn massing in the east her melancholy army
> Attacks once more in ranks on shivering ranks of gray,
>   But nothing happens.[6]

Owen's and Remarque's works were strongly critical of war, but others reached different conclusions. The English composer Edward Elgar's best wartime work, a song cycle for choir and soloists entitled *The Spirit of England*, is set to poems by Laurence Binyon. One of the stanzas became quite famous and is linked in the minds of many people with Elgar's musical setting:

> They shall not grow old as we that are left grow old.
> Age shall not weary them, nor the years condemn.
> At the going down of the sun and in the morning,
> We shall remember them.

Here Elgar and Binyon make a clear association between the soldiers and the natural spectacle of the rising and setting of the sun. These were particularly poignant for the British soldiers who associated dawn with attacks and who, stuck in trenches for weeks and deprived of natural scenery, became keen observers of the sky. As successful as this piece became, even Elgar had regrets about it. Before the war, his music had been appreciated by many people in Germany. He hesitated about aspects of the poetry that were propagandistic, while soldiers who listened to it believed that the piece was too sentimental.[7]

Oversentimentality affected the works of numerous wartime composers. It is possible that the process of musical composition was hindered by ambivalence about nationalism. Classically trained musicians typically traveled and studied internationally. The violinist and composer Fritz Kreisler fought in the Austrian army. In 1915, he wrote in a letter that "my devotion to my own land is well known. I have many friends in France, Belgium, England, and Russia. How could I change my feeling towards them? How could any personal enmity enter in? To bridge over the abysses of hatred that this war will leave behind it—that must be the mission of the artist."[8] One of the only composers to respond to the war successfully, Maurice Ravel, was one of the few to embrace patriotism—at the start of the war he enlisted in the French army at the age of thirty-nine. One of his best choral compositions, "Three Birds of Paradise," is a tasteful and plaintive song in which three different birds, colored in the red, white, and blue of France, fly over people at home who are missing their loved ones because they have gone to war. The birds traditionally represent hope. The song's focus is on the natural world of sky and birds, while the people on the ground struggle to interpret the absence of their loved ones, all without sentimentality or bellicosity. Ravel was fascinated by the natural world and also by modern technology, particularly airplanes. The concluding sixth section of his work for piano, *The Tomb of Couperin*, is not only dedicated to a heroic French officer, but it is a thumping, rhythmic depiction of an aircraft engine. Ravel describes an important technology in one of his most famous virtuoso pieces, while refraining from any sentimentality that could be associated with the war.[9]

The war's impact inspired many works of music, art, and fiction. There are also powerful depictions in personal memoirs. In one of the most martial memoirs to come out of the war, *Storm of Steel*, the German veteran Ernst Junger described how soldiers survived a shelling.

> You cower in a heap alone in a hole and feel yourself the victim of a pitiless thirst for destruction. With horror you feel that all your intelligence, your capacities, your bodily and spiritual characteristics, have become meaningless and absurd. While you think of it, the lump of metal that will crush you to a shapeless nothing may have started on its course. . . . You know that not even a cock will crow when you are hit. Well, why don't you jump up and rush into the night till you collapse in safety behind a bush like an exhausted animal? Why do you hang on there all the time, you and your braves? There are no superior officers to see you. Yet some one watches you. Unknown perhaps to yourself, there is some one within you who keeps you to your post by the power of two mighty spells: Duty and Honour. . . . You clench your teeth and stay.[10]

For Junger, the war tested human nature and confirmed its strength. After describing the shelling for several paragraphs, he concludes that "human nature is indeed indestructible." This may be true, but the First World War helped to change humanity's view of nature and the material world. Veterans remembered a landscape that had become ominous, even surreal, while pre-war visions of technological progress were complicated by the experience of mass, industrialized killing.

Notes

2. EMPIRES, TECHNOLOGIES, AND THE ORIGINS OF WAR

1. Michael Adas, *Machines as the Measure of Man: Science, Technology, and Ideologies of Western Dominance* (Ithaca: Cornell University Press, 1989).

2. Many studies examine the connections between liberalism and imperialism. Two of the best-known works are Thomas Holt, *The Problem of Freedom: Race, Labor, and Politics in Jamaica and Britain, 1832–1938* (Baltimore: Johns Hopkins University Press, 1992), and Ronald Robinson and John Gallagher, *Africa and the Victorians: The Official Mind of Imperialism*, 2nd ed. (London: Macmillan, 1981).

3. For an excellent survey, see Frederick Cooper and Jane Burbank, *Empires in World History: Power and the Politics of Difference* (Princeton: Princeton University Press, 2009).

4. Winston Churchill, *The River War: An Account of the Reconquest of the Soudan* (New York: Scribner's, 1933), 273–74.

3. EUROPEAN RIVALRIES

1. Max Arthur, *Forgotten Voices of the Great War: A History of World War I in the Words of the Men and Women Who Were There* (Guilford, CT: Lyons Press, 2002), 11.

2. Gordon Martel, *The Origins of the First World War*, 3rd ed. (London: Pearson Longman, 2003), 18–21.

3. Frank B. Tipton, *A History of Modern Germany since 1815* (Berkeley and Los Angeles: University of California Press, 2003), 175–77, 249–51.

4. Martel, *Origins of the First World War*, 19–20.

5. Samuel R. Williamson and Russel Van Wyk, *July 1914: Soldiers, Statesmen, and the Coming of the Great War: A Brief Documentary History* (Boston: Bedford St. Martin's, 2003), 80–81.

6. Niall Ferguson, *The Pity of War: Explaining World War I* (London: Allen Lane, 1998), 8–10.

7. John Keegan, *The First World War* (New York: Knopf, 1999), 30–36.

8. Keegan, *First World War*, 36–40.

9. Robert K. Massie, *Dreadnought: Britain, Germany, and the Coming of the Great War* (New York: Random House, 1991), 151.

4. THE CRISIS OF 1914

1. Samuel R. Williamson and Russel Van Wyk, *July 1914: Soldiers, Statesmen, and the Coming of the Great War: A Brief Documentary History* (Boston: Bedford St. Martin's, 2003), 37–38.
2. Fritz Fischer, *Germany's Aims in the First World War* (New York: W.W. Norton, 1967).
3. Sean McMeekin, *The Russian Origins of the First World War* (Cambridge, MA: Harvard University Press, 2011).
4. Michael S. Neiberg, ed., *The World War I Reader: Primary and Secondary Sources* (New York: New York University Press, 2007), 48.
5. Williamson and Van Wyk, *July 1914*, 143.
6. John Keegan, *The First World War* (New York: Knopf, 1999), 68–69.
7. Williamson and Van Wyk, *July 1914*, 147.

5. THE WESTERN FRONT, 1914–1915

1. Max Arthur, *Forgotten Voices of the Great War: A History of World War I in the Words of the Men and Women Who Were There* (Guilford, CT: Lyons Press, 2002), 11.
2. Trans. by Stanley Kunitz and Max Hayward in Jon Silkin, ed., *The Penguin Book of First World War Poetry* (London: Penguin, 1979), 274.
3. John Keegan, *The First World War* (New York: Knopf, 1999), 93.
4. Harold A. Winters et al., *Battling the Elements: Weather and Terrain in the Conduct of War* (Baltimore: Johns Hopkins University Press, 1998), 39–44.
5. Byron Farwell, *Armies of the Raj: From the Mutiny to Independence, 1858–1947* (New York: Viking, 1989), 248–53; David E. Omissi, *The Sepoy and the Raj: The Indian Army, 1860–1940* (New York: Macmillan, 1998), 114–20.
6. Keegan, *First World War*, 135–36.
7. Arthur, *Forgotten Voices*, 46.
8. Michael S. Neiberg, ed., *The World War I Reader: Primary and Secondary Sources* (New York: New York University Press, 2007), 227.
9. Silkin, *Penguin Book of First World War Poetry*, 129–30.
10. James Hannah, ed., *The Great War Reader* (College Station: Texas A&M University Press, 2000), 117.
11. The Latin is from the poet Horace: "How sweet and fitting it is to die for one's country." Silkin, *Penguin Book of First World War Poetry*, 192–93.
12. Arthur, *Forgotten Voices*, 103.

6. THE WAR IN EASTERN AND
SOUTHERN EUROPE, 1914–1915

1. Sean McMeekin, *The Russian Origins of the First World War* (Cambridge, MA: Harvard University Press, 2011), 83–85.
2. John Keegan, *The First World War* (New York: Knopf, 1999), 142.
3. Keegan, *First World War*, 151–55.
4. Keegan, *First World War*, 166–70.

5. Michael S. Neiberg, ed., *The World War I Reader: Primary and Secondary Sources* (New York: New York University Press, 2007), 118.

6. Keegan, *First World War*, 170.

7. Norman Stone, *The Eastern Front, 1914–1917* (New York: Scribner, 1975), 92–94.

8. Shelley Baranowski, *Nazi Empire: German Colonialism and Imperialism from Bismarck to Hitler* (Cambridge: Cambridge University Press, 2011), 86–89.

9. Mark Thompson, *The White War: Life and Death on the Italian Front, 1915–1919* (London: Faber & Faber, 2008).

10. Svetlana Palmer and Sarah Wallis, eds., *Intimate Voices from the First World War* (London: Simon & Schuster, 2003), 155–56.

7. THE WORLD WAR IN AFRICA, 1914–1916

1. John Morrow, *The Great War: An Imperial History* (London: Routledge, 2004), 43.

2. Robin W. Kilson, "Calling Up the Empire: The British Military Use of Non-Western Labor in France, 1916–1920" (PhD diss., Harvard University, 1990).

3. Shelley Baranowski, *Nazi Empire: German Colonialism and Imperialism from Bismarck to Hitler* (Cambridge: Cambridge University Press, 2011), 46–63.

4. Hew Strachan, *The First World War in Africa* (Oxford: Oxford University Press, 2004), 13–18.

5. Strachan, *First World War in Africa*, 19–60.

6. Albert Grundlingh, *Fighting Their Own War: South African Blacks and the First World War* (Johannesburg: Ravan Press, 1987).

7. Bill Nasson, *Springboks on the Somme: South Africa in the Great War, 1914–1918* (Johannesburg: Penguin, 2007), 35–59.

8. Nasson, *Springboks on the Somme*, 63–88.

8. THE WAR AT SEA, 1914–1915

1. Paul G. Halpern, *A Naval History of World War I* (Annapolis: Naval Institute Press, 1994), 70-84.

2. Halpern, *Naval History of World War I*, 21–50.

3. Halpern, *Naval History of World War I*, 223–38.

4. Robert K. Massie, *Castles of Steel: Britain, Germany, and the Winning of the Great War at Sea* (New York: Random House, 2003), 123.

5. Halpern, *Naval History of World War I*, 287–304.

9. THE WAR IN THE MIDDLE EAST, 1914–1916

1. For an excellent overview of the Dardanelles Campaign, see Peter Hart, *Gallipoli* (Oxford: Oxford University Press, 2011).

2. Max Arthur, *Forgotten Voices of the Great War: A History of World War I in the Words of the Men and Women Who Were There* (Guilford, CT: Lyons Press, 2002), 118.

3. Jill Hamilton, *From Gallipoli to Gaza: The Desert Poets of World War One* (East Rosedale, Australia: Simon and Schuster, 2003), 79.

4. Arthur, *Forgotten Voices*, 119.

5. Jon Silkin, ed., *The Penguin Book of First World War Poetry* (London: Penguin, 1979), 81–82.

6. John Keegan, *The First World War* (New York, Knopf, 1999), 222–25; Hew Strachan, *The First World War* (New York: Viking, 2003), 109–15.

7. David Fromkin, *A Peace to End All Peace: The Fall of the Ottoman Empire and the Creation of the Modern Middle East* (New York: Owl Books, 1989), 173–99.

10. THE OFFENSIVES OF 1916

1. John Keegan, *The First World War* (New York: Knopf, 1999), 275–76.

2. Keegan, *First World War*, 278; Hew Strachan, *The First World War* (New York: Viking, 2003), 188.

3. Harold A. Winters et al., *Battling the Elements: Weather and Terrain in the Conduct of War* (Baltimore: Johns Hopkins University Press, 1998), 133–39.

4. Strachan, *First World War*, 189.

5. Henri Barbusse, *Under Fire*, trans. Robin Buss (London: Penguin, 2003), 189–90.

6. Barbusse, *Under Fire*, 205.

7. Mark Thompson, *The White War: Life and Death on the Italian Front, 1915–1919* (London: Faber & Faber, 2008), 163–8.

8. Strachan, *First World War*, 190–91.

9. Robin Prior and Trevor Wilson, *The Somme* (New Haven: Yale University Press, 2005), 112–18.

12. THE STRAINS OF TOTAL WAR

1. Max Arthur, *Forgotten Voices of the Great War: A History of World War I in the Words of the Men and Women Who Were There* (Guilford, CT: Lyons Press, 2002), 68.

2. Margaret Higonnet, ed., *Lines of Fire: Women Writers of World War I* (New York: Plume Books, 1999), 194.

3. Higonnet, *Lines of Fire*, 185.

4. Higonnet, *Lines of Fire*, 232–33.

5. Susan Grayzel, *Women and the First World War* (London: Pearson, 2002), 27–43.

6. Avner Offer, *The First World War: An Agrarian Interpretation* (Oxford: Oxford University Press, 1998), 368–76.

7. David Stevenson, *Cataclysm: The First World War as Political Tragedy* (New York: Basic Books, 2004), 179–81.

8. Stevenson, *Cataclysm*, 181–83.

9. Stevenson, *Cataclysm*, 183–84.

10. Stevenson, *Cataclysm*, 184–86.

11. Michael S. Neiberg, ed., *The World War I Reader: Primary and Secondary Sources* (New York: New York University Press, 2007), 246.

12. Offer, *First World War*, 23–31, 45–53.

13. The previous section on comparative domestic politics in Europe and the United States relies on Stevenson, *Cataclysm*, 215–32.

14. Justin McCarthy, *The Ottoman Peoples and the End of Empire* (London: Arnold, 2001), 95–112.

13. THE OFFENSIVES OF 1917

1. John Keegan, *The First World War* (New York: Knopf, 1999), 329–31. Hew Strachan, *The First World War* (New York: Viking, 2001), 245–48.
2. Mark Thompson, *The White War: Life and Death on the Italian Front, 1915–1919* (London: Faber & Faber, 2008), 249–60.
3. A. M. J. Hyatt, *General Sir Arthur Currie: A Military Biography* (Toronto: University of Toronto Press, 1987), 77–89; Keegan, *First World War*, 360–69.
4. David Stevenson, *Cataclysm: The First World War as Political Tragedy* (New York: Basic Books), 264–67, 365–68.
5. Michael S. Neiberg, ed., *The World War I Reader: Primary and Secondary Sources* (New York: New York University Press, 2007), 189.

14. ALLIED EMPIRE-BUILDING, 1916–1918

1. Bill Nasson, *Springboks on the Somme: South Africa in the Great War, 1914–1918* (Johannesburg: Penguin, 2007), 89–122.
2. Svetlana Palmer and Sarah Wallis, eds., *Intimate Voices from the First World War* (London: Simon & Schuster, 2003), 178–79.
3. Palmer and Wallis, *Intimate Voices*, 184–85.
4. Hew Strachan, *The First World War* (New York: Viking, 2001), 85–92; Hew Strachan, *The First World War in Africa* (New York: Oxford University Press, 2004), 131–84.
5. David Killingray, "The War in Africa," in Hew Strachan, *The Oxford Illustrated History of the First World War* (Oxford: Oxford University Press, 1998), 92–102.
6. David Fromkin, *A Peace to End All Peace: The Fall of the Ottoman Empire and the Creation of the Modern Middle East* (New York: Owl Books, 1989), 308–14.
7. Fromkin, *A Peace to End All Peace*, 291–99.
8. Fromkin, *A Peace to End All Peace*, 257.

15. THE WAR'S END, 1918

1. John Keegan, *The First World War* (New York: Knopf, 1999), 372–73.
2. Svetlana Palmer and Sarah Wallis, eds., *Intimate Voices from the First World War* (London: Simon & Schuster, 2003), 319–20.
3. John M. Barry, *The Great Influenza: The Epic Story of the Deadliest Plague in History* (New York: Viking, 2004), 171.
4. Alfred W. Crosby, *Epidemic and Peace, 1918* (Westport, CT: Greenwood Press, 1976), 156–66; Barry, *Great Influenza*.
5. Erich Maria Remarque, *All Quiet on the Western Front*, trans. A. W. Wheen (New York: Fawcett, 1958), 286.

16. THE PEACE SETTLEMENTS

1. Niall Ferguson, *The Pity of War: Explaining World War I* (London: Allen Lane, 1998), 337; Gerd Hardach, *The First World War, 1914–1918* (Berkeley and Los Angeles: University of California Press, 1977), 153.

2. David Stevenson, *Cataclysm: The First World War as Political Tragedy* (New York: Basic, 2004), 442–43.

17. UNDERSTANDING AND REMEMBERING THE WAR

1. Richard P. Tucker, "The World Wars and the Globalization of Timber Cutting," in *Natural Enemy, Natural Ally*, ed. Richard P. Tucker and Edmund Russell (Corvallis: Oregon State University Press, 2004).

2. The works of art described here may be easily found in art history textbooks and on Internet sites. An Internet site that contains many of the works of art discussed here is "Art of the First World War: 100 Paintings from International Collections to Commemorate the 80th Anniversary of the End of the First World War," http://www.memorial-caen.fr/10EVENT/EXPO1418/gb/visite.html.

3. Erich Maria Remarque, *All Quiet on the Western Front*, trans. A. W. Wheen (New York: Fawcett, 1958), 110–11.

4. Remarque, *All Quiet on the Western Front*, 55–56.

5. Remarque, *All Quiet on the Western Front*, 204.

6. Paul Fussell, *The Great War and Modern Memory* (Oxford: Oxford University Press, 1975), 62.

7. Glenn Watkins, *Proof through the Night: Music and the Great War* (Berkeley and Los Angeles: University of California Press, 2003), 54–55.

8. Watkins, *Proof through the Night*, 357.

9. Watkins, *Proof through the Night*, 172–80.

10. James Hannah, ed., *The Great War Reader* (College Station: Texas A&M University Press, 2000), 296.

Sources on the First World War

This book is a short interpretation of the First World War, a subject that has been written about by thousands of authors. The following section makes suggestions for further reading, followed by a bibliography of works that I found most helpful in writing this book. The suggestions and bibliography offered here are not extensive. A very good and more substantial introductory bibliography may be found in John Morrow's book *The Great War: An Imperial History*. A comprehensive guide to reading and research may be found in Robin Higham's *Researching World War I* as well as *A Companion to World War I*, edited by John Horne. The best overview of how historians have interpreted the First World War is *The Great War in History*, co-authored by Jay Winter and Antoine Prost.

SUGGESTIONS FOR FURTHER READING

In recent years, there have been a number of books written that provide good overviews of the war. The most readable is *The First World War* by John Keegan, who also provides many insights about how soldiers imagine and experience geography and landscape. A somewhat more academic and analytical approach is taken by Hew Strachan in his own survey history, *The First World War*, which is also highly recommended. Four other books—John Morrow's *The Great War*, Michael Neiberg's *Fighting the Great War*, Eric Brose's *A History of the Great War*, and Lawrence Sondhaus's *World War I: The Global Revolution*—also present balanced scholarship in readable prose, while paying careful attention to global aspects of the war. Students who begin to develop a serious interest in the First World War should read David Stevenson's *Cataclysm*, my personal favorite survey of the war. Stevenson's book is longer than the others listed, and it contains fewer colorful stories about the human experience of the war. Yet Stevenson writes well, and he presents a superior, detailed, and nuanced overview of the war's politics and economics. The next step for serious students of the war will be to read the formidable three-volume *Cambridge History of the First World War*, edited by Jay Winter. Winter and the other contributors survey all aspects of the war, ranging from strategy to mourning practices. And finally, the survey work that does the best job of introducing the excitement of interpreting and debating the war is Niall Ferguson's *The Pity of War*. In this book, as in his other books, Ferguson excels at challenging the received wisdom of fellow historians.

Students who wish to explore the history of the war will also want to read about the war from the perspective of the participants. There are some very good edited collections of primary sources. I highly recommend Michael Neiberg's *The World War I Reader*, James Hannah's *The Great War Reader*, and Susan Grayzel's *The First World War*. There are also some very memorable interviews collected by Max Arthur in his two books, *Forgotten Voices of the Great War* and *Last Post*. One collection is especially good on the war's outbreak, *July 1914*, edited by Samuel R. Williamson and Russel Van Wyk.

After reading these introductory surveys and collections, readers may wish to stoke their imaginations by watching films. There are two excellent video series about the First World War. One, called *The Great War and the Shaping of the Twentieth Century*, was conceived mainly by Jay Winter and Blaine Baggett and released in 1996. It is particularly insightful about the psychology of the people who experienced the war. Another excellent video series titled *The First World War* was produced in 2004 by Jonathan Lewis. It is based on the survey book *The First World War* by Hew Strachan and adds much to it, not only by using standard archival footage of the war and interviews with experts, but also by presenting the landscapes of the war as they may be seen today, thereby linking the past to the present.

Documentary series are not the only ways to explore the visual side of the war. The war has been the subject of many feature films. In the interest of space and time, I will recommend my personal favorites, all of which should be easy to locate. *The Grand Illusion* (1938) by Jean Renoir is the story of two French pilots, captured by the Germans, who join together in an effort to escape in spite of their different class backgrounds. The film raises questions about class loyalties and also about race—the pilots are joined in prison by a French Jew and a French African—while presenting war as senseless. A similar argument about war's senselessness is made in Stanley Kubrick's 1957 film *Paths of Glory*, which tells the story of French mutineers, some of whom are put on trial as examples to their comrades. Kubrick, like Renoir, shows soldiers who begin the war as willing participants and then change their minds when encountered with the evidence of the war's perverse logic.

The opposite approach is taken by Howard Hawks, the director of *Sergeant York* (1941). In this film, a backwoods American, Alvin York, is persuaded to abandon his pacifist idealism and participate in the war. He goes on to become an enthusiastic soldier and a hero, responsible for single-handedly capturing more than a hundred German soldiers. Howard Hawks hoped that York's example would persuade isolationist Americans to participate in the Second World War, while his near-contemporary, Jean Renoir, used *The Grand Illusion* to urge his countrymen to avoid another world war. The conflict between duty and idealism, on the one hand, and war's senselessness, on the other hand, is drawn out very well by Peter Weir in *Gallipoli* (1981), a movie about two Australian friends who are caught up in a senseless attack on Ottoman positions in the film's final scene. Instead of resisting their orders, their entire unit goes "over the top" and is sacrificed. Finally, when the war becomes unbearably depressing, I recommend watching the Marx Brothers' spoof of early-twentieth-century diplomacy and warmaking, the hilarious film titled *Duck Soup* (1933). Groucho plays Rufus T. Firefly, the prime minister of "Freedonia," who starts and participates in a needless war against the neighboring country of "Sylvania."

Comic and tragic films about the First World War have done much to support the interpretation that the war was a senseless slaughter. So have numerous works of fiction. Henri Barbusse's *Under Fire* was written in the final years of the war and published in newspapers. It provides an unsparing account of the lives of French soldiers caught up in the terrible fighting along the Western Front. A German perspective is presented by Erich Maria Remarque in *All Quiet on the Western Front* (1928). Both books are famous indictments of warfare, as are the wartime poems of the British officers Robert Graves, Wilfred Owen, and Siegfried Sassoon, which have been collected in many anthologies. These poets feature prominently in one of the best works of historical fiction about the war, *Regeneration* (1993) by Pat Barker. In this novel, Barker explores the psychological traumas of war and their influences over the officers' sense of duty. The most richly detailed historical fiction about the war, Aleksandr Solzhenitsyn's *August 1914* (1972), analyzes the reasons for the Russian army's failures at Tannenberg, while providing rich characterizations of officers and men.

BIBLIOGRAPHY

Adas, Michael. *Machines as the Measure of Man: Science, Technology, and Ideologies of Western Dominance.* Ithaca: Cornell University Press, 1989.

Anderson, Scott. *Lawrence in Arabia: War, Deceit, and Imperial Folly in the Making of the Modern Middle East.* New York: Doubleday, 2013.

Arthur, Max. *Forgotten Voices of the Great War: A History of World War I in the Words of the Men and Women Who Were There.* Guilford, CT: Lyons Press, 2002.

————. *Last Post: The Final Word from Our First World War Soldiers*. London: Weidenfeld and Nicolson, 2005.

Audoin-Rouzeau, Stéphane, and Annette Becker. *14–18: Understanding the Great War*. Trans. Catherine Temerson. New York: Hill and Wang, 2002.

Baranowski, Shelley. *Nazi Empire: German Colonialism and Imperialism from Bismarck to Hitler*. Cambridge: Cambridge University Press, 2011.

Barbusse, Henri. *Under Fire*. Trans. Robin Buss. London: Penguin, 2003.

Barry, John M. *The Great Influenza: The Epic Story of the Deadliest Plague in History*. New York: Viking, 2004.

Bennett, Geoffrey. *Naval Battles of the First World War*. London: Batsford, 1968.

Berg, A. Scott. *Wilson*. New York: G. P. Putnam's Sons, 2013.

Bourke, Joanna. *An Intimate History of Killing: Face-to-Face Killing in Twentieth-Century Warfare*. New York: Basic Books, 1999.

Brose, Eric. *A History of the Great War: World War One and the International Crisis of the Early Twentieth Century*. Oxford: Oxford University Press, 2010.

Burbank, Jane, and Frederick Cooper. *Empires in World History: Power and the Politics of Difference*. Princeton: Princeton University Press, 2010.

Byerly, Carol R. *Fever of War: The Influenza Epidemic in the U. S. Army during World War I*. New York: New York University Press, 2005.

Chickering, Roger, and Stig Förster. *Great War, Total War: Combat and Mobilization on the Western Front, 1914–1918*. Washington, DC: German Historical Institute; Cambridge: Cambridge University Press, 2000.

Churchill, Winston. *The River War: An Account of the Reconquest of the Soudan*. New York: Scribner's, 1933.

Clark, Christopher. *The Sleepwalkers: How Europe Went to War in 1914*. New York: Harper, 2013.

Cooper, John Milton. *Woodrow Wilson: A Biography*. New York: Knopf, 2009.

Crosby, Alfred W. *Epidemic and Peace, 1918*. Westport, CT: Greenwood Press, 1976.

Diamond, Jared. *Guns, Germs, and Steel: The Fates of Human Societies*. New York: W. W. Norton, 1999.

Dunn, J. C. *The War the Infantry Knew, 1914–1919: A Chronicle of Service in France and Belgium*. London: Abacus, 1994.

Edgerton, David. *The Shock of the Old: Technology and Global History since 1900*. Oxford: Oxford University Press, 2007.

Emmerson, Charles. *1913: In Search of the World before the Great War*. New York: Public Affairs, 2013.

Evans, Martin Marix. *American Voices of World War I: Primary Source Documents, 1917–1920*. Chicago: Fitzroy Dearborn Publishers, 2001.

Farwell, Byron. *Armies of the Raj: From the Mutiny to Independence, 1858–1947*. New York: Viking, 1989.

Ferguson, Niall. *The Pity of War: Explaining World War I*. London: Allen Lane, 1998.

Fewster, Kevin, Vecihi Başarın, and Hatice Hürmüz Başarın. *Gallipoli: The Turkish Story*. Crow's Nest, Australia: Allen and Unwin, 1985.

Finnegan, Terrence. *Shooting the Front: Allied Aerial Reconnaissance and Photographic Interpretation on the Western Front—World War I*. Washington, DC: National Defense Intelligence College, 2006.

Fischer, Fritz. *Germany's Aims in the First World War*. New York: W. W. Norton, 1967.

————. *War of Illusions: German Policies from 1911 to 1914*. New York: W. W. Norton, 1975.

Forty, Simon. *Historical Maps of World War I*. New York: Sterling, 2002.

Fromkin, David. *Europe's Last Summer: Who Started the Great War in 1914?* New York: Alfred A. Knopf, 2004.

————. *A Peace to End All Peace: Creating the Modern Middle East, 1914–1922*. New York: Henry Holt, 1989.

Fussell, Paul. *The Great War and Modern Memory*. Oxford: Oxford University Press, 1975.

Gatrell, Peter. *Russia's First World War: A Social and Economic History.* London: Pearson Longman, 2005.

Gilbert, Martin. *The Routledge Atlas of the First World War.* 2nd ed. London: Routledge, 1994.

Glover, Jon, and Jon Silkin, eds. *The Penguin Book of First World War Prose.* London: Penguin, 1989.

Grayzel, Susan R. *The First World War: A Brief History with Documents.* Boston: Bedford, 2013.

———. *Women and the First World War.* London: Pearson, 2002.

Hamilton, Jill. *From Gallipoli to Gaza: The Desert Poets of World War One.* East Rosedale, Australia: Simon & Schuster, 2003.

Hamilton, Richard F., and Holger Herwig, eds. *The Origins of World War I.* Cambridge: Cambridge University Press, 2003.

Hannah, James, ed. *The Great War Reader.* College Station: Texas A&M University Press, 2000.

Hardach, Gerd. *The First World War, 1914–1918.* Berkeley and Los Angeles: University of California Press, 1977.

Hart, Peter. *Gallipoli.* Oxford: Oxford University Press, 2011.

Hastings, Max. *Catastrophe 1914: Europe Goes to War.* New York: Alfred A. Knopf, 2013.

Herman, Judith. *Trauma and Recovery: The Aftermath of Violence—from Domestic Abuse to Political Terror.* New York: Perseus Books, 1992.

Higham, Robin, ed., with Dennis Showalter. *Researching World War I: A Handbook.* Westport, CT: Greenwood Press, 2003.

Higonnet, Margaret, ed. *Lines of Fire: Women Writers of World War I.* New York: Plume Books, 1999.

Holt, Thomas. *The Problem of Freedom: Race, Labor, and Politics in Jamaica and Britain, 1832–1938.* Baltimore: Johns Hopkins University Press, 1992.

Horne, John, ed. *A Companion to World War I.* Oxford: Wiley-Blackwell, 2011.

Hubert C. Johnson, *Breakthrough! Tactics, Technology, and the Search for Victory on the Western Front in World War I.* Novato, CA: Presidio Press, 1994.

Hyatt, A. M. J. *General Sir Arthur Currie: A Military Biography.* Toronto: University of Toronto Press, 1987.

James, Robert Rhodes. *Gallipoli.* London: Batsford, 1965.

Joll, James. *The Origins of the First World War.* 2nd ed. London: Pearson, 1992.

Keegan, John. *The First World War.* New York: Alfred A. Knopf, 1999.

Keene, Jennifer. *The United States and the First World War.* London: Pearson, 2000.

Kilson, Robin W. "Calling Up the Empire: The British Military Use of Non-Western Labor in France, 1916–1920." Ph.D. diss. Harvard University, 1990.

Korte, Barbara, and Ann-Marie Einhaus, eds. *The Penguin Book of First World War Stories.* New York: Penguin Books, 2007.

Leed, Eric. *No Man's Land: Combat and Identity in World War I.* Cambridge: Cambridge University Press, 1979.

Livesey, Anthony, with H. P. Willmott. *The Historical Atlas of World War I.* New York: Henry Holt, 1994.

MacDonald, Lyn. *1914–1919: Voices and Images of the Great War.* London: Michael Joseph, 1988.

Macleod, Jenny. *Reconsidering Gallipoli.* Manchester: Manchester University Press, 2004.

Macmillan, Margaret. *Paris 1919: Six Months That Changed the World.* New York: Random House, 2001.

———. *The War That Ended Peace: The Road to 1914.* New York: Random House, 2013.

Martel, Gordon. *The Origins of the First World War.* 3rd ed. London: Pearson, 2003.

Mason, Philip. *A Matter of Honour: An Account of the Indian Army, Its Officers and Men.* London: Macmillan, 1974.

Massie, Robert K. *Castles of Steel: Britain, Germany, and the Winning of the Great War at Sea.* New York: Random House, 2003.

———. *Dreadnought: Britain, Germany, and the Coming of the Great War.* New York: Random House, 1991.

McCarthy, Justin. *The Ottoman Peoples and the End of Empire.* London: Arnold, 2001.

McMeekin, Sean. *July 1914: Countdown to War.* New York: Basic Books, 2013.

Metcalf, Thomas R. *Imperial Connections: India in the Indian Ocean Arena, 1860–1920.* Berkeley and Los Angeles: University of California Press, 2007.

Mommsen, Wolfgang J. *Imperial Germany, 1867–1918: Politics, Culture, and Society in an Authoritarian State.* London: Arnold, 1995.

Morrow, John H. *German Air Power in World War I.* Lincoln: University of Nebraska Press, 1982.

———. *The Great War in the Air: Military Aviation from 1909 to 1921.* Washington, DC: Smithsonian, 1993.

———. *The Great War: An Imperial History.* London: Routledge, 2004.

Nasson, Bill. *Springboks on the Somme: South Africa and the Great War, 1914–1918.* Johannesburg: Penguin, 2007.

Neiberg, Michael S. *Fighting the Great War: A Global History.* Cambridge, MA: Harvard University Press, 2005.

———, ed. *The World War I Reader: Primary and Secondary Sources.* New York: New York University Press, 2007.

Offer, Avner. *The First World War: An Agrarian Interpretation.* Oxford: Oxford University Press, 1998.

Page, Melvin E. *Africa and the First World War.* London: Macmillan, 1987.

———. *The Chiwaya War: Malawians and the First World War.* Boulder, CO: Westview Press, 2000.

Palazzo, Albert. *Seeking Victory on the Western Front: The British Army and Chemical Warfare in World War I.* Lincoln: University of Nebraska Press, 2000.

Palmer, Svetlana, and Sarah Wallis, eds. *Intimate Voices from the First World War.* London: Simon & Schuster, 2003.

Prior, Robin, and Trevor Wilson. *The Somme.* New Haven: Yale University Press, 2005.

Reeves, Nicholas. *The Power of Film Propaganda: Myth or Reality?* London: Cassell, 1999.

Remarque, Erich Maria. *All Quiet on the Western Front.* Trans. A. W. Wheen. New York: Fawcett, 1958.

Robertson, Linda R. *The Dream of Civilized Warfare: World War I Flying Aces and the American Imagination.* Minneapolis: University of Minnesota Press, 2003.

Robinson, Ronald, and John Gallagher. *Africa and the Victorians: The Official Mind of Imperialism.* 2nd ed. London: Macmillan, 1981.

Rose, Lisle A. *Power at Sea: The Age of Navalism, 1890–1918.* Columbia: University of Missouri Press, 2007.

Russell, Edmund. *War and Nature: Fighting Humans and Insects with Chemicals from World War I to "Silent Spring."* Cambridge: Cambridge University Press, 2001.

Sheffield, Gary, ed. *War on the Western Front: In the Trenches of World War I.* Oxford: Osprey Publishing, 2007.

Showalter, Dennis E. *Tannenberg: Clash of Empires.* Hamden, CT: Archon Books, 1991.

Silkin, Jon, ed. *The Penguin Book of First World War Poetry.* London: Penguin, 1979.

Smith, Leonard V., Stéphane Audoin-Rouzeau, and Annette Becker. *France and the Great War, 1914–1918.* Trans. Helen McPhail. Cambridge: Cambridge University Press, 2003.

Sondhaus, Lawrence. *World War One: The Global Revolution.* Cambridge: Cambridge University Press, 2011.

Stevenson, David. *Cataclysm: The First World War as Political Tragedy.* New York: Basic Books, 2004.

———. *With Our Backs to the Wall: Victory and Defeat in 1918.* Cambridge, MA: Harvard University Press, 2011.

Stone, Norman. *The Eastern Front, 1914–1917.* New York: Charles Scribner's Sons, 1975.

Strachan, Hew. *The First World War.* New York: Viking, 2003.

———. *The Oxford Illustrated History of the First World War.* Oxford: Oxford University Press, 1998.

Tipton, Frank B. *A History of Modern Germany since 1815.* Berkeley and Los Angeles: University of California Press, 2003.

Travers, Tim. *Gallipoli 1915*. Stroud, UK: Tempus Publishing, 2001.

Tucker, Richard P., and Edmund Russell, eds. *Natural Enemy, Natural Ally: Toward an Environmental History of War*. Corvallis: Oregon State University Press, 2004.

Watkins, Glenn. *Proof through the Night: Music and the Great War*. Berkeley and Los Angeles: University of California Press, 2003.

Williamson, Samuel R., and Russel Van Wyk. *July 1914: Soldiers, Statesmen, and the Coming of the Great War: A Brief Documentary History*. Boston: Bedford St. Martin's, 2003.

Winter, Jay. *Sites of Memory, Sites of Mourning: The Great War in European Cultural History*. Cambridge: Cambridge University Press, 1995.

———, ed. *The Cambridge History of the First World War*. 3 vols. Cambridge: Cambridge University Press, 2013.

Winter, Jay, and Antoine Prost. *The Great War in History: Debates and Controversies, 1914 to the Present*. Cambridge: Cambridge University Press, 2005.

Winters, Harold A., et al. *Battling the Elements: Weather and Terrain in the Conduct of War*. Baltimore: Johns Hopkins University Press, 1998.

Index

active defense, 96
aerial intelligence, 139
Afghanistan, 1
Africa: colonialism in, 5, 6, 7, 8, 13, 25; early in war, 64, 65–71, 67; effects of war on, 147; labor supply of, 64, 146; later in war, 143–147; war participation of, 64
agricultural production, 117
aircraft: at Battle of Verdun, 96; bombers, 140–142; fighter planes, 139–140, 141; and infantry tactics, 95; military impact of, 139–142, 158; in Nivelle offensive, 131; technology of, 139–142; and trench warfare, 46; zeppelins, 37, 142, 143
Akhmatova, Anna, "July 1914," 35–36
Albert, King of Belgium, 37, 41, 156
Albert, Prince, 24
Alexandra, Tsarina, 124
Allenby, Edward, 148, 149
Allies: alliances with, 112–113; command structure of, 154; and communications, 53; conclusion of war, 151–153; financing of war, 164; goals of, 34; imperialism of, 84, 91–92, 143–150; imperialist advantages of, 81; later in war, 129; manpower of, 131, 154; objectives of, 151–153; and Ottoman Empire, 84–92; and peace settlements, 166–171; relative strength of, 34; and Russian civil war, 170; strategy of, 94; U.S. attitudes toward, 109; and war finances, 119–120

Alsace-Lorraine, 14–15, 20, 22, 23, 37, 64, 167
American First Army, 159
American Second Army, 159
American Second Division, 157
American Third Division, 157
Anglo-Boer War (1899–1902), 38, 46, 69
Anglo-Persian Oil Company, 87
Arabs, 92, 149
architecture, 166
Argentina, 26
Armenia and Armenians, 91, 165, 169
art, representations of war in, 166, 175–179
artillery: aiming of, 82, 137–138; at Battle of Verdun, 104; British methods of, 130; halting of, at mealtimes, 43; infantry tactics' effect on, 95; poison gas delivered by, 49; shell production for, 56; technological advances in, 9, 130, 137–138, 158; technology of, 82; and trench warfare, 46, 48, 100; used in sieges, 37. *See also* cannons
Artois, Battle of (1915), 49
Asia: colonialism in, 5, 6, 7, 8, 13; labor supply of, 64
Asquith, Herbert, 122
atrocities, 37

attrition strategy, 94, 96, 105, 131, 134, 157
Auda (sheik), 149
Audoin-Rouzeau, Stéphane, 2, 165
Australia: casualties of, 131; government of, 7, 70; war participation of, 84, 87, 105, 131, 133, 135, 158, 161; wartime production of, 117
Australian and New Zealand Army Corps (ANZAC), 84
Austria, 170
Austro-Hungarian Empire: attitudes toward war in, 123; and Bosnia, 29; casualties of, 55, 56, 57, 99, 100, 133; collapse and division of, 161, 170; conclusion of war, 161; early in war, 52, 55–59; German relations with, 15, 16, 27, 30; impact of war on, 51; imperialism of, 7, 13; later in war, 94, 98–102, 132, 136–137; manpower of, 57; navy of, 26; and origins of war, 29–30, 31; prewar, 5, 14; and war finances, 118, 119, 120

Balfour, Arthur, 149
Balfour Declaration, 149
Balkans, 29–34
Baltic countries, 127
Baltic Sea, 26, 77
barbed wire, 49
Barbusse, Henri, 97
Baster, 69
battleships, 25–26, 27, 73
Bavaria, 14, 15
Bean, C. E. W., 84
Beatty, David, 108
Becker, Annette, 2, 165
Beckmann, Max, 176
BEF. *See* British Expeditionary Force
Belgian Congo, 68, 144
Belgium: casualties of, 43; conclusion of war, 154, 156, 160; early in war, 36–38, 39, 40–43; environmental destruction in, 174; German war planning concerning, 20, 22, 23, 34; later in war, 133–135; and origins of war, 32–33, 34
Belorussia, 127
Berchtold, Leopold, 31
Bernhardi, Friedrich von, 17–19

Bethmann-Hollweg, Theobald von, 31, 110
Binyon, Laurence, 178
Bismarck, Otto von, 14, 16–17, 24
Black Sea, 76
Bloch, Ivan, 19
blockades, 73, 78–79, 110, 118, 152, 167
blood transfusions, 165
Blücher, Evelyn, 121
Boccioni, Umberto, 175
Boers, 24, 26, 69–70, 144
Boer War. *See* Anglo-Boer War
Bolsheviks, 125, 126, 127, 149, 170–171
bombers, 140–142
Bonamore, Virgilio, 61
Bosnia, 29
Botha, Louis, 69, 70, 71
Boughton, Harold, 85
Bourke, Joanna, 165
Brazil, 26, 112
breakthrough attacks, 94–95, 96, 98, 100, 102–103, 131, 134, 137–138
Breslau (ship), 76
Brest-Litovsk, Treaty of (1918), 127
Britain: and Africa, 64, 65–71, 144–145, 146; aircraft of, 142; and Anglo-Boer War, 69; attitudes toward war in, 122–123; casualties of, 43, 49, 104–105, 109, 131, 133–134, 135, 138; conclusion of war, 153–160, 161–162; early in war, 37, 38, 39–43, 43–44, 45–49, 59; French relations with, 23, 32; German relations with, 15, 20, 24, 27; imperialism of, 5, 7, 63–64, 65, 69–70, 89, 146, 147, 149–150, 169; later in war, 94, 99, 102–105, 129–135, 137–142; liberalism in, 6; manpower of, 93, 103; military planning of, 23; navy of, 25–26, 27, 74–76, 77–79, 82, 87, 107–109; and origins of war, 32; and Ottoman Empire, 82–92, 147–149; and peace settlements, 166–171; Portuguese relations with, 79; prewar, 5; Russian relations with, 23; strategy and tactics of, 131; U.S. attitudes toward, 109; and war finances, 118, 119–120; and war in Africa, 65, 68
British East Africa, 68

British Expeditionary Force (BEF), 37, 38, 39, 41, 42, 130, 133, 158
British Fifth Army, 134, 154
British First Army, 49, 156, 158
British Fourth Army, 103, 158
British Second Army, 47, 133, 134, 156
British Third Army, 103, 158
Brittain, Vera, 45
Brooke, Rupert, 86–87
Brusilov, Alexei, 56, 100, 102, 126
Bulgaria, 59, 102, 112, 144, 161, 170
bulges. *See* salients
Bülow, Bernhard von, 25
Bülow, Karl von, 39
Byng, Julian, 137

Cadorna, Luigi, 59, 61, 99–100, 137
Cambodia, 13
Cambrai, Battle of (1917), 137–138
Cameroon, 25, 66
Canada: casualties of, 131; government of, 7, 70; war participation of, 47, 63, 105, 131, 135, 158; wartime production of, 117
cannons, 9, 25, 26. *See also* artillery
Caprivi, Leo von, 17
Caproni (bomber), 141
Caribbean, labor supply of, 64
Carranza, Venustiano, 111
Caspian region, 170
Caspian Sea, 87
casualties: causes of, 174; early in war, 43, 49, 55, 56, 56–57, 64, 91; from influenza epidemic, 159; later in war, 98, 99, 100, 102, 104–105, 109, 131, 132, 133–134, 135, 138, 154, 157, 159; total, 163–164, 164
cattle disease, 66
Caucasus, 90, 127, 170
cavalry, 138, 149
censorship, 122, 123, 124
Central Powers: and communications, 53; financing of war, 164; goals of, 34; Italian offensive by, 136–137; and peace settlements, 166–171; relative strength of, 34; victory eluding, 56–59; and war finances, 119, 120
Chagall, Marc, 175
Champagne, Battle of (1915), 49

Chile, 74
China: declining empire of, 13; entry into war, 113; German imperialism in, 25; Japanese war gains in, 167; labor supply of, 64
chlorine gas, 47, 49, 58
Christmas Day truce (1914), 43
Churchill, Winston, 10–11, 82, 87
civilians, in war effort, 115–116
Civil War, U.S., 9, 11, 19
Clemenceau, Georges, 166
coal, 74, 87
codes, 53, 76, 108
Cold War, 1, 30
combat, nature of, 10–11
Committee on Public Information (U.S.), 123
communications: aircraft as aid to, 139, 158; problems in, 46, 53, 135, 158; radio, 53
communism, 170–171
Constantine, King of Greece, 112
convoys, naval, 139
creeping barrage, 104
cruiser rules, 78, 110
Cuba, 13
cubism, 175
cuesta, 95
Currie, Arthur, 135
Curzon, George, 134
Czechoslovakia, 170

Dahomey, 66
Dardanelles, 82, 83, 152, 161
death: descriptions and artistic representations of, 48, 86, 116, 175; mourning and memorialization of, 165–166. *See also* casualties
defense in depth, 130, 132
defensive fighting: "active defense" strategy, 96; by British, 38; by France, 131–132; by Germany, 44, 46, 48; new weapons advantageous for, 11, 34, 44; by Ottoman Empire, 82; planning for, 20, 23
Denmark, 119
Deppe, Ludwig, 145
Dervishes, 10–11
Diamond, Jared, 8

Diaz, Armando, 137
Dietz, Lothar, 45
disease: cattle disease, 66; dysentery, 86,
   145; influenza, 157, 158, 164; malaria,
   9, 59, 144, 146; medicine and, 164;
   sleeping sickness, 144; trench warfare
   and, 44, 85, 85–86
Dix, Otto, 176
domestic politics, 121–123, 160, 162
Dreadnought (ship), 26
drug addiction, 117
Dual Alliance, 16
Dutch East Indies (Indonesia), 87
dysentery, 86, 145

East Africa, 66–68, 144–145, 146
Eastern Front: early in war, 49, 51–61, 54;
   later in war, 98–102; Western compared
   to, 57
East Prussia, 52
Ebert, Friedrich, 162
economics: blockades and, 73, 78–79, 110,
   118, 152, 167; and free trade, 152; in
   Germany, 14; imperialism and, 5;
   laissez-faire, 6; liberalism and, 6;
   money supply, 118; prewar, 6; of war,
   118–120, 164, 168. *See also* industrial
   production
Edward VII, King of England, 25
Elgar, Edward, *The Spirit of England*, 178
Emden (ship), 74
Emmanuel III, King of Italy, 59
Engels, Friedrich, 19
Entente Powers. *See* Allies
environment: in Africa, 68, 70, 144, 145;
   Allied offense against Ottoman Empire,
   84–85; attitudes toward, 3; for Battle of
   Verdun, 95; on Eastern Front, 52; of
   First World War, 2–3; in Flanders, 41;
   historiography of, 2–3; impact of war
   on, 163, 173–174; imperialism and,
   8–9; of Italian front, 59–61; in Middle
   East, 148; naming practices of soldiers
   for, 86, 87; sacrifice zones in, 36; of
   trench warfare, 44–45, 85, 97, 134–135
Espèrey, Franchet d', 39
Espionage Act (United States, 1917), 123
Europe: postwar, 169; prewar, 5, 7, 18, 29;
   and race, 7

explosives, manufacture of, 118
expressionism, 176

Falkenhayn, Erich von, 40, 94–95, 95, 97,
   98, 102, 105, 148
Falkland Islands, 74
Feisal (son of Sharif of Mecca), 149
Ferguson, Niall, 2, 164
Fernando Po, 66
fighter planes, 139–140, 141
Finland, 127, 170
firearms, technological advances in, 9
First World War: artistic/humanistic
   representations of, 166, 175–179;
   attitudes toward, 35–36, 43, 86, 96,
   119, 121–123, 160, 162, 177; domestic
   politics during, 121–123; Europe after,
   169; financing, 118–120, 164, 168;
   histories of, 2, 3, 30–31, 33, 84; impact
   of, 1, 163–166, 173–179; imperialism
   in relation to, 63–65, 91–92, 143–150;
   lessons of, 1; mobilizations for, 31–33;
   origins of, 29–34, 51; planning for,
   19–27; strains of total war, 115–118
Fischer, Fritz, 31
Flanders, 41–42, 133–135, 156
Foch, Ferdinand, 39, 154
Fokker, Anton, 140
food rationing, 121
forts, 19, 20, 36, 82, 94, 95, 96
France: and Africa, 63–64, 146; African
   labor employed by, 147; aircraft of,
   141; attitudes toward war in, 121;
   British relations with, 23, 32; casualties
   of, 43, 49, 98, 105, 131; conclusion of
   war, 153–154, 156–160, 161; early in
   war, 37–38, 39–42, 43, 44, 45–49, 59;
   environmental destruction in, 174;
   German relations with, 14–15, 16, 17;
   German war planning concerning,
   19–22; imperialism of, 5, 7, 13, 63–64,
   65, 117, 146, 147, 149, 169; industrial
   production in, 93; later in war, 93,
   94–98, 102–105, 129–130, 131–132,
   137; manpower of, 93; military
   planning of, 19, 23, 37; nationalism in,
   14, 15; navy of, 26, 77, 82; and origins
   of war, 31, 32; and Ottoman Empire,
   82–84, 91–92; and peace settlements,

166–171; prewar, 5; Russian relations with, 17; and war finances, 118, 119, 120; and war in Africa, 66

Franz Ferdinand, Archduke of Austria, 29

Franz-Joseph, Emperor, 123

free trade, 152

French, John, 37, 49

French Fifth Army, 38, 39, 40

French First Army, 134, 158

French Fourth Army, 49, 159

French Ninth Army, 39

French Revolution, 5

French Second Army, 41, 49, 96

French Sixth Army, 39, 40

French Tenth Army, 41, 49

French Third Army, 95, 96

Friedrich, Kaiser, 16

Fussell, Paul, 177

futurism, 175

Gallipoli, 84–86, 87, 122

Gandhi, Mahatma, 175

gas attacks. *See* poison gas

German Eighth Army, 52, 53, 127

German Fifth Army, 95

German First Army, 39

German Fourth Army, 40

German Second Army, 138

German Sixth Army, 49

German Tenth Army, 99

German Third Army, 49

Germany: and Africa, 65–71, 143–144; aircraft of, 142; arms production in, 118; atrocities committed by, 37; attitudes toward war in, 121–122, 160, 162; Austrian relations with, 15, 16, 27, 30; British relations with, 15, 20, 24, 27; casualties of, 43, 49, 98, 99, 100, 105, 109, 138, 154, 157; conclusion of war, 151, 153, 154–160, 155; domestic situation in, 160, 162, 167; early in war, 36–41, 43, 43–44, 45–49, 51–53, 56–59; on the Eastern Front, 51–53, 56–59; French relations with, 14–15, 16, 17; imperialism of, 5, 7, 14, 24, 64–65, 65–71, 91, 168; industrial production in, 14; Italian relations with, 27; later in war, 94–105, 126–127, 130–142; liberalism in, 6; manpower

of, 17, 157; and Middle East, 148; military planning of, 19–22, 25–27, 34, 38–39, 44; nationalism in, 64; navy of, 25, 26, 27, 68, 74–79, 107–109, 162; and origins of war, 30, 30–34; Ottoman relations with, 76; and peace settlements, 160, 166–171; prewar, 5, 14–19; Prussian, 14–16; Russian relations with, 15, 16, 17, 127; U.S. attitudes toward, 109; and U.S. entry into war, 110–111; and war finances, 118, 119, 120; and war in Africa, 65–71

Germany Second Army, 39

germ theory of disease, 165

Ghana, 65

Gibbs, Philip, 141

Gneisenau (German offensive), 157

Goeben (ship), 76

Gold Coast Regiment (Britain), 65

gold standard, 118

Gotha (bomber), 142

Gough, Hubert, 134, 135, 154

Great Depression, 168, 173

Greece, 92, 112, 169–170

guerrilla tactics, 144

Hague Convention, 47

Haig, Douglas, 49, 103, 130, 131, 133–135, 137, 147, 154, 156

Handley-Page (bomber), 142

Hardach, Gerd, 164

Harding, Warren, 171

Headrick, Daniel, 8–9

Herbert, A. P., 85

Herero, 68

Hindenburg, Paul von, 53, 56, 98, 100, 105, 110–111, 122, 156, 160

Hindenburg Line, 130, 131

Hitler, Adolf, 168

Hochschild, Adam, 2

Hoffman, Maximilian, 53

Hohenzollern family, 14

Horne, Henry, 156

horses, 174

hospitals, 164

Hötzendorf, Conrad von, 32, 55, 98, 100

Hub, Paul, 156

Hughes, Charles Evans, 110

Hungary, 170

Hussein, Sherif, 92

Il'ya Murometz (airplane), 141
immigrants, 123
imperialism: Allied, 84, 91–92, 143–150;
    Austro-Hungarian, 7, 13; Balfour
    Declaration and, 149; colonial
    manpower used in war, 42, 45, 63, 117,
    129, 133, 135, 144, 146, 149, 157, 161;
    environment and, 8–9; European, 7–8;
    First World War in relation to, 63–65,
    91–92, 143–150; French, 5, 7, 13;
    German, 14, 24; impact of, 5; industrial
    production and, 5–6; Japanese, 5, 7, 13;
    and labor supply, 64; later in war,
    143–150; liberalism and, 6; Ottoman, 7,
    13; outcome of war and, 163, 169;
    postwar decline of, 34; prewar, 5–9, 13;
    Russian, 5, 7, 13; technology and, 8–9;
    U.S., 5, 7, 13; weapons technology and,
    9
India: German naval attacks on, 74;
    Muslim population of, 89; nationalism
    in, 89; war participation of, 42, 45, 63,
    89–90, 161
Indian Sixth Division, 89
Indian Twelfth Division, 89
industrial production and industrialization:
    attitudes toward, 163; in communist
    Russia, 171; in Germany, 14;
    imperialism and, 5–6; in nineteenth-
    century Europe, 5; war affected by, 56,
    93, 125
inflation, 119, 168
influenza epidemic, 157, 158, 164
insects, 85
intelligence. *See* aerial intelligence; codes
interrupters, 140
Iraq: in First World War, 87–90, 147–148,
    161; imperial control of, 92, 169; U.S.
    war in (2003–2011), 2
Ireland: British relations with, 70, 109,
    122–123; nationalism in, 122–123; war
    participation of, 63, 133
Irish Volunteers, 123
irony, 86
Isonzo, Tenth Battle of (1917), 132
Italian Front, 60
Italian front, 59–61, 98, 132, 136–137, 161

Italy: aircraft of, 141; attitudes toward war
    in, 122; casualties of, 99, 132;
    conclusion of war, 161; early in war,
    59–61; German relations with, 27;
    imperialism of, 5, 7, 84, 91; later in
    war, 98–99, 132, 136–137; liberalism
    in, 6; navy of, 26; and origins of war,
    33, 51; and peace settlements, 167, 170;
    prewar, 5; and war finances, 118, 119,
    120
"It's a Long Way to Tipperary" (song), 86

Japan: and China's entry into war, 113;
    imperialism of, 5, 7, 13; liberalism in,
    6; navy of, 26, 27, 74; and peace
    settlements, 167; prewar, 5
Jasanoff, Sheila, 3
Jellicoe, John, 107, 108
Jews: Britain and, 148–149; Russian
    oppression of, 13, 58, 109, 120, 148;
    U.S. support for, 109, 120, 148;
    widespread persecution of, 165; and
    Zionism, 14, 148–149
jihad, 89
Joffre, Joseph, 23, 33, 38, 39, 94, 96, 98,
    130
Jordan, 169
Junger, Ernst, *Storm of Steel*, 179
Jutland, Battle of (1916), 73, 108–109

Karl, Emperor, 161
Karlsruhe (ship), 74
Keegan, John, 2, 33, 93, 95, 131, 154
Kemal, Mustafa, 87, 170
Kenya, 68, 144
Kerensky, Alexander, 126–127
Kiel Canal, 26
Kitchener, Horatio, 93
Kluck, Alexander von, 36, 39
Koch, Robert, 165
Königsberg (ship), 68, 74
Korea, 13
Kornilov, Lavr, 127
Kreisler, Fritz, 178
Krupp 420 howitzers, 37

labor, colonial supply of, 64
laissez-faire economics, 6
Laos, 13

Latour, Bruno, 3
Lawrence, T. E., 149
League of Nations, 34, 110, 152–153, 168, 169, 171
Lebanon, 92, 169
Léger, Fernand, 175
Leighton, Roland, 45
Lenin, Vladimir Ilyich, 127
Lettow-Vorbeck, Paul von, 68, 144, 145, 146
liberalism, and imperialism, 6
Lippett, Charles, 49
Lister, Joseph, 165
literature, representations of war in, 166, 175–179
Lithuania, 58
Lloyd George, David, 122, 134, 135, 147, 148, 149, 154, 166
Lossberg, Fritz von, 105
Ludendorff, Erich, 53, 56, 110–111, 122, 153, 154–157, 158, 160, 161, 162
Lusitania (ship), 79, 110
Luxembourg, 20, 23, 36–37
Lvov, Georgy Yevgenyevich, 125

machine guns, 9, 131, 140
Mackensen, August von, 102
Mahdists, 10–11
Maji-Maji, 68
malaria, 9, 59, 144, 146
Malawi, 68, 146
manpower: Allied, 131, 154; Austrian, 57; British, 93, 103; colonial, 42, 45, 63, 117, 129, 133, 135, 144, 146, 149, 157, 161; and composition of the military, 17, 57; diseases' effect on, 157, 158; French, 93; German, 17, 157; logistics concerning, 22; Russian, 56, 93, 129; strategy concerning, 19, 103, 105; U.S., 129, 154, 157, 159, 160. *See also* casualties
Marinetti, Filippo, 175
Marne, Battles of, 39, 40, 157
Marwitz, Georg von der, 138
Maude, Frederick Stanley, 147–148
Maunoury, Michel-Joseph, 39
Max, Prince of Baden, 162
Maxim, Hiram, 10
McMahon, Henry, 92

McMeekin, Sean, 31, 52
medicine, 164
Mehmet V, 89
Meiji, Emperor, 6
Meinertzhagen, Richard, 145
memoirs, 179
Mensheviks, 125
mental illness, 165
merchant vessels, sinking of, 138–139
Mesopotamia Campaign, 87–90, 147
Messimy, Adolphe, 33
Mexico, 111, 112
Michel, Victor, 23
Middle East: and peace settlements, 169; present-day, 1; war in (1914–1916), 81–92, 88; war in (1916–1918), 147–150
military strategy. *See* war plans
Milner, Alfred, 134
mines (explosives): landmines, 71, 77; in naval and submarine warfare, 27, 74, 78, 82, 139; in trench warfare, 104, 133
minesweepers, 82
modernism, 166
Moltke, Helmuth von, 19
Moltke, Helmuth von, the Younger, 22, 31, 33, 39, 40, 53
money supply, 118
morale. *See* psychology and morale
Morgan, J. P., 120
morphine addiction, 117
Morrow, John, 2
mourning, 165
Mozambique, 144, 146
Mudros armistice (1918), 161
Mueller, Lauro, 112
Murray, Joe, 85–86
Muslims, 43, 89, 124
mustard gas, 135

Naepflin, Maria, 117
Nama, 69
names, given by soldiers to geography, 86, 87
Namibia, 25, 68, 147
Napoleon Bonaparte, 5, 19
Napoleon III, 14
nationalism: in Alsace-Lorraine, 15; and anti-colonialism, 34; in art and

literature, 177, 178; in the Balkans, 29; critique of, 177; in France, 14, 15; in Germany, 64; in Greece, 112; in India, 89; in Ireland, 122–123; in Russia, 13, 126; in Turkey, 170
Natives Land Act (South Africa, 1913), 69
natural resources, 8
nature, effect of war on attitudes toward, 177–178, 179
navies: early in war, 73–79; later in war, 107–109; prewar arms race in, 25–27; protection of merchant vessels by, 138–139; and rules of warfare, 78, 110; ship construction, 25; strategies and tactics of, 73, 78; technological advances in, 25–26, 73, 87; vulnerability of, 73. *See also* submarines
Neiberg, Michael, 2
Netherlands, 21, 22, 119
Neuilly, Treaty of (1919), 170
Neuve Chapelle, Battle of (1915), 45–46
Nevinson, C. R. W., 175
New Zealand: government of, 7, 70; war participation of, 84, 87, 105, 133, 135
Nicholas II, Tsar, 31, 32, 33, 34, 58, 124–125, 126
nitrates, 118
Nivelle offensive, 130–132
Nivelle, Robert, 98, 130, 131–132
Nixon, John, 90
no-man's-land, 104, 177
North, Katherine Hodges, 116
Northern Rhodesia, 68, 146
North Sea, 26, 40, 41, 75, 76, 77, 108
Norway, 119
nostalgia, 86
nurses, 116–117
Nyasaland, 68, 146

oil, 87–89, 89, 90, 161
Omdurman, Battle of (1898), 10–11
Operation Blücher-Yorck, 156
Operation Georgette, 156
Operation Michael, 154–156
Ottoman Empire: Allied offense against, 81–92; attitudes toward war in, 123; casualties of, 91; conclusion of war, 161; early in war, 43, 76; German

relations with, 76; imperialism of, 7, 13, 91; later in war, 147–149; and peace settlements, 169; prewar, 5; and war finances, 118
Ovambo, 69
Owen, Wilfred: "Dulce et Decorum Est," 48; "Exposure," 177–178

Pacific, colonialism in, 5, 8, 25
Pact of London (1915), 84
Pale of Settlement, 58
Paléologue, Maurice, 32
Palestine, 92, 148, 149, 161, 169
pals battalions, 93, 103
Pan German League, 64
Papua New Guinea, 25
Passchendaele, Battle of (1917), 134–135
Pasteur, Louis, 165
peace negotiations and settlements, 160, 161–162, 166–171
Pershing, John, 154, 159
Persia (Iran), 87
Pétain, Philippe, 96–97, 98, 132, 153
Peter, King of Serbia, 59
Peters, Karl, 65
Petrograd Soviet, 125–126
Philippines, 13
phosgene gas, 98, 136
Picot, François, 92
Plan XVII, 23, 37
Plumer, Hubert, 133, 134, 135, 156
plunder, 145, 156
pogroms, 58
poison gas, 2, 47–49, 58, 98, 131, 135, 136, 154, 156, 160
Poland: Austrian-Russian conflict in, 55; German attitudes toward, 58, 64; German war planning concerning, 20; postwar creation of, 168, 170; Russian cession of, to Germany, 127
population, impact of war on, 164
porters, 144, 145, 146, 165
Portugal, 5, 70, 79
Potiorek, Oskar, 55
Poustis, Robert, 14, 35
Princip, Gavrilo, 29
Prittwitz, Maximilian von, 52, 52–53
propaganda, 37, 47, 79, 90

Provisional Government (Russia), 125–126, 127

Prussia, 14–16. *See also* East Prussia

psychology and morale: of air attacks, 142; of British army, 153; challenges to, 117, 165, 179; defensive fighting and, 96; of French army, 131–132; of German army, 130, 153, 158, 159, 162; impacts of war, 165; of Indian soldiers, 43; of Italian army, 60, 136–137; mental illness resulting from war, 165; of pilots, 140; reinforcements important to, 96; of Russian army, 126, 132; of U.S. army, 154

public opinion, and war strategy, 96, 99, 112. *See also* First World War: attitudes toward

Puerto Rico, 13

Al-Qaida, 1

race, imperialism and, 7

radio, 53, 65, 108

Rasputin, Grigorii, 34, 124–125

Ravel, Maurice, 178

Rawlinson, Henry, 103

realism, 176

registration, artillery, 137–138, 158

reinforcements, 96

Reinsurance Treaty (1887), 16, 17

religion, 43, 90

Remarque, Erich Maria, *All Quiet on the Western Front*, 160, 176–177

Rennenkampf, Pavel von, 52, 53

Republican Party (U.S.), 6

resistance to war, 43

Riga, Latvia, 127

rinderpest (cattle disease), 66

Rivers, W. H., 165

Robertson, William, 134, 147

Romania, 100–102, 161, 170

Rothschild, Walter, 149

Royal Naval Division, 42

rules of warfare: Hague Convention, 47; naval, 78, 110

Ruskin, John, 175

Russia: aircraft of, 141; British relations with, 23; casualties of, 56, 57, 99, 100; early in war, 39, 44, 48, 51–53, 55–59; exit from war, 127, 129; French relations with, 17; German relations with, 15, 16, 17, 127; German war planning concerning, 20–22; impact of war on, 51; imperialism of, 5, 7, 13, 89, 91; industrial production in, 56, 93, 125; later in war, 93, 98–100, 126–127; manpower of, 56, 93, 129; military planning of, 19, 23; nationalism in, 13; navy of, 26, 76; and origins of war, 30, 31–32; and Ottoman Empire, 82, 90–92; postrevolutionary, 170–171; prewar, 5, 13; revolution in, 124–127; U.S. attitudes toward, 109; and war finances, 118, 119, 120

Russian First Army, 52, 53

Russian Revolution, 124–127

Russian Second Army, 52, 53, 99

Russian Twelfth Army, 127

Russo-Japanese War (1904–1905), 11, 13, 19, 77

sacrifice zones, 36

Saint Germain-en-Laye, Treaty of (1919), 170

Salandra, Antonio, 59, 122

salients, 41, 95, 96, 105

Samoa, 25

Samsonov, Aleksandr, 52, 53

Sanders, Liman von, 148

saps, 100

Sassoon, Siegfried, "Counter Attack," 45

Sazonov, Sergei Dmitrievich, 30

Scheer, Reinhard, 108, 109

Schlieffen, Alfred von, 20–22, 163

Schlieffen Plan, 20–22, 21, 31, 33, 34, 38–39, 44, 55, 94

Second World War, 174

Sedition Act (United States, 1918), 123

self-determination, national, 109, 150, 152, 169

September 11, 2001, terrorist attacks, 1

Serbia: casualties of, 55; conclusion of war, 161; early in war, 48, 55, 59; and origins of war, 29–30, 31

Sèvres, Treaty of (1920), 169

ship construction, 25

shortages of goods, 120

Sikorsky, Igor, 141

Skoda 305 howitzers, 37

sleeping sickness, 144

Smuts, Jan, 69, 70, 134, 144, 145

socialism: in France, 132; in Germany, 15, 17, 122, 162; in Italy, 122; in Russia, 125; in United States, 123

Socialist Revolutionaries, 125

Somme, Battle of (1916), 102–105

South Africa: African labor employed by, 147; German support for, 24, 69; government of, 7; war participation of, 70–71, 105, 154

South African National Party, 69, 70

Southern Africa, 68–71

South-West Africa, 68–69, 70–71

Spain, 13, 26, 66

Spee, Maximilian Graf von, 74

Stevenson, David, 2, 120, 164

St. Mihiel, Battle of (1918), 159

storm troopers, 95, 96, 127, 136, 138, 154, 156

Strachan, Hew, 2, 95, 103

strikes, 125, 131, 137

submarines: attitudes toward, 77, 79, 81, 94, 112; as new technology of war, 27, 74, 77; and rules of warfare, 78, 110; warfare using, 77–79, 110–111, 130, 138–139

Sweden, 119

Sykes, Mark, 92

symbolism in war, 96

Syria, 2, 92, 169

Taiwan, 13

Taliban, 1

tanks, 105, 131, 137–138, 158, 174

Tanzania, 25, 144, 146

taxes, 118

technology: of aircraft, 139–142; of artillery, 9, 130, 137–138, 158; artists' attitudes toward, 175, 178; attitudes toward, 3, 163, 175; of First World War, 2–3, 174; historiography of, 2–3; imperialism and, 8–9; military tactics affected by, 137–138; nature of warfare changed by, 10–11, 34, 35, 36, 38; naval, 25–26, 73, 87; poison gas, 47–49; radio, 53; submarine, 27, 74, 77; tanks, 105

Three Emperors League, 16

Tirpitz, Alfred von, 26

Togo, 65

Tolstoy, Leo, 175

torpedoes, 74

totalitarianism, 165, 171

total war, 115–118

Townshend, Charles, 90

Toynbee, Arnold, 91

Transylvania, 100–102

trauma, 165

Treitschke, Heinrich von, 18, 19

trench warfare: on Eastern Front, 57; Eastern vs. Western, 57; environment of, 44–45, 85–86, 97, 134–135; examples of, 45–49; at Gallipoli, 84, 85–86, 87; German preparations for, 48, 105, 130, 134; literary representations of, 176–177; mines used in, 133; new weaponry and, 19, 42, 44, 47; strategy for, 44, 46, 48, 100, 130; on Western Front, 42, 44–45, 48, 103–104, 105

triage, 165

Trianon, Treaty of (1920), 170

Triple Alliance, 16, 17

Trotsky, Leon, 127, 171

trypanosomiasis, 144

Tucker, Richard, 173

Turkey, 87, 152, 161, 169

turnips, 121

U-boat campaign (1917), 138–139

Uganda, 68

Ukraine, 127

United States: attitudes toward war in, 123; Bill of Rights, 6; casualties of, 159; Civil War, 9, 11, 19; conclusion of war, 154, 156–160; contributions of, 129; entrance of, into war, 79; entry into war, 109–113, 120, 150, 151; imperialism of, 5, 7, 13; liberalism in, 6; manpower of, 129, 154, 157, 159, 160; navy of, 26, 27, 129; oil in, 87; and peace settlements, 166–171; prewar, 5; and war finances, 120; wartime production of, 117

U.S. Congress, 111, 166, 171

Venizelos, Eleutherios, 112

Verdun, Battle of (1916), 94–98
Versailles, Treaty of (1919), 30, 167–168, 171
Victoria, Queen of England, 24
Vietnam, 13
Villa, Pancho, 111
Vimy Ridge, breakthrough at (1917), 130–131
violence, 165

war bonds, 119
warfare: nature of, changed by technology, 10–11, 34, 35, 36, 38; statehood and, 18–19. *See also* psychology and morale
War Industries Board (U.S.), 123
war plans, 19–27; Allied offense against Ottoman Empire, 82, 84; of Britain, 23; decision-making influenced by, 29; of France, 19, 23, 37; of Germany, 19–22, 21–27, 31, 34, 38–39, 44; of Russia, 19, 23. *See also* attrition strategy
weapons: effects of new, 10–11, 19, 34, 35, 36, 37, 38; imperialism and, 9; technological advances in, 9
weather, 95, 131, 135
West Africa, 65–66, 146
Western Front: conclusion of war, 153–160; early in war, 36–49; Eastern compared to, 57; environmental impact

on, 163, 174; later in war, 42, 129–142
West Indies, 13
Wilhelm, Crown Prince, 95
Wilhelm I, Kaiser, 16, 25
Wilhelm II, Kaiser, 17, 24–25, 26, 27, 31–32, 33, 94, 98, 108, 110, 111, 156, 160, 162, 163
Williams, Lloyd, 157
Williamson, Henry, 44
Wilson, Henry, 23
Wilson, Woodrow, 79, 109–110, 111, 111–112, 113, 120, 123, 150, 151–153, 154, 159, 162, 167, 170, 171; Fourteen Points, 150, 151–153, 160, 162, 166
Winter, Jay, 2, 166
women: as nurses, 116–117; as soldiers, 117; various war experiences of, 117; in wartime workforce, 115–116

Ypres, Battles of, 41, 46–47, 134–135
Yudenich, Nikolai, 92
Yugoslavia, 170

Zakharova, Lidiya, 116–117
Zambia, 68, 146
Zeppelin L.59, 143–144
zeppelins, 37, 142, 143
Zimmerman, Arthur, 110–111
Zionism, 14, 148–149